M000251200

Hitler's Generals
in America

HITLER'S GENERALS IN AMERICA

Nazi POWs and Allied Military Intelligence

DEREK R. MALLETT

UNIVERSITY PRESS OF KENTUCKY

Copyright © 2013 by The University Press of Kentucky

Scholarly publisher for the Commonwealth,
serving Bellarmine University, Berea College, Centre College of Kentucky, Eastern
Kentucky University, The Filson Historical Society, Georgetown College, Kentucky
Historical Society, Kentucky State University, Morehead State University, Murray State
University, Northern Kentucky University, Transylvania University, University
of Kentucky, University of Louisville, and Western Kentucky University.
All rights reserved.

Editorial and Sales Offices: The University Press of Kentucky
663 South Limestone Street, Lexington, Kentucky 40508-4008
www.kentuckypress.com

17 16 15 14 13   5 4 3 2 1

Library of Congress Cataloging-in-Publication Data

Mallett, Derek R., 1969-
  Hitler's generals in America : Nazi POWs and allied military intelligence / Derek R.
Mallett.
     pages cm
  Includes bibliographical references and index.
  ISBN 978-0-8131-4251-7 (hardcover : alk. paper) — ISBN 978-0-8131-4253-1 (pdf) —
ISBN 978-0-8131-4252-4 (epub)
  1. World War, 1939-1945—Prisoners and prisons, American. 2. Prisoners of war—
Germany—History—20th century. 3. Prisoners of war—United States—History—20th
century. 4. Generals—Germany—History—20th century. 5. World War, 1939-1945—
Military intelligence. 6. Cold War—Military intelligence. I. Title.
  D805.U5M34 2013
  940.54'7273—dc23   2013029397

This book is printed on acid-free paper meeting the requirements of the American
National Standard for Permanence in Paper for Printed Library Materials.

Manufactured in the United States of America.

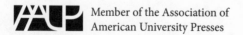 Member of the Association of
American University Presses

For my mother's quiet strength and subtle leadership;
for her solid, principled example;
and for her having always been there.

And for my father's satirical view of the world;
for his firm, father's hand;
and for his reminder that life is not always what it seems.

Contents

Abbreviations

BA-MA	Bundesarchiv-Militärarchiv, Freiburg
CAD	Civil Affairs Division, U.S. War Department
CSDIC	Combined Services Detailed Interrogation Centre
GMDS	German Military Document Section
MIRS	Military Intelligence Research Section
MPEG	Military Police Escort Guard
NARA	National Archives and Records Administration, College Park, Maryland
NCO	noncommissioned officer
OKH	Oberkommando des Heeres (German Army High Command)
OKW	Oberkommando der Wehrmacht (German Armed Forces High Command)
PMGO	Provost Marshal General's Office
SD	Sicherheitsdienst
TNA	National Archives of the United Kingdom
USFET	U.S. Forces European Theater

Introduction

Discussions of World War II German generals often bring to mind names like Erwin Rommel or Heinz Guderian. Undoubtedly, these men and officers like them played significant roles in the conduct of the war. Scholars have paid less attention to the fates of hundreds of senior German officers taken prisoner by the Allies, with the exception of Wehrmacht officers in Soviet hands, those issuing anti-Nazi propaganda from Russian prisoner-of-war camps being of particular note.

What seem to have been of least interest are the general officers captured by the Western Allies who spent anywhere from a few months to a few years in England or North America. Indeed, little has been written about the fifty-five German general officers who were held as prisoners of war in the United States during World War II.[1] Yet the collective story of these men's experiences as prisoners of war reveals a great deal about the differences in American and British perceptions of these men, and even more about the differences in America's national security concerns in the summer of 1943, when the army first brought Wehrmacht general officers to the United States, and the summer of 1946, when it repatriated the last of them.

From the earliest stages of the war, providing for captured enemy soldiers increasingly burdened Allied authorities. When General Hans Jürgen von Arnim surrendered the Axis's North African forces in May 1943, 250,000 German and Italian soldiers became the responsibility of the British and American governments. This represented the first massive influx of prisoners of war into Allied custody. These prisoners included not only the usual German and Italian enlisted men and lower-ranking officers but seventeen German general officers as well, including General von Arnim himself. Washington and London engaged in a great deal of discussion regarding who should take responsibility for these select prisoners. The two Allies agreed that Britain's Combined Services Detailed Interrogation Centre (CSDIC), the agency charged with interrogating important prisoners of war in England, "should act as advanced echelon" for their collaborative effort. But the ultimate question of "ownership" of these prisoners was immaterial, as transfers of some of the generals to the United States could be easily effected. As if to demonstrate this, CSDIC sent four generals and a colonel awaiting promotion to the United States on the first of June, a little more than two weeks after their capture in North Africa, with more to follow as the war progressed.[2]

The U.S. War Department most likely deferred to the British in dealing with the general officer prisoners because London had far more experience handling prisoners of war. During the First World War, the British learned a great deal about caring for war prisoners, which provided a model for efficient and well-managed treatment of POWs during World War II. Britain graduated from temporarily housing the Kaiser's men aboard ships in the winter of 1914–1915 to the establishment of land-based camps both in the British Isles and in France the following year. Prisoners of the British enjoyed a bountiful food allotment of forty-six hundred calories a day through most of the war, and even when Britons themselves struggled with food shortages in the spring of 1917, POWs still consumed three thousand calories a day.[3]

Other staples of World War II British POW policy developed out of the trials and errors of the Great War as well. The use of prisoner labor, while not practiced at all until the spring of 1916, quickly expanded until almost one-third of the German prisoners in Britain were working at various agricultural jobs by war's end. And, not unlike their successors in the Second World War, World War I German officer prisoners found themselves in stately mansions like Donington Hall in Derby, enjoyed the use of adjacent acres of land for regular walks, and were aided by enlisted prisoners who acted as servants and orderlies.[4]

Historian Richard Speed contends that "British camps [during the Great War] more nearly matched the prewar ideal of captivity than did those of any other European belligerent." The British government heavily weighed the often vague requirements of the Hague Conventions that governed the treatment of war prisoners during World War I and sought to incorporate the spirit of this existing international law to provide humane treatment for all POWs. At the onset of the Second World War, twenty years later, the British simply had to reincarnate the system for accommodating prisoners of war that they had worked out during World War I.[5]

The American experience with prisoners, like the country's experience with the First World War in general, was unique. Whereas the other belligerents began dealing with prisoners of war in 1914, the United States did not officially enter the war until 1917, and even then American troops did not see their first major engagement until Cantigny in May of the following year. Only then, almost four years after the start of World War I, did the Americans begin to establish some kind of apparatus to handle prisoners of war. Prior to becoming an active belligerent, however, the United States had served as the protecting power for the war prisoners of Germany, Austria-Hungary, France, Great Britain, and Russia. In this capacity, American officials inspected the camps of these respective nations to ensure humane treatment of prisoners. Thus, when U.S. authorities began to develop their own POW policy they at least possessed some well-formulated ideals if no practical experience.[6]

When the first American units arrived in France in 1917, they served under French command and, consequently, turned any captured prisoners over to French control. As the American Expeditionary Force fully mobilized in Europe and entered the war as an independent entity in 1918, the Americans insisted on handling their own war prisoners. This enabled them to better negotiate with the German government in regard to the treatment of American POWs. Near the end of the war, American authorities even demanded that the French transfer any prisoners captured by American forces back to U.S. control.[7]

The American experience with handling World War I POWs was also unique in that circumstances largely compelled U.S. authorities to intern the overwhelming majority of their prisoners on foreign soil. The U.S. Army established ten base camps and seventy-six smaller labor camps throughout France, placing the Department of the Provost Marshal General and its newly created Prisoner of War Division in charge of overseeing the entire operation. The Provost Marshal General's Office (PMGO) initially considered sending captured German officers to the United States. But, after quickly being overwhelmed with prisoners before adequate arrangements could be made to transport them across the Atlantic, the Americans decided to keep the officers in France instead. They eventually established quarters for all of these men at the Chateau Vrillays at Richelieu in November 1918. The 85 highest-ranking officers, out of a total of 874 prisoners at Richelieu, were quartered in the chateau itself, while the remaining prisoners lived in barracks constructed on the chateau grounds. In scenes similar to those in World War II POW camps in the United States, almost all of the German officer prisoners occupied themselves by engaging in educational courses, many of them taken for credit at German universities.[8]

Washington established four internment camps in the United States during the First World War, but only one of these held prisoners of war. Fort

McPherson, on the outskirts of Atlanta, Georgia, housed 1,356 German naval officers and enlisted men. These prisoners, mostly U-boat crewmen, had all been captured near the Atlantic coast and thus could more easily be kept in the United States than shipped back to Europe for confinement.[9]

The Americans dealt with prisoners of war fairly well during World War I, considering the relatively short span of time they had to develop any kind of system and appropriate apparatus. Yet the Americans' use of tents to house prisoners during a rainy French spring in 1918, when the other belligerents had long since established permanent facilities, and the deaths of dozens of prisoners employed in the disposal of munitions after the war marred the American effort. Furthermore, the hastily assembled American system of camps and logistics might well have been overwhelmed had the war not concluded only a few months after the American military took responsibility for its own prisoners.[10]

Given the U.S. military's limited experience in dealing with prisoners of war during World War I, it is not surprising that the United States initially followed the British lead in handling POWs during the Second World War. Additionally, by the time America entered World War II, Great Britain had been dealing with prisoners of war in this conflict for more than two years. Also, British authorities already had experience in dealing with German generals, the first being Major General Hans Friemel, captured in the Netherlands in May 1940. Generals Hans von Ravenstein and Artur Schmitt soon joined Friemel, and London sent all three to POW camps in Canada, where they remained until 1946.[11] The British also had established facilities in England for two other German generals, Ludwig Crüwell and Wilhelm Ritter von Thoma, who had been in captivity for several months prior to the end of the North African campaign.

In addition to following British experience in establishing facilities for prisoners of war, the Americans sought to emulate British intelligence practices; consequently, the two Allies increasingly combined their intelligence operations as the war progressed. Initially, the United States and the United Kingdom operated prisoner-of-war interrogation teams independently in North Africa, with each attempting to gather information from its own captures. By February 1943, however, they had pooled their staff and resources to form the Allied Captured Intelligence Centre in Algiers. By the climax of the war in North Africa in May 1943, American authorities had replicated British methods, assigning interrogators to work with British personnel in London to gain "practical experience" under the guidance of British operatives.[12]

Despite the Americans' initial willingness to learn from their British allies, the U.S.-British joint handling of POW matters proved cumbersome, if not contentious, at times. P. H. Gore-Booth, a senior official in the British Foreign Office, blamed the American State and War Departments' administration of prisoner affairs for much of the problem. He characterized both as "bottle-neck departments," observing that all American POW issues filtered through a small number of key personnel who were greatly overworked. He observed that J. H. Keeley, head of the State Department's Special War Problems Division, "always [had] more special war problems on his desk than he [could] cope with," and Bernard Gufler, who served as Keeley's "No. 2," was "in a similar situation." The result, according to the British official, was that neither man could devote his attention to any particular matter.[13]

Gore-Booth stated that this was even more pronounced in the case of the principal War Department representative in the joint Anglo-American meetings. He described Lieutenant Colonel M. C. Bernays as "desperately overworked" and a man whose "superiors have paid no attention to his complaints on this score." He praised Colonel Bernays as a "tiger for work" and a "demon for thoroughness" who considered everything in minute detail before approving it. Unfortunately, this meticulous approach often led to delays in the joint meetings, as compromises had to be reached regarding the wording of documents. The British official wryly noted that all drafts had to read "quaintly," as he put it, "since they [were] written in that curious mongrel, the Anglo-American language."[14]

In assessing the relationship between the two Allied nations, Gore-Booth ultimately concluded that the U.S.-British collaboration worked successfully, albeit slowly, thanks in part to the American personnel not sparing any effort to make the procedures a success. In particular, he lauded both Bernays and Gufler for doing "everything possible within the framework of the rather rigid American official procedure to keep things moving." But even the Americans, Gore-Booth added, were "acutely conscious of the difficulties which their system sometimes presents."[15]

If the observations of Gore-Booth are accurate, the American prisoner-of-war administration was dogged by a lack of necessary personnel and overwhelming workloads that bred inefficiency and delay. Yet despite the "machinery" of Washington, as the British official termed it, the two countries learned to work together. When the United States entered the war in December 1941, the two Allies established a fifty-fifty agreement for the disposal of prisoners of war. This meant that every few months the two nations would simply divide all newly captured prisoners of war into two equal halves, regardless of who captured whom, with each being responsible for the internment of its portion. This arrangement remained in effect until September 1944 when, after being inundated with prisoners of war in the months following D-Day, Britain could no longer properly house an equal share of the prisoners and asked the United States to abrogate the agreement. The Americans agreed to take responsibility for an additional 175,000 German prisoners of war on behalf of the British government. Consequently, the United States returned these men to British custody in 1946 rather than repatriating them directly to Germany, causing a great deal of resentment among the prisoners.[16]

Despite these postwar complications, the two Allies established a working relationship regarding POW matters during the war. They shared a great deal of information and regularly passed prisoners of war back and forth. Indeed, it appears that the British even provided American military intelligence with copies of the transcripts of the generals' interrogations and the conversations recorded by CSDIC personnel, as the existing CSDIC reports regarding the German generals are stamped "Most Secret (British)—Secret (American)."[17] That British intelligence staff offered their American counterparts access to these files may further explain American willingness to allow the British to take the lead in holding and interrogating the German generals. U.S. intelligence likely saw no need to expend precious American resources to operate eavesdropping machinery or conduct interrogations of those generals who were later transferred to U.S. custody when CSDIC had already done a capable job for them.

Nonetheless, this seemingly one-way transfer of intelligence highlights a major difference in the manner in which the two Allies initially viewed the German POW generals. The British appear to have viewed these senior officers as potentially valuable from the start. In addition to interrogations and secretly recorded conversations, in mid-November 1943, only six months after the generals' arrival in England, the Historical Branch of the British War Cabinet decided that there was "a wealth of valuable material . . . emanating from the German and Italian generals" and quickly assigned an officer to go through it in detail. The Americans, by contrast, interrogated only the first parcel of generals sent to the United States in June 1943. Once these men departed the U.S. interrogation center at Byron Hot Springs, California, American officers barely spoke to the German generals in their custody, much less actively interrogated them, and no attempts were ever made at Camp Mexia, Texas; Camp Clinton, Mississippi; Camp Dermott, Arkansas; or Camp Ruston, Louisiana, to secretly record any of the generals' conversations. Even American interest in the generals for strictly historical purposes did not emerge until after the war ended in 1945. Whereas the British valued the generals as important "guests," as they referred to them, the Americans largely viewed them much as they did any other German prisoners of war.[18]

This discrepancy between the two Allies' views of the generals was reflected in their treatment of these prisoners. Unlike the British, the Americans did not feel compelled to provide these distinguished prisoners with the extra amenities that the generals thought appropriate to their rank and status. Consequently, a great deal of resentment developed early on among the German generals toward their American captors. At the heart of this resentment were some inherent cultural differences that may have initially made the British better suited than the Americans to accommodate German generals as prisoners of war, at least in the eyes of the generals themselves.

The German officer corps evolved from a feudal tradition in which gentlemen of noble birth commanded men in the field.[19] While feudalism itself had long since declined in Germany by the time of the Second World War, a significant portion of the aristocracy still existed and a number of individual German officers descended from one of these aristocratic families. For example, sixteen men held the rank of *Generalfeldmarschall* (field marshal; equivalent to a U.S. five-star general) in the German Army as of May 1, 1944, of whom ten belonged to the aristocracy.[20] Of these ten aristocratic generals, nine were descended from German generals or high-ranking officers. Thus, the elite heads of the Wehrmacht were not only aristocrats but members of an aristocracy who had also inherited a strong militaristic tradition.[21]

Similarly, one-third of the *Generalobersten* and *Generalen der Infanterie* (equivalent to U.S. four-star and three-star generals, respectively) could be counted as members of the German aristocracy or held aristocratic family connections through their wives or mothers. Moreover, these men were highly decorated, with 85 percent of them having been awarded the Knight's Cross of the Iron Cross. Even the lower echelons of the cadre of German general officers, *Generalleutnants* and *Generalmajore* (equivalent to American two- and one-star generals, respectively) reflected German aristocratic traditions. Of the 470 *Generalleutnants* in the German Army in May 1944, 152, or 29 percent, descended from aristocratic families. Similarly, 176, or 31 percent, of the 565 *Generalmajore* held aristocratic family ties.[22]

As prisoners of the British, the aristocratic German generals found themselves in the hands of gentlemen similar to themselves. Prior to the First World War, professional military castes had influenced the development of both the German and the British officer corps to a great extent. At the turn of the twentieth century, over 80 percent of German and 40 percent of British generals and admirals were noblemen, demonstrating that the move toward more middle-class officers had only begun following World War I. Further illustrating the similarities between the two nations' military leaders, British officers, like their German counterparts, often inherited their military tradition. From 1870 until the end of the 1950s, almost 40 percent of British generals and admirals had fathers who had been military officers themselves, most of them holding the rank of lieutenant colonel or above.[23]

Historian Correlli Barnett contends that during the 1940s and 1950s "the social gulf—the gulf in status—between the British officer and his non-commissioned officers and men . . . remained far wider than in European or North American armies." Indeed, the British officer corps developed from much the same feudal military traditions as did the German. British general officers, like their German counterparts, came from the upper and upper-middle classes. In the 1930s half of the general officers in the British Home Army still hailed from the aristocracy or landed gentry. Even after the Second World War, as late as 1952, the share of British general officers with aristocratic heritage remained at almost 40 percent, at a time when the rest of the officer corps had been professionalized and become almost entirely middle class in nature.[24]

Therefore, during World War II, German prisoner-of-war generals and their British captors had a great deal more in common, at least in terms of the social heritage of the military, than did either group with the Americans. Perhaps these men could understand each other on a social and cultural level that neither group shared with their Yankee counterparts. The British decision to devote significant resources and attention to German general officer prisoners and provide them with special privileges does not appear to have been controversial. It was simply assumed that British authorities would accommodate their social equals in a manner they thought befitting their own aristocratic general officers.

The Americans, by contrast, shared neither their enemy's nor their ally's aristocratic officer corps traditions. Thomas Jefferson founded the U.S. Military Academy at West Point on the basis of the "natural aristocracy," military cadets ostensibly being chosen mostly by talent and natural intelligence rather than by wealth or social status. Dr. Andrew Goodpaster, former NATO commander and West Point commandant, once observed that "since [the founding of the U.S. Military Academy] America has never had a military caste, either social or political. The officer corps has been drawn from all corners and all levels of society. If the academy admitted enough sons of high officials, civil and military, to raise the hackles of a few, it always also included a significant number of lads whose fathers were cobblers, mechanics, and farmers."[25]

During the American Civil War, many officers gained appointments for political reasons as well as out of necessity when both the Union and Confederacy created more military units than could be accommodated by graduates of the military academy. But the U.S. officer corps further professionalized in the late nineteenth and twentieth centuries as an increasing percentage of peacetime army and marine corps officers obtained their commissions by graduating from a federal military school and not by political appointment. The social origins of the American officer corps during the U.S. war with Spain in 1898 reflected this more democratic composition. At a time when 40 percent of German military officers could tout their noble birth, more than half of U.S. Army officers in the Spanish-American War had been appointed from the ranks of enlisted men or as veterans of volunteer units. Four decades later, this democratic heritage prompted one U.S. Marine Corps major to brag that "the professional soldiers and sailors of this country are . . . connected in no way with any one region or caste, but constituting in fact a cross section of the whole population."[26]

The perception has long existed, at least among members of the American military establishment, that the U.S. officer corps reflects the democratic ideals of the civilian population. Historian Russell Weigley describes America's first army, Washington's Continental Army during the Revolutionary War, as "a product of a middle-class society" and distinguishes it from contemporary European armies that "remained largely the products of a feudal age." He argues that "this distinction made for profound differences of spirit, discipline, and organization." In regard to officers in particular, Weigley concludes that from its inception "the American officer corps came from the same general social strata as the American soldiery, while European officer corps were composed overwhelmingly of noblemen, or among the British at least of members of the gentry."[27]

In addition to the unique social composition of the U.S. military officer corps, American perceptions of German generals during the Second World War may well have been influenced by America's long-standing societal distrust of professional militaries in general. The American colonies inherited a citizen-soldier tradition from England in the form of popular militias. The militias fell out of favor in England after the English Civil War, much as they did in the rest of Europe, and by the early eighteenth century the European powers relied almost exclusively on professional armies. The United States, by contrast, continued to utilize short-service militia and volunteers who served only during wartime. These "citizen soldiers" proved useful time and again in American wars, whether fighting to win American independence, routing British troops under Andrew Jackson at the Battle of New Orleans, or defeating a Mexican army under Colonel Alexander Doniphan—a volunteer himself—during the U.S.-Mexican War.

American suspicions of professional militaries even affected the development of the U.S. Military Academy. Not only was admission to West Point structured to admit a cross-section of the American population, the school's curriculum was designed as much for practical concerns as it was for strictly military ones. As Russell Weigley observes, "In a country not immediately imperiled by foreign enemies and jealous of standing armies, the academy had to justify itself by preparing officers who could do useful work in peace, so it became largely a school of civil engineering."[28]

Despite going through a period of military professionalization in the late nineteenth century, the United States entered World War II with its belief in a small regular army and the virtues of citizen soldiers intact. This does not solely account for the differences between American and British treatment of German generals. It does, however, illustrate the potential for American military personnel to be reluctant to pay homage to what they saw as an unnecessarily aristocratic and professional German military hierarchy by providing these German officer prisoners with special privileges.

The cultural and intellectual climate of the two decades preceding U.S. entry into the Second World War may have further aggravated American skepticism of professional military institutions, the officer corps in particular. Widespread disillusionment following the First World War bred a generation of antiwar writers and intellectuals on both sides of the Atlantic, including Erich Maria Remarque, Henri Barbusse, and Ernest Hemingway. During the 1920s and 1930s, the portrayal of U.S. military officers by American intellectuals and professional academics reflected this sense of disillusionment. Historian C. Robert Kemble argues that some American writers and filmmakers in the two decades leading up to the Second World War attacked the quality of West Point as an academic institution and thus the quality of officers it could produce. Yet, simultaneously, critics of American military officers expressed their fear of an "undemocratic military caste," labeling the American officer as "a Prussianistic professional who had been trained to his autocratic ways . . . rather than the nineteenth-century ersatz aristocrat who was despotic by class instinct."[29]

Kemble contends that John Dos Passos's novel *Three Soldiers,* originally published in 1921, established the prototype that two decades of novelists followed. Dos Passos's antimilitary formula, according to Kemble, portrayed "sensitive, humanitarian, intelligent" men of peace, frequently represented as Ivy League graduates, beaten down by cruel, military authoritarians, often portrayed as West Point graduates. Kemble notes that despite the later proliferation of American military heroes in World War II–era films and novels, the most preferred protagonist was a "patriotic but uncontaminated civilian at heart," rather than a professional soldier. Indeed, a *New York Times Book Review* summation of American World War II novels written throughout the decade of the 1940s found the common assumption that "all officers are cads, or worse." The analysis continued by observing that, in most of these novels, "the rule is that an officer's capacity for evil is in direct ratio to his rank; the higher the rank, the greater the scope for villainy." The reviewer concluded that "the officer caste in [American] World War II fiction [fulfilled] a symbolic function: In these antifascist novels the officer is the fascist, the authoritarian."[30]

Consequently, Americans seemed predisposed to distrust professional military officers, whether their own or those of another nation. In the American mind, who best exemplified autocratic militarism if not an aristocratic, "Prussianistic professional" general? If Americans heavily criticized the "undemocratic military caste" of their own officer corps, one that had not developed from an aristocratic tradition, they would undoubtedly oppose providing German general officers with what they may have viewed as aristocratic treatment in the form of privileges that often exceeded the basic requirements of international law.

Nevertheless, the German generals arrived in Allied custody expecting to be treated like aristocrats. They encountered fellow gentlemen in England. The similarly aristocratic British officer corps provided the generals with extra amenities and paid the prisoners considerable respect and attention. The Americans, on the other hand, whether because they lacked an aristocratic tradition or were influenced by a long-standing suspicion of professional militaries, or simply because they allowed their anti-Nazi animosity to temper their judgment, initially refused to offer the generals anything more than that required by the Geneva Convention.

This discrepancy between British and American treatment of German general officer prisoners slowly began to change following the successful Allied invasion of Normandy in June 1944. The slow, steady advance of Allied troops across Western Europe brought thousands more prisoners of war into Allied hands, including dozens of German generals. Along with these prisoners came the realization that Allied victory was likely and that Britain and the United States would bear significant responsibility for the fate of Europe at the end of the war.

Allied authorities, aware of the prominent status of the prewar German military, believed that German prisoners of war might wield considerable influence in the postwar years. Thus it behooved the Allies to "re-educate" the well over half a million German men in their custody, some of whom undoubtedly still subscribed to the tenets of National Socialism. In the fall of 1944 the British War Office and the American Provost Marshal General's Office initiated "intellectual diversion" programs designed to subtly introduce German prisoners of war to the merits of Western democracy.

If ordinary soldiers were being prepared for leadership roles in a new, democratic German society, how much more important and influential might the general officers be? In conjunction with the intellectual diversion program, a great deal of discussion ensued in the United States in the fall of 1944 regarding the potentially influential roles these men might be able to play in postwar Germany. For the first time, Allied perceptions of which general officer prisoners were "Nazis" and which "anti-Nazis," something CSDIC had been eager to determine during the first two years of the generals' stay in England, now became a paramount concern for American authorities.

One of the first tests of the political orientation of the generals had come in the form of the National Committee "Free Germany" and its affiliated organization, the League of German Officers, created in the Soviet Union during the late summer and early fall of 1943. After Field Marshal Friedrich Paulus surrendered the German Sixth Army at Stalingrad, the Soviet Union sought to make use of the twenty-three general officers and the thousands of newly captured German POWs in its custody to undermine morale among German troops still fighting on the Eastern Front and to encourage active resistance to the Hitler regime among the German population. The National Committee and League of German Officers, collectively known as the Free Germany Committee, consisted of German political exiles, enlisted prisoners of war, and about a hundred Wehrmacht officers headed by General Walter von Seydlitz. The committee published a newspaper, *Freies Deutschland,* broadcast anti-Hitler appeals on the radio, worked to recruit German prisoners in the Soviet camps, and even broadcast to German troops at the front via loudspeakers.[31]

The committee's overall effect on German troops, the German home front, and the outcome of the war was negligible. But British officials utilized their captive generals' reactions to news of the committee's activities to gauge each individual prisoner's level of sympathy toward the Nazi regime, as well as to evaluate the possibility of creating a similar organization in Britain.

While no such organization emerged among the prisoners of war in either Britain or the United States, the possibility provoked a great deal of discussion about the generals' individual political views and potential value to Allied plans for postwar Germany.

This work examines those generals who were at some point prisoners of war in the United States and looks largely at American treatment of these men from initial capture in 1943 until the last of them departed American soil in mid-1946. The narrative largely focuses on those general officer prisoners who seemed to most capture the interest of American authorities. Because many of these general officers spent time in the respective camps of both Britain and the United States, their experiences serve as an interesting comparison between American and British treatment and perceptions of these prisoners of war. Furthermore, these prisoners best illustrate the dramatic American change of heart in the postwar era. Having been largely disregarded as POWs during the course of the war, these generals developed relationships with American authorities after the war that demonstrate the evolution of American national security interests in the immediate postwar years and how this evolution was reflected in U.S. POW policy.

British and American authorities each, at different times, attempted to gauge their prisoners' respective levels of commitment to the National Socialist government. Both Allies found the prospect of making accurate determinations tricky, at best, and few prisoners better illustrated the complicated nature of this endeavor than the general officers under consideration here. Comparing the captivity and postwar careers of these men reveals both significant similarities and fascinating divergences. After the war, one of the "Nazis" emerged as one of the strongest pro-Western politicians in West Germany, while Allied authorities eventually came to suspect one of the "anti-Nazis" to be a militaristic threat to postwar peace.

Had these men undergone a change of heart? Did opposition to Nazism in an American POW camp represent an opportunistic attempt to land on the right side of Germany after the war? Or was there something more to these stories than originally met British and American eyes? How much did considerations of families living under the Nazi regime affect prisoner behavior? Did the Allies recognize any difference between German patriotic loyalty on the one hand and an actual belief in National Socialism on the other? How much did the Allies' perceptions of who was and who was not a Nazi influence their decision making? And were the prisoners that Allied authorities deemed to be the most open to a democratic message and perhaps the best suited for postwar leadership positions really the most democratically minded or were they simply opportunists? The story of these generals in American custody suggests that any assessment of an enemy's loyalties requires very careful, individual consideration.

The broadest of the questions to be addressed deals with why American authorities changed their ideas about the value of the German generals in their custody and how these changes affected the respective Allied relationships with these prisoners. Almost immediately when the war ended, the British seemingly lost interest. While they retained custody of these senior officers for another three years, the British moved the generals' camp to a different location and ceased all eavesdropping and interrogation operations. The Americans, by contrast, found German generals far more useful after the war than they ever had before.

The end of the war in Europe transformed the American perception of the importance of the German generals. The Grand Alliance of Britain, the United States, and the Soviet Union had been an uneasy one at best. While the three nations successfully worked together to defeat Nazi Germany, mutual distrust and suspicion had plagued their relationship from the beginning. With the war coming to an end in the spring of 1945, those suspicions resurfaced and led the Americans and British to question who actually posed the greatest threat to Western Allied interests.

The British, likely because of larger concerns about rebuilding their own war-torn nation, now allowed the Americans to take the lead in the two Allies' relationship with Wehrmacht generals. Despite a lack of interest in these senior officers during the war, U.S. authorities suddenly began to appreciate their potential value to U.S. national security. Thus began a relationship between U.S. civilian and military officials and German general officers that would eventually see the U.S. Army, Navy, Air Force, Joint Chiefs of Staff, and Central Intelligence Agency make use of former Wehrmacht officers for intelligence, leadership roles in the Federal Republic of Germany, the writing of a comprehensive history of the Second World War, and even a revision of U.S. Army doctrine.

The American perspective on the German generals who had come and gone from the United States between June 1943 and June 1946 changed from one of neglect and disregard to one of respect and admiration. Curiously, these senior officers became far more valuable to American interests after the war ended than they had been before. Indeed, these prisoners of war emerged as allies in the early years of the Cold War. Unlike the British, American perceptions of the value of the generals directly correlated to changes in American beliefs about who the "enemy" was at war's end. For the United States, the "German question" had been answered and a new threat had emerged.

1

Afrikaner and *Französen*

The first large group of German generals to arrive in Allied hands came from the massive German surrender in Tunisia in May 1943. In September 1940 Italian dictator Benito Mussolini initiated a campaign against the British in North Africa. He met with only limited success before British forces drove the Italians out of Egypt and into western Libya by early 1941. In an effort to save his ally, German chancellor Adolf Hitler sent German forces to North Africa under the leadership of General Erwin Rommel, who promptly regained most of the territory the Italians had lost. The subsequent struggle between British general Bernard Montgomery's Eighth Army and the "Desert Fox's" Afrika Korps is well documented. The British drove the Germans back through Libya by January 1942 only to have Rommel, freshly reinforced, conquer much of British-controlled Egypt over the next five months. But with Montgomery's victory at El Alamein in November, Axis fortunes finally entered into a decline from which they could not recover.

The Allies initiated a pincer movement in November 1942 with Operation Torch, landing sixty-five thousand men at Oran, Algiers, and Casablanca on the western coast of North Africa. The Germans initially responded well to the Allied offensive, crushing previously untested American forces at Kasserine Pass in February 1943. However, insufficient resources and a dispute between Rommel and General Hans Jürgen von Arnim, commander of the Fifth Panzer Army, halted the German advance. Following the British attack on the Mareth Line in March and Rommel's departure from North Africa because of his declining health, von Arnim's remaining Armee Gruppe Afrika found itself hemmed into a small area around Tunis and Bizerte. Short of supplies and unable to retreat any further, von Arnim finally capitulated on May 12, 1943, surrendering all of Germany's forces in Tunisia.

Hans Jürgen von Arnim (Courtesy
of the Mississippi Armed Forces
Museum)

The end of Germany's campaign in North Africa began with the surrender of Lieutenant General Gustav von Vaerst, a recipient of the Knight's Cross
of the Iron Cross, one of the highest honors bestowed by the German military.[1] Von Vaerst had only been in command of the Fifth Panzer Army for
two months when he was forced to surrender his unit to American general
Omar Bradley on May 9, 1943. In the next three days, sixteen of von Vaerst's
fellow general officers would follow suit.

Later the same day, Brigadier General Fritz Krause, commander of the
334th Infantry Division, sent three members of his staff bearing a white flag
to the headquarters of the American First Armored Division and negoti-
ated his surrender.[2] Krause arrived at American headquarters only shortly
ahead of another of his colleagues, Major General Willibald Borowietz.
Borowietz had earned rapid promotion as commander of the Fifteenth
Panzer Division due to his superb leadership during the last days of the
German Tunisian campaign. He was promoted to brigadier general on January 1, 1943, and then major general a scant four months later, on the first
of May. Already a decorated soldier bearing the Knight's Cross, he received
the Oak Leaves on May 10, 1943, for having counterattacked and destroyed
two-thirds of a large British tank force in Tunisia with a depleted tank force

German prisoner-of-war generals at Trent Park, November 1943. *Front row, left to right:* Generalleutnant Friedrich von Broich, Generalleutnant Theodor Graf von Sponeck, Generalmajor Kurt Freiherr von Liebenstein, and Generalmajor Gerhard Bassenge. *Back row, left to right:* Oberst Hans Reimann, Generalmajor Georg Neuffer, Generalmajor Fritz Krause, Oberst Otto Köhnke, and Oberstleutnant Ernst Wolters. (German Federal Archive [Bundesarchiv], Bild 146-2005-0130 / Photographer: Unknown)

of his own. Yet, despite this earlier success, he now found himself a prisoner of war.[3]

Major General Karl Robert Max Bülowius quickly joined von Vaerst, Krause, and Borowietz as an Allied POW when he too surrendered his unit, the Manteuffel Division, on May 9, 1943. As the North African campaign continued to collapse, other German generals from Armee Gruppe Afrika arrived in Allied hands as well, including Major General Carl Peter Bernard Köchy. This Luftwaffe general and Afrika Korps air commander's previous experience in the German navy made him a particularly interesting and potentially valuable prisoner. The communications specialist and former commandant of Tobruk, Brigadier General Ernst Schnarrenberger, and the Austrian captain Paul Meixner, chief of staff for the German and Italian naval command in Tunisia, also found themselves prisoners of war of the British and Americans.[4]

Of the seventeen German generals who fell into Allied hands from the Tunisian surrender, Brigadier General Kurt Freiherr von Liebenstein and Major General Theodor Graf von Sponeck seemed to raise the greatest interest in both London and Washington. The well-heeled "Baron" von Liebenstein, with his prominent mustache and Knight's Cross, surrendered to the Allies in the final hours of the North African campaign. Earlier in his career he served as chief of staff for the renowned panzer leader Colonel General Heinz Guderian and commanded the 164th Light Division from December 1942 until he too was forced to surrender to the Allies on May 12, 1943.[5]

"Count" von Sponeck, whose uniform was also adorned with a Knight's Cross, had assumed command of the 90th Light Africa Division in September 1942. He "performed brilliantly" in the German retreat, fighting "nearly 2,000 miles from Egypt to Enfidaville." On May 12, 1943, after being informed that he must surrender unconditionally, von Sponeck first replied that his men would fight to the last bullet. Given time to further contemplate his alternatives, however, von Sponeck surrendered to the British Eighth Army's New Zealand Division. He later explained, "Most of my tanks were immobile through lack of fuel and our air support was negligible. I held out for 48 hours, but by then, we had received such a terrific battering, that I thought 'Hitler or no Hitler,' I will surrender. There's no sense in prolonging this needless slaughter."[6]

By contrast, British and American authorities would later take a dimmer view of Generals Heinrich-Hermann von Hülsen and Gotthard Frantz. Von Hülsen assumed command of the 21st Panzer Division near the end of April 1943 and received a promotion to brigadier general only a few days later on the first of May. Thus he was forced to surrender after having been in command of the 21st Panzer for less than two weeks. Likewise, Gotthard Frantz had recently been promoted to major general at the time of his surrender in May 1943. Frantz, however, had commanded the 19th Flak Division for six months before its surrender on May 13, 1943.[7]

The biggest catch and the senior officer among the generals captured in North Africa was Colonel General Hans Jürgen von Arnim. At the time of his surrender, he was one of the most prominent German prisoners of war in Allied hands. Von Arnim, descended from a long line of Prussian military officers, was a highly decorated veteran of both fronts in the First World War. In spite of having no previous experience with armor, he was given command of the 17th Panzer Division in autumn 1940 and distinguished himself on the Eastern Front. Field Marshal Ernst Busch praised von Arnim's "strong relationship with the troops" and his ability to remain "unruffled and strong-nerved . . . in the most difficult situations." He too was awarded the Knight's Cross in September 1941 and promoted to full general a little more than a year later. Upon awarding von Arnim command of the Fifth Panzer Army in North Africa, Hitler promised the general that he would receive all the supplies necessary for his operations in the desert, a promise soon to be broken and one that von Arnim would not forget.[8]

Despite von Arnim's earlier success in Russia, the North African campaign revealed the limits of his command skills. Indeed, historian Correlli Barnett characterizes von Arnim as an "excellent tactician" who was responsible for a number of "important local victories" but an overly conservative officer who "had been promoted above his ceiling." Part of the problem was the aristocratic von Arnim's relationship with Erwin Rommel. Rommel intended to use their combined forces in an offensive strategy against the Allies in the spring of 1943. Von Arnim, who envied the success and notoriety of the Desert Fox while disdaining his middle-class background, refused to cooperate. Complicating matters, Berlin had established no clear chain of command before von Arnim arrived in North Africa. Consequently, on the third day of the generals' coordinated attack in February 1943, von Arnim withheld parts of the Tenth and Twenty-First Panzer Divisions instead of following a prearranged plan. Despite Rommel's pleas to the German military command and its subsequent reprimand of von Arnim, the Prussian would not release all the tanks necessary for the operation and Rommel's offensive had to be aborted. Von Arnim's subsequent "ill-conceived and unsuccessful" Operation Ox Head resulted in heavy losses and only served to further delay Rommel's attack against the British. Eventually, having been stymied by both von Arnim and the British Army, Rommel departed North Africa on March 9, 1943, exhausted and in poor health.[9]

This left von Arnim, Rommel's replacement, in command of Armee Gruppe Afrika, which was outnumbered and lacking the necessary provisions to face the Allies—Hitler's promises notwithstanding. Von Arnim notified Berlin that he would require 140,000 tons of supplies per month to mount a successful defense against the Allies in North Africa. In January 1943 von Arnim had received approximately 46,000 tons of supplies, considerably less than he had expected. This figure dropped even further, to about 33,000 tons the following month, owing to Allied bombing of Axis supply ships in the Mediterranean and Hitler's focus on the Eastern Front. When Berlin criticized von Arnim for "squinting over [his] shoulder," referring to the general's conservative retreat in Tunisia, von Arnim bitterly replied that he was "squinting at the horizon" for ships that never arrived.[10]

After the Allies launched their final offensive on May 6, Hitler sent word that von Arnim's forces were to fight to the last man. The general chose to interpret this directive as requiring them to fight to the last bullet or, more specifically, the last tank shell. Thus, with the supply of tank shells exhausted on May 12, 1943, von Arnim destroyed what was left of his tanks and guns and surrendered. For the official ceremony, von Arnim donned his finest uniform and submitted his pistol and knife—although grudgingly and in French, despite his proficiency in English—to the British. He packed his remaining personal items, delivered a brief speech to his subordinate officers, and concluded by shaking each of their hands and exchanging salutes. He was then escorted through long lines of his devoted men chanting "Von Arnim! Von Arnim! Von Arnim!"[11]

The British initially received von Arnim with a great deal more cordiality than did the Americans. In fact, von Arnim's surrender serves as an interesting comparison of the two Allied nations' initially differing attitudes toward their captive German generals. American general Dwight Eisenhower broke with customary protocol and refused to meet von Arnim or accept his sword in surrender, citing Germany's wartime atrocities and apparent unwillingness to resist the leadership of a man like Adolf Hitler. By contrast, British field marshal Harold Alexander hosted von Arnim in his tent and later expressed regret that he had not been "more chivalrous" and complimentary of the German general's forces.[12]

Following his meeting with Alexander, von Arnim and his subordinate generals remained in temporary camps in North Africa for three days awaiting their transportation to England. Due to the Anglo-American arrangement regarding the German general officers, the British first took custody of all of these senior prisoners of war. Before departing North Africa, the generals enjoyed a three-hour excursion through a valley famous for its wildlife and a tea party at the residence of an anonymous English lady. General von Sponeck later recalled how much the generals appreciated these friendly gestures.[13]

The British began transferring the generals from North Africa to north London on May 15, 1943. While en route, they passed through Gibraltar, where the military governor, Lieutenant General Frank Macfarlane, accommodated von Arnim in the governor's palace. The other generals stayed in rooms prepared for them in the local military hospital. The following day von Arnim proceeded to England alone, with his fellow officers scheduled

Generaloberst (Colonel General) Hans Jürgen von Arnim (*far left*) arrives at Hendon Airport south of London to begin his stay as a British prisoner of war, May 16, 1943. He is accompanied by Oberstleutnant V. Glasow and General der Panzertruppe Hans Cramer. (German Federal Archive [Bundesarchiv], Bild 146-2005-0132 / Photographer: Unknown)

to follow within a few days. He arrived on May 16, a day when Britain happened to be celebrating the Allied victory in Tunisia by ringing church bells all over England, Scotland, and Northern Ireland. It must have added insult to von Arnim's injury to be driven from Hendon Airport south of London to Trent Park in the north part of the city to the sound of a national celebration honoring his defeat.[14]

Once in England, the British interned the German generals at Camp No. 11, located at Trent Park, a private estate in the north London suburb of Cockfosters. British authorities organized Camp No. 11 as part of the Combined Services Detailed Interrogation Centre, the agency charged with the interrogation of important prisoners of war. Considering the number of potentially valuable German and Italian prisoners, CSDIC commandeered several splendid homes, including Wilton Park and Latimer House. The British hoped these stately accommodations would alleviate some of the prisoners' anxiety and coax them into cooperating. German general officers sometimes temporarily transited through Wilton Park, but Trent Park remained the generals' designated residence throughout the war.[15]

The Trent Park estate, a remnant of the once-vast Enfield Chase royal hunting grounds, featured a stately mansion dating to the end of the eighteenth century. Numerous renovations and additions over the years had enlarged the mansion and the estate, culminating in the luxurious touches added by Philip Sassoon, the owner for almost three decades before his death in 1939. Sassoon constructed a terrace and a swimming pool and located Renaissance statues around the grounds to complement the existing airfield and nine-hole golf course. The palatial grounds had hosted the likes of Winston Churchill, George Bernard Shaw, Charlie Chaplin, Lawrence of Arabia, numerous members of the English royal family, and the king and queen of Belgium, as well as once serving as a honeymoon retreat for the Duke and Duchess of Kent.[16]

The generals, fresh from Tunisia, joined distinguished company upon their arrival in England. Lieutenant General Ludwig Crüwell had been in British custody since May 1942, when his plane was shot down over the Italian lines in North Africa. Before his capture, Crüwell had earned a reputation as an excellent tactical commander. He first led the Eleventh Panzer Division in Yugoslavia, where he was credited with the capture of Belgrade in April 1941. For this he was awarded the Knight's Cross and later became the first divisional commander to be awarded the additional Oak Leaves on September 1, 1941, for his command of the Eleventh Panzer on the Russian Front. This distinction elevated Crüwell, along with his colleague General Borowietz, into elite company. These men were two of fewer than nine hundred recipients of the Knight's Cross with Oak Leaves during the entire war.[17]

After a brief respite on the continent in the spring of 1942, Crüwell returned to North Africa in May and assumed responsibility for a combined German and Italian force.[18] In a meeting with Hitler in 1942, Crüwell expressed concern about the condition and morale of his Italian forces in North Africa. Curiously, his apprehension about the Italian contingent would be his undoing. With his new position came the responsibility to monitor the Italian Front. He arranged to be flown in a Fieseler Storch reconnaissance plane over the Italian lines on May 29, 1942, with soldiers on the ground charged with lighting flares to indicate the front's location. In a bizarre turn of events, the officer in charge of lighting the flares was called to the telephone moments before Crüwell's plane flew over, and the flares were never lit. By the time Crüwell figured out that he had overflown his intended target, British

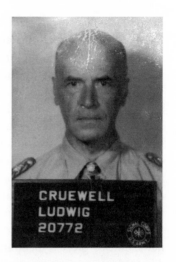

General der Panzertruppe Ludwig Crüwell
(Courtesy of the Mississippi Armed Forces
Museum)

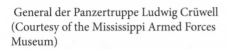

antiaircraft shells sent his plane into a crash landing. Miraculously, the Storch held together well enough for the general to emerge relatively unscathed, although now a British prisoner of war. His capture was a substantial loss to Rommel's effort in North Africa.[19]

Crüwell's British captors first housed him near Cairo in a single room with a balcony, but they transferred him to Trent Park in early September 1942. A few weeks after his arrival, Crüwell informed a Swedish camp inspector that he did not have the slightest grounds for complaint with his treatment by the British. The inspector noted that Trent Park offered the general a "spacious cottage" situated on extensive grounds and adorned with beautiful trees and a "well-kept park." He also complimented the large, comfortable, well-furnished bedroom, bathroom, living room, and dining room and praised British willingness to allow the general two-hour, daily walks around the estate and occasional sightseeing trips outside the camp. The inspector was most impressed, however, with the level of respect with which the British guard detail treated the distinguished prisoner.[20]

Also a "guest" of the British in May 1943 was General Ritter von Thoma, who had been captured in North Africa two months after Crüwell's arrival at Trent Park. General Montgomery, the British victor at El Alamein, had invited von Thoma to dine with him after the opposing general's capture. The two discussed their moves of the preceding battle over dinner and von Thoma later graciously thanked Montgomery for the chivalry that the British general had displayed. He even invited Montgomery to join him on his estate in Germany following the conclusion of the war. Upon learning of this, the

British press heavily criticized Montgomery for having been too cordial with the enemy. But Prime Minister Winston Churchill stemmed the controversy with a snide remark to the British House of Commons: "Poor von Thoma," he said, "I too have dined with Montgomery."[21]

The primary function of CSDIC at Trent Park was, of course, gathering information, and this it did with proficiency. The Cockfosters estate allowed the British government to house its German generals in rather grand surroundings, albeit surroundings that had been enhanced to allow British officers to glean important information from the prisoners. The generals' rooms were bugged, with microphones in the light fixtures. These listening devices all connected to a central "switchboard" where the British eavesdroppers at Camp No. 11, nicknamed Mother by the staff, surreptitiously listened to conversations among their guests. Von Thoma and Crüwell, hungry for news, quickly greeted incoming POWs to discuss the latest battles and war developments. Consequently, both were of "considerable value to the British." Crüwell's conversations with U-boat commander Wolfgang Römer in late 1942, for instance, provided the British with valuable information about German submarine tactics.[22]

Von Thoma and Crüwell had also previously been interrogated at the London District Cage, a somewhat notorious British military intelligence interrogation center in Kensington Palace Gardens. Here the two generals, during a "bugged" conversation, discussed their surprise at seeing most of London still standing. One explained to the other about the German testing of unmanned flying machines that could inflict very heavy damage. This admission prompted an investigation by British intelligence that eventually uncovered the existence of the German research program developing the deadly V-1 and V-2 rockets.[23]

These two were far from the only generals to provide the British with valuable information about German leaders and German military organization or, later, with interesting divulgences about war crimes or the generals' views on the German resistance. In addition to simple eavesdropping, the British obtained such information in part because of their ingenious techniques to loosen the prisoners' tongues. The most interesting of these was Lord Aberfeldy. Lord Aberfeldy's real name was Ian Munroe, and he was, in reality, an agent of MI19, the British intelligence division responsible for enemy prisoners of war. Aberfeldy lived at Trent Park with the prisoners, ostensibly as an interpreter. He acted the part of a British officer and aristocrat who took the generals not only on long walks around the Cockfosters estate but also occasionally on dining or shopping trips into London. He also ran errands for them, making regular trips into the city to purchase items for the generals that they could not obtain at the camp canteen. Along the way, Munroe attempted to win the generals' trust and maneuver them into conversations that could provide information of value to British intelligence.[24]

Aberfeldy's efforts among the prisoners facilitated Mother's work behind the scenes. German and Austrian refugees manned Mother's eavesdropping equipment and subsequently translated the German text of the generals' recorded conversations into English for dissemination.[25] These agents monitored daily conversations from the time of Crüwell's arrival in 1942 until the end of the war in Europe in May 1945. During this time, CSDIC routinely circulated reports on information received from the generals to the intelligence departments of the three branches of the British military and, at times, even to U.S. military intelligence as well.

With playing cards, board games, table tennis and billiards, or painting and reading as their only distractions, the generals at Trent Park had a great deal of time for conversation. CSDIC operatives learned the generals' feelings on an array of topics, including the reasons for the failed German offensive in North Africa, the current state of the war, and the generals' respective views of the Allies, Hitler, and the German High Command. Many of the comments recorded during their first weeks at Trent Park consisted of the generals' attempts to justify their recent surrender, mock their Italian allies, or disparage the Allied victors.[26]

Despite these divulgences and the more revealing ones that followed over the course of the next two years, it is difficult not to conclude that the generals suspected their conversations were being monitored by British intelligence. Berlin had previously issued strict rules of conduct for German prisoners of war in British hands that specifically mentioned the possibility of hidden microphones and the use of stool pigeons like Lord Aberfeldy.[27] But if the generals, in fact, suspected that Mother was listening, this raises interesting questions about what their comments were intended to achieve. Complaints about insufficient supplies and defiant criticisms of the character and fighting ability of both the British and American armies sound a lot like sour grapes, intended to inform their enemy that if only the Germans had had sufficient supplies they would have bested the "astonishingly slow" Allied army. And it is unlikely that the general officers cared whether Mussolini found out about their low opinion of Italian soldiers.

Yet what is puzzling is that, once ensconced in the stately Trent Park mansion, the generals offered some detailed information about the ongoing German offensive against the Soviet Union. If they suspected they were being recorded, as it seems quite likely they did, the generals must certainly have realized that statements about German commanding officers and the German order of battle, logistics, and their Romanian, Bulgarian, and Hungarian allies could easily have been transmitted to the Allied army general staff. Most curiously, however, the prisoners also offered some fairly revealing comments about Adolf Hitler and certain members of the German High Command.

For example, General Krause insinuated that Hitler would be "obstinate" and "stupid" not to consider uniting with either the British and Americans against the Russians or vice versa, even though this would mean "modifying his demands considerably." Von Arnim referred to the German failure in North Africa as "this whole catastrophe" that occurred "because no one really dared to say, 'It just won't work.'" The generals intimated that Hitler and the German High Command shifted the responsibility for any failure entirely to the troops in the field, even when they had not been properly supplied. The officers contended that battlefield commanders felt they had no choice but to simply follow the orders they received from higher authorities without question because disagreeing with the Führer was not tolerated. They cited the example of General Franz Halder, chief of the German General Staff, who had openly disagreed with Hitler and subsequently been removed from his post.[28] Generals von Arnim and Bülowius also made derogatory remarks about the Hitler Youth, observing how it made them sick to see their own children marching with the "H.J.s" and that they were beginning to "realize the stupidity of it."[29]

Assuming the generals knew their British captors monitored all of their conversations, their comments insisting that Hitler and the Wehrmacht High Command made all of the important decisions and that none of the general officers were allowed to question them suggests that the origins of the myth of the clean Wehrmacht began at Trent Park. Much like their fellow German general officers who provided the U.S. Army Historical Division with accounts of the war after its conclusion in 1945, the generals at Camp No. 11 attempted to absolve themselves of any responsibility for their part in the war. Perhaps following their surrender in North Africa, coming on the heels of the capitulation of von Paulus's Sixth Army at Stalingrad a few months earlier, the prisoners at Camp No. 11 determined that the war was lost. Perhaps the generals believed that by offering small amounts of useful intelligence about the Eastern Front, they could convince British eavesdroppers to trust the veracity of the information they supplied them, especially their criticisms of Hitler and their insinuation that the Führer bore sole responsibility for the war. Instances also abounded where prisoners who refused to provide British interrogators with information promptly returned to their rooms and told their fellow officers exactly what information they had withheld.[30] Perhaps this too was designed to inspire British trust in the information that was spoken directly into Mother's microphones.

Yet some questions remain. As new faces emerged at Trent Park in the months following the successful Allied invasion of France, the generals at Trent Park turned their conversations to discussions of war crimes in which a few of them admitted to questionable, even criminal behavior. It seems puzzling that some of the prisoners would make such admissions knowing they were speaking into British microphones and that their remarks would be sent to British and American military authorities. Furthermore, in his memoirs, written some time after the war, von Sponeck claimed that the generals at Trent Park did not suspect Lord Aberfeldy. Von Sponeck described the "special advantage" of having an English officer who was fluent in German and who obliged the generals' special requests on his frequent shopping trips to London. Aberfeldy earned the generals' trust, according to von Sponeck, and they did not learn of his real identity until some years after the war.[31]

Again, perhaps the admissions of war crimes and even von Sponeck's comments in his memoirs were designed to further a political agenda, which may have included feigned ignorance of Aberfeldy's identity to justify having shared information with him. It may also be that, given a certain amount of time in captivity, the generals had grown comfortable at Trent Park and ceased to care about the presence of microphones in their quarters. Either way, comfortable that the information the generals provided was of some value, CSDIC operatives continued their work unabated.

Indeed, CSDIC seemed to particularly value the generals' evaluations of various German military leaders. One report lauded the assessments the generals had provided the British of men like Field Marshal Albert Kesselring, Germany's commander in chief south; Field Marshal Erwin Rommel; Reichsmarschall Hermann Göring, commander in chief of the Luftwaffe; and his second in command, Deputy Reich Commissioner for Aviation Erhard Milch, among others.[32] Unfortunately, the report did not state exactly what the British learned about these German leaders or how the information was used.

Much of this activity had been conducted with a small, unchanging population of prisoners beginning in June 1943 and continuing for almost a year. Generals von Vaerst, Borowietz, Bülowius, and Köchy departed for the United States on June 1, 1943, and four more German generals from North Africa took their place at Trent Park. These four generals, Schnarrenberger, von

Liebenstein, von Sponeck, and Friedrich von Broich, had journeyed from Gibraltar to London aboard the British battleship HMS *Nelson* and had been temporarily interned a few miles away at Wilton Park until space could be made available for them at Camp No. 11. Their arrival brought Trent Park's total population of German prisoner-of-war generals to thirteen, eight of whom would also eventually be transferred to American custody.[33]

Aside from attempting to glean operational and tactical intelligence from the general officer prisoners, the British also took a particular interest in the prisoners' political orientations. For example, shortly after the prisoners arrived at Trent Park, they began to divide themselves into cliques that CSDIC labeled "anti-Nazi" and "pro-Nazi." The two cliques centered around the two men who had been in camp the longest, Ritter von Thoma and Ludwig Crüwell. British intelligence labeled von Thoma's group, which included generals von Sponeck, Hans Cramer, Gerhard Bassenge, Georg Neuffer, von Liebenstein, and von Broich, as "Anti-Nazi and Defeatist." Von Thoma openly espoused "violent anti-Nazi views" and took great pains to antagonize his pro-Nazi opponents by verbally chastising them as well as circulating German-language, anti-Nazi literature that had been supplied to him by British camp authorities.[34]

The British labeled Ludwig Crüwell's clique, politically opposite from von Thoma, "Anti-Defeatist" and pro-Nazi. In addition to Crüwell, this group included generals Frantz and von Hülsen. Trent Park authorities found these three to be a nuisance, noting that they were "always moaning and demanding the impossible. They seem to consider this a sanatorium for tired German generals rather than as a [prisoner-of-war] camp. They even go out of their way to complain."[35]

Not surprisingly, British intelligence at Trent Park viewed the members of von Thoma's anti-Nazi clique in a significantly more favorable light. A CSDIC report from June 1943 noted, "The defeatist section comprises all those who are most intelligent, most traveled and who have [the] most culture. They never complain about conditions in the camp and continue to tell us how grateful they are for the excellent treatment which is meted out to them here."[36] These types of statements illustrate as much about the British observers as they do about the German prisoners and reveal a common Allied misperception. Throughout the war, British and American officials alike often confused prisoner cooperativeness with anti-Nazi views and vice versa. Consequently, Trent Park officers would certainly have seen von Thoma's clique as more intelligent, cultured, and politically savvy simply because they showed gratitude and did not complain.

Also indicative of British perceptions are the revealing character studies of each of the generals compiled by CSDIC officers at Trent Park in June and July 1943. These evaluations again demonstrate some Allied misperceptions and exaggerations. For instance, the "pro-Nazi" generals are largely portrayed as buffoons or insidious agitators, while the members of the "anti-Nazi" clique appear as intelligent, educated men of culture.

Significantly, these British evaluations of the early general officer prisoners compiled in 1943 provided some of the foundation for the American relationship with the Wehrmacht general officers who were later sent to the United States and, consequently, for some Allied decisions made about the generals in the postwar era. Indeed, until May 1945, the majority of the general officer prisoners sent to the United States had first been assessed by CSDIC at Trent Park. And the group of senior officers who were the focus of these character studies would be the next parcel of general officer POWs delivered to the Americans, even though it took almost a year before this occurred. Without doubt, these initial British judgments influenced American perceptions of the generals at least to some degree, especially considering that the Americans expended no time or resources evaluating these men for themselves. It is unlikely to have been pure coincidence that two of the five generals later chosen by American officials for reeducation and groomed to be potential leaders for postwar Germany, von Sponeck and von Liebenstein, were two British favorites from the beginning. This, in turn, raises questions about how much von Sponeck's and von Liebenstein's "anti-Nazism"—and that of other generals like them—was calculated to achieve just such an end.

Noteworthy in evaluating these British character studies are the German Army evaluations of specific prisoners' political orientations, conducted prior to their capture. German historian Sönke Neitzel discounts these assessments as "not particularly useful," citing a criticism by Major General Rudolf Schmundt, head of the German Army High Command Personnel Office in 1943 about the overuse of vague expressions like "he stands on National Socialist ground." Undoubtedly, evaluations like that of General Schnarrenberger as possessing a "positive attitude toward National Socialism" fall into this useless category. However, a few comments may be more illustrative of the difficulty of adequately assessing the generals' real political views. For example, General von Liebenstein, whom both the British and Americans came to greatly admire, had been described by his German superiors in October 1942 as an officer who "epitomizes the greater ideals of National Socialism" and "communicates this body of thought to others."[37]

Perhaps von Liebenstein's superior officer simply chose to embellish in an effort to win the baron favor with the German High Command. Perhaps von Liebenstein intentionally chose to communicate the greater ideals of National Socialism to his superiors in an effort to gain promotion. It is also not inconceivable that von Liebenstein may have seen the handwriting on the wall, so to speak, by 1943 and have begun to change his political stripes. Regardless, by the 1950s von Liebenstein must have come to epitomize the greater ideals of representative democracy because he obtained a position as major general in the Bundeswehr with the blessings of the U.S. government.

Despite this inability to adequately determine the prisoners' political orientations, the British took a keen interest in the generals' views of the postwar balance of power. A report prepared by the British officers at Trent Park in January 1944 stated the importance of the generals' comments in shaping British postwar policy. In some ways, British intelligence officers admired the German generals. They remarked on the Germans' "strong sense of duty," praised them as "good leaders of men with a feeling of responsibility for the welfare of those under their command," and acknowledged their widespread condemnation of Nazi brutality, sincere or otherwise. Yet CSDIC cautioned that despite their "superficial quarrels and personal animosities" the generals were united in one fundamental belief: "the greatness of the German Reich." What made the generals potentially dangerous, as the British saw it, was their ability to inspire this belief in generations of Germans to come. British intelligence recognized that the German officer corps as a whole had for generations been "the most influential body of men in Germany, representing one of the few cohesive traditions of leadership in the country." The generals' influential status, coupled with their grandiose aims, made it imperative that something be done to prevent yet another reemergence of German militarism like that which had occurred after the First World War. The British report of January 1944 placed the generals at the forefront of British postwar concerns by declaring that it was "impossible to read this series of conversations without feeling that the question of how to handle these men in such a way as to prevent them from leading yet another attempt at world domination [was] one of the most important of those to be faced after the war."[38]

Clearly, the British had no intention of allowing the general officers to play substantial roles in the postwar reconstruction of Germany. Because of the long-term observations of the German generals in their custody, the British realized as early as January 1944 that allowing any of these men to obtain positions of leadership, or allowing Germany to extricate itself from the war without an unconditional surrender, was out of the question. CSDIC observed that "however defeatist the talk of the prisoners may appear, how-

A group picture of the German generals at Trent Park, November 1943. *Note:* Although a few of the generals are recognizable, the Bundesarchiv caption for this photo does not identify specific individuals. (German Federal Archive [Bundesarchiv], Bild 146-2005-0133 / Photographer: Unknown)

ever hopeless about the outcome of the war and angry and even ashamed at the actions of the Nazis they may be, [the generals] are still thinking of the next war and how to prepare for it." In this regard, British intelligence placed von Arnim and von Thoma, who seemingly represented opposite ends of the political spectrum, in the same category. Both hoped that Germany could achieve a stalemate or armistice arrangement, similar to the one that had ended the First World War, as opposed to being forced into unconditional surrender and foreign occupation. This would allow Germany to maintain some kind of foundation upon which to rebuild.[39]

Their observations of the generals certainly recognized what the British saw as the senior officers' pragmatism. Both von Arnim and von Thoma, as well as most of their fellow generals, founded their concerns about preserving Germany's influential political position on their fear of the Soviet Union. The British report observed that discussions of the Russian threat were the "most persistent theme of the [generals'] conversations." The German generals at Camp No. 11 feared, somewhat presciently, that if the Allies agreed to allow the Soviets to establish control over part of Germany the Russians would "never let go." The German generals foresaw the coming Cold War struggle between communist Russia and Western capitalism and believed that Germany's greatest chance of retaining its influential position in the world, and the only hope of survival for the German officer class, was to support the West.[40]

British intelligence clearly realized that most of the German prisoner-of-war generals based their political views more in pragmatic concerns than in ideological adherence. By the time analysts compiled the report in January 1944, the British observed that there seemed to be "an almost unanimous anti-Nazi feeling among the generals." But they believed that this anti-Nazism sprang from wartime frustration, not from any real ideological opposition. As with von Arnim, the animosity most of the generals felt for Hitler and the Nazis could be attributed solely to the regime's handling of the war and, consequently, Germany's impending defeat. General von Broich summed up the feelings of most of the generals in, once again, placing the blame squarely on Hitler and the Nazis. He stated that by the spring of 1942 the German Army "realized that Germany could not win and should endeavor to negotiate, but [Hitler] and the Party would not hear of it."[41]

By early 1944, the German general officers in British custody already harbored thoughts of allying themselves in some capacity with the Western Allies. Given the opportunity, the German officers of course preferred rebuilding the Fatherland and reoccupying a prominent position on the global stage. Yet, if faced with the prospect of Soviet domination at the end of the war, the "Nazi" generals indicated that they were already prepared to throw in their lot with the British and Americans well over a year before the war in Europe had ended.

American military authorities, who would soon inherit a significant number of these general officer prisoners, might have done well to consult more closely with their British allies in this regard. By eavesdropping on the generals at Trent Park, the British realized the importance of combating any resurgent postwar German militarism by January 1944. American authorities would struggle to reach a similar conclusion over a year later and only after repeating a great deal of the same work the British had already completed.

For the British, detailed observation of the prisoners at Camp No. 11 became more difficult as their numbers grew following the Allied invasion of northwest France in June 1944. An influx of new prisoners in the months following D-Day and continuing throughout the remainder of the war necessitated the departure of many of the existing internees, who, by this point, had been in British custody for over a year. On D-Day, ten German generals resided at Trent Park. By the end of 1944, the camp had become home to twenty-six more generals, five admirals, and twenty-one of their aides-de-camp.[42] Eventually, CSDIC had more occupants than it could accommodate at Trent Park, and a second camp, Grizedale Hall, was established a short distance away.

Perhaps not surprisingly, the British noted a significant difference between their first group of general officer prisoners, the so-called *Afrikaner*—those captured in North Africa—and the *Französen*—the officers taken in Western Europe after D-Day. The majority of the *Afrikaner* Wehrmacht generals had long and distinguished careers in the German military prior to the rise of the Nazi regime. Moreover, the Allies captured them at a time when German fortunes had not yet sunk to an abysmal level. By contrast, Hitler had rapidly promoted some of the *Französen* generals out of necessity, and many of these men had less impressive credentials. Indeed, CSDIC operatives observed that "those recently captured are not such good types, physically or mentally, and have by no means the same degree of culture. None of them is what has become known as the German officer type."[43]

However, British operatives continued eavesdropping on their guests, despite, or perhaps because of, the changing faces at Trent Park. Replacing many of the original occupants of Trent Park were senior officers captured

Generalmajor Robert Sattler (Courtesy of the Mississippi Armed Forces Museum)

at Cherbourg in the early days of the Allied invasion. The first of this new crop of senior German officers was Rear Admiral Walter Hennecke, the commander of German naval forces in Normandy, and Brigadier General Robert Sattler, the second in command at Fortress Cherbourg.[44] A sense of impending German defeat seemed to accompany these *Französen* generals to Trent Park. British camp personnel observed how the Allied invasion weighed heavily on their prisoners of war and "led to considerable pessimistic talk during these days." This defeatist attitude became characteristic of the prisoners, who largely seemed to believe by the fall of 1944 that Germany's war had been lost.[45]

The flood of senior officers who poured into Trent Park in the late summer and fall of 1944 only added to the prisoners' growing malaise. On August 8, the American First Army captured Major General Karl Spang, commanding officer of the 266th Infantry Division, near Brest. His capture marked the first of a flurry of general officers taken prisoner during August and September as the Allies advanced east from the Normandy coast into the French interior. One week later, Brigadier General Ludwig Bieringer surrendered. Bieringer had spent most of his career in the supply branch of the German Army. By mid-1944, he was serving as field commander of the military administration headquarters at Draguignan in southern France, about twenty miles from the Mediterranean coast. After receiving word of the approach of French partisans early on the morning of August 15, Bieringer and his staff barricaded themselves into the headquarters villa. They held off the resistance forces until the following day. But, fearing that the French were "out for blood," Bieringer quickly abandoned his original order to fight to the last bullet and instructed a member of his staff to immediately surrender at the first sight of American troops.[46]

On the same day, the French partisans had also driven Lieutenant General Ferdinand Neuling, commander of the Sixty-Second Reserve Corps, out of Draguignan into the hills north of town. American airborne troops surrounded Neuling's headquarters early on August 17 and cut off all communications to his subordinate units. At eight in the morning, as a show of good faith to his American captors, General Bieringer arrived in the company of an American officer, informed Neuling of his own surrender the previous day, and advised the latter to follow suit. Neuling "wildly proclaimed his intention to hold out and then kill himself with his last bullet." Even after American artillery shelled his position, he still refused to capitulate. But by the next morning, with all of his ammunition exhausted and an American tank advancing on the house in which he was holed up, Neuling finally relented. "I

Generalleutnant Curt Badinski
(Courtesy of the Mississippi Armed
Forces Museum)

knew that my position was hopeless," he explained to his American captors, "but I had orders to hold all positions to the last cartridge. One must do one's duty. Besides, a general who does not obey such orders nowadays is shot out of hand, so I simply had to hold on until all my ammunition was gone."[47]

During the next three days, three more senior Wehrmacht officers, Brigadier General Hans Schuberth and Major Generals Curt Badinski and Erwin Menny, joined Neuling and Bieringer as Allied prisoners of war. Schuberth commanded Feldkommandatur (field command) 792 in southern France and surrendered in Digne, about an hour's drive north of Draguignan. Badinski commanded the 276th Infantry Division holding a small sector of northwest France, and Erwin Menny, in command of the 84th Infantry Division, was captured at Magny in northwest France on August 21, 1944.[48]

Notably, Menny was one of the few residents of Camp No. 11 who had had direct contact with General Seydlitz and the Free Germany Movement in Russia. At one point during his service on the Eastern Front, Soviet forces encircled Menny's unit. Captured German soldiers arrived under a flag of truce and delivered a handwritten letter from General Seydlitz. The letter read, "Dear Menny, you must realize yourself that it's no use. You know the Russians are already in your rear; tomorrow you'll be cut off and no one from your 'division' will escape. Surrender. The whole war is senseless and should be brought to an end as soon as possible to enable us to spare a great number of people's lives." Perhaps because of his fear of the Russians, Menny was unfazed by Seydlitz's pleas for surrender. Amazingly, Menny escaped, but he was the only person from his division who did.[49]

The capture of Bieringer, Neuling, Schuberth, Badinski, and Menny highlighted a noteworthy change in Allied procedure regarding high-ranking Wehrmacht officers. After D-Day, CSDIC in England no longer took the primary role in interrogating captured general officers as it had done in the past. American and British intelligence now cooperated on the effort through a joint operation in France labeled "CSDIC West." Important military intelligence could be immediately gleaned from these prisoners while they were still at the front where the information was most needed. While Mother continued listening to the generals' conversations at Trent Park, prisoners now arrived there having already been interrogated by combined Allied personnel. Moreover, as part of the new Allied POW procedures, Bieringer, Neuling, and Schuberth immediately departed for the United States, while Badinski and Menny joined their colleagues in England.[50]

At the time of the capture of Badinski and Menny in August 1944, the Allies had almost reached Paris. The commander of Allied forces, General Dwight D. Eisenhower, and his staff originally planned to skirt the city and continue their eastward advance, forcing the capital's German occupiers to continue providing food and fuel for its French residents. At the last minute, however, Eisenhower opted to retake Paris after all, both because of an uprising by French resistance forces within the city and because of the actions of the German military governor of Paris, General der Infanterie Dietrich von Choltitz.

General Wilhelm Burgdorf, the chief of personnel of the Oberkommando der Wehrmacht (OKW), had personally recommended von Choltitz to Hitler as the man best able to take command of Paris because he was "an officer who had never questioned an order no matter how harsh it was." As a lieutenant colonel in May 1940, von Choltitz had been responsible for the destruction of the Dutch city of Rotterdam. After seizing control of the city's essential bridges, he tried to encourage the city's military commander to surrender by sending Dutch civilians in to persuade him. When the commander could not be found, von Choltitz grew impatient and ordered a large-scale bombing attack. The Germans virtually obliterated the heart of the city, killing over seven hundred people and leaving almost eighty thousand civilians wounded, homeless, or both.[51]

Two years later, in July 1942, von Choltitz had taken the Russian city of Sevastopol with similar destructiveness. Afterward, he reputedly bragged about the humor he found in requiring Russian prisoners of war to load the cannons that were used to destroy their own homes. Even after German fortunes on the Russian Front turned against them in 1943, von Choltitz observed that it was his fate "to cover the retreat of our armies and to destroy the cities behind them." Subsequently, von Choltitz took part in the Battle of Kharkov and the Kursk Offensive as commanding officer of the Forty-Eighth Panzer Corps in 1943 and led the Eighty-Fourth Army Corps in France in 1944 before assuming command of the German occupation of Paris in early August 1944. He replaced Lieutenant General Hans Wilhelm Freiherr von Boineburg-Lengsfeld, who had been relieved of his command for refusing to destroy the Parisian bridges over the Seine River. Hitler was confident that he would not face this kind of insubordination from von Choltitz.[52]

Yet, upon taking command in the French capital, von Choltitz, the reputed "destroyer of cities," appears to have been transformed. He took command of Paris as the Allies were closing in and received orders from Hitler on August 14 to destroy all forty-five of the Seine River bridges as well as most of the city's industrial capacity and public utilities. Von Choltitz refused, for the practical reason that he and his fellow Germans, who were still occupying the city, required utility service as well. Three days later, on August 17, he again received orders to detonate the charges that had previously been set on the bridges and again he refused, contending that this action would make it impossible to maintain control of the Parisians. Hitler had also reportedly instructed von Choltitz to "stamp out without pity" any acts of rebellion or sabotage. On August 19 von Choltitz spurned this directive as well by aborting a planned attack against the French resistance movement that had initiated armed resistance to German control earlier in the day.[53]

Twice more von Choltitz's superiors ordered him to initiate the destruction of Paris and twice more the general refused or simply ignored the command. Von Choltitz even prodded the Swedish consul general, Raoul Nordling, to travel through the German lines outside Paris in hopes that the Swede would contact the Allied command and encourage them to liberate Paris before von Choltitz was forced to follow orders or risk Hitler's wrath.[54] Why would von Choltitz develop such reluctance to carry out the demolition of the French capital when he had so eagerly carried out Hitler's previous orders to destroy cities in Holland and Russia?

The general later claimed that he was "simply appalled" by the order to destroy Paris. He believed that the wanton destruction of one of the most beautiful cities in Europe lacked any military justification. Moreover, von Choltitz now suspected that Hitler was insane and that the Führer wanted von Choltitz to destroy the French capital "and then sit in its ashes and accept the consequences." It seems much more likely, however, that by mid-1944 von Choltitz must have seen the end of the war approaching and realized that the unnecessary destruction of Paris would win him no favor from the Western Allies. His fellow prisoners at Trent Park later summed up von Choltitz's political persuasion by noting that he had been "very much 'Third Reich'" earlier in the war but had "become something quite different in the meantime." He knew on "which side his bread [was] buttered." Likewise, British camp personnel found von Choltitz to be not only "a cinema-type German officer, fat, coarse, bemonocled and inflated with a tremendous sense of his own importance." More importantly, they also quickly realized that the general was "very much concerned with appearing in the most favorable light possible."[55]

In spite of von Choltitz's apparent change of heart, regardless of his motives, he nonetheless continued to defend Paris against the Allied advance. By late August, however, French resistance forces had completely taken over the city, according to von Choltitz, and "were even driving about in tanks in front of his hotel," and the Americans and French were on the outskirts of the city. Lacking the manpower and inclination to continue the struggle, and having satisfied his soldier's honor by putting up token resistance, von Choltitz surrendered to General Jacques Philippe Leclerc of the French Second Armored Division on August 25.[56]

Upon arriving at Camp No. 11 in late August 1944, the garrulous von Choltitz claimed that he had been a defeatist for a couple of years because he had "spent too much time at HQ" and, he explained sarcastically, "seen the masterly way in which difficult problems [were] solved there." The British did not find von Choltitz's contributions to be "of any tremendous value," although they did find his conversations with his fellow prisoners entertaining; he was apparently somewhat of a comedian. Notably, his descriptions of meetings with the German High Command showed "the incredible state of mind of Hitler" and gave the impression that Germany was now a "mad house."[57]

As the Allies advanced eastward following von Choltitz's surrender of Paris, they quickly captured dozens more Wehrmacht general officers, including Brigadier General Hans-Georg Schramm. Schramm served as field commander of German forces at Troyes, southeast of Paris, and was captured on August 26, the day after the fall of the French capital. Three days later,

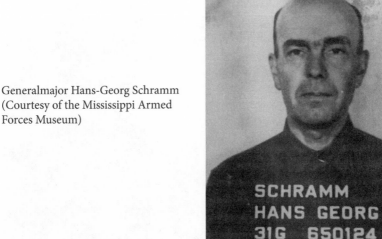

Generalmajor Hans-Georg Schramm
(Courtesy of the Mississippi Armed
Forces Museum)

Brigadier General Alfred Gutknecht, commander of motorized units on the Western Front, was ordered to bring important documents and report to his superiors in Soissons. While on the road from Rheims on August 29, he rounded a curve only to find himself in the middle of an American brigade. Despite his attempts to quickly turn his car around, he was captured and slightly wounded in the process. Gutknecht represented an important source of information about German motorized vehicles and the Wehrmacht's ability to replace and repair them. The papers in his possession included information about recent relocations of maintenance parks, tables detailing the location and capacity of available supply and repair depots, lists of the types of vehicles that could be repaired in particular depots, and the number of personnel available in each location.[58] Also on August 29, the American 36th Infantry Division captured Brigadier General Otto Richter, an engineering officer in command of the 198th Infantry Division in southern France. Richter, like his colleagues Bieringer, Neuling, and Schuberth, went directly to the United States, bypassing any British interrogation or eavesdropping at Trent Park.[59]

On the first of September 1944, Lieutenant General Erwin Vierow, military commander of northwest France and commanding general of the newly formed corps the Generalkommando z.b.V. Somme, fell into Allied hands.[60] Three days later, the British captured Brigadier General Christoph Graf zu

General der Infanterie Erwin Vierow
(Courtesy of the Mississippi Armed
Forces Museum)

Generalmajor Christoph Graf zu
Stolberg-Stolberg (Courtesy of the
Mississippi Armed Forces Museum)

Stolberg-Stolberg in Antwerp, where he served as military commander. Prior
to his appointment in Antwerp, Stolberg had commanded Special Employment Division Staff 136, responsible for battalions largely composed of Soviet
prisoners of war who had offered their services to Nazi Germany either out
of a strong conviction to fight communism or simply to escape a German
POW camp.[61]

At about the same time, the Allies also captured Brigadier General Hubertus von Aulock and Major Generals Rüdiger von Heyking and Paul Seyffardt. The Allies captured all three of these senior officers in the vicinity of
Brussels as they pushed eastward out of northern France.[62] CSDIC assumed
responsibility for both von Heyking and Seyffardt and sent them to Trent
Park. Von Aulock, on the other hand, was quickly transferred to the United
States. He visited Camp No. 11 for a few hours to see his brother, Andreas
von Aulock, the "Mad Colonel of St. Malo," who was a resident of Trent Park
at this time.[63] But General von Aulock did not remain at the camp and spent
only a few weeks in British custody before being transferred to the Americans by the end of September.[64]

The "egocentric" and opportunistic Brigadier General Detlef Bock von

Generalleutnant Paul Seyffardt
(Courtesy of the Mississippi Armed
Forces Museum)

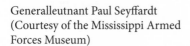

Wülfingen, military commander of Liege, and Rear Admiral Hans von Tresckow, German naval commander along the northwest coast of France, also surrendered in early September.[65] But the biggest prize for the Allies in the month of September was the capture of the fortress of Brest and its "fanatical defender," General der Fallschirmtruppe Bernhard-Hermann Ramcke. Called "Papa" by his men, Ramcke was one of the most decorated German officers captured by the British and Americans. Ramcke began his military career as a marine in the German Imperial Navy of the First World War. He finished the war as a second lieutenant, having earned the Iron Cross, both first and second classes, as well as the Prussian Military Service Cross for his bravery. After serving in the Reichswehr under the Weimar Republic and obtaining the rank of colonel, Ramcke volunteered for parachute training school in 1940 at the age of fifty-one. Completion of this training normally required six jumps in six days; Ramcke did all six in three days.[66]

In May 1941 Ramcke parachuted onto Crete with what he thought were five hundred paratroopers to restore order to an ongoing German invasion of the island. Upon landing, he discovered that he had only half the expected number of men and that the ship bringing most of the Mountain Division to support him had been sunk by the British Royal Navy. Displaying his usual ingenuity, Ramcke and his small force captured an airfield and used an abandoned British tank to clear the runway for German planes bringing reinforcements, munitions, and supplies. The Germans subsequently captured the island, including over seventeen thousand prisoners of war, on June 2, and in August Ramcke received the Knight's Cross for his role in the operation. Alarmingly, and perhaps displaying what would become Ramcke's customary brutality, the general condemned the treatment he believed his men had received at the hands of the Cretans and admitted taking revenge against the people in villages where mutilated German paratroopers were found. He believed this behavior was justified to maintain order among the Cretan civilian population.[67]

After a brief stint as a parachute instructor, Ramcke assumed command of the parachute brigade bearing his name in the spring of 1942. Berlin quickly sent the Ramcke Parachute Brigade to support Rommel in North Africa in July, and Ramcke only added to his reputation in this theater of the war as well. During the German retreat following the Battle of El Alamein, Ramcke's brigade was separated from Panzer Armee Afrika and forced to proceed on foot for several miles through hostile terrain. During this trek, Ramcke and his men happened upon a British tank supply column that included vehicles, fuel, water, and a large supply of food and cigarettes. Crawling to the vehicles under the cover of darkness, Ramcke's unit hijacked the entire column without firing a shot. One can only imagine the reaction that Ramcke must have received from Rommel and the rest of the German Army when he and his men proudly rolled up in British vehicles. For this bold move and for returning his men to safety, Ramcke received the Oak Leaves to his Knight's Cross on November 11, 1942.[68]

In the spring of 1943 Ramcke formed the Second Parachute Division and was promptly sent to Rome to oppose the Allied invasion of Italy. He then led this unit to the Russian Front and fought at Zhitomir and Kirovograd in the Ukraine in the winter of 1943–1944. Following the successful Allied landing at Normandy in early June 1944, the Americans needed the French port city of Brest, located on the tip of the Breton Peninsula, as a conduit for supplies for their men in western France. Consequently, Hitler sent Ramcke and thirty thousand men to shore up the city's defenses in mid-June.[69]

In the last week of August the Americans began an assault on the French port city that would last for over three weeks. During this time Ramcke and his chief of staff, Brigadier General Hans von der Mosel, who had been the commandant of the fortress of Brest before Ramcke's arrival, refused American demands to surrender. The two sides conducted fierce house-to-house fighting in the city streets before the Americans finally forced the Germans back into the fortress.[70]

Generalmajor Hans von der Mosel
(Courtesy of the Mississippi Armed
Forces Museum)

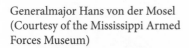

By September 13, American forces had surrounded the fortress and offered the Germans a chance to surrender "with honor," but the fanatical Ramcke steadfastly held out for another week. Finally, having exhausted all avenues for victory or escape, Ramcke chose to surrender rather than risk the lives of any more of his men. Remarkably, considering his dogged defense of the French fort, Ramcke seemed well prepared to be a prisoner of war when he emerged to officially surrender to American general Troy Middleton on September 19, 1944. As if expecting a luxurious vacation, the general arrived with "eight large, well-packed suitcases, a complete set of delicate china, an elaborate box of expensive fishing tackle together with four long rods, and a thoroughbred setter dog."[71]

In an interesting twist, on September 19 Ramcke became both the ninety-ninth recipient of the Swords and the twentieth of only twenty-seven recipients of the Diamonds to add to the Knight's Cross with Oak Leaves he had already earned. Hitler decorated Ramcke both for his bravery and for his "continuous tenacious struggle" to hold Brest Fortress. The Führer normally awarded the Diamonds personally but, considering Ramcke's situation at the time, ordered that they be parachuted into the fortress and awarded to Ramcke there.[72]

Upon arriving at Trent Park, Ramcke and four of his accompanying subordinates became the most vocal Nazi supporters that British officers had

Generalleutnant Erwin Rauch
(Courtesy of the Mississippi Armed
Forces Museum)

RAUCH
ERWIN
31 G 21300

seen since the departure of Ludwig Crüwell. Like their commander, Major General Erwin Rauch, Brigadier General Hans von der Mosel, Vice Admiral Alfred Schirmer, and Rear Admiral Otto Kähler had been captured following the surrender of Brest.[73] It quickly became obvious that the attitudes of these four subordinates reflected that of their commanding officer. The American officer who interrogated Ramcke in France following his surrender summed up the general as "an egotistical, conceited Nazi." The officer found the general to be "a firm believer in Hitler and greatly inclined towards the [Nazi] Party." Ramcke espoused the belief that Germany was "a clean, innocent nation greatly wronged by other nations" and that, following the war, Germany would "rise again in 10 to 30 years." He defiantly stated that he would return home and prepare his five sons "to revive and free Germany again." The British officers at Trent Park gained the same "deplorable impression of him as a man." They agreed that "if there [was] to be such a thing as a list of especially dangerous men to be kept under surveillance [after the war], General Ramcke ought to qualify as one of the very first candidates."[74] They would not realize how correct their impressions were until several years after the war had ended.

There seemed to be little doubt that Ramcke genuinely supported the Nazi regime. Aside from his political orientation, he also benefited from financial ties to Hitler and Goebbels. The propaganda minister ordered that each German mayor purchase a copy of Ramcke's book, *Vom Schiffsjungen zum Fallschirmjäger-General* (From cabin boy to paratroop general), for his city. The book had been published by Eher Publishing, the Nazi Party press that controlled the overwhelming majority of German publications, including the infamous daily party newspaper, *Völkischer Beobachter*. When four hundred thousand copies of the book sold, both Ramcke, who earned two reichsmarks per sale, and Hitler, who owned a significant interest in Eher, profited handsomely.[75]

At the end of September, following Ramcke's surrender of Brest, the Allies also captured Rear Admiral Carl Weber and Brigadier General Botho Elster. Weber had been apprehended in the vicinity of Beaugency, France, located partway between Paris and the coastal city of Bordeaux, where Weber had served as commandant of the German arsenal. Upon capture, he joined the senior Wehrmacht officers at Trent Park in England. The following day, September 17, 1944, and in the same area of the Loire Valley, the Allies also captured General Elster. He served as commanding officer of Feldkommandatur 541, which oversaw the transfer of Spanish supplies through France to Germany. Elster, who had been dogged for some time by the French resistance, ceremoniously surrendered his pistol as well as munitions, machinery, and twenty thousand men to Major General Robert C. Macon of the American Eighty-Third Infantry Division on Beaugency Bridge on the Loire River. For deciding to capitulate rather than unnecessarily send hundreds more men to their deaths, a Nazi court condemned Elster to death in absentia in March 1945. Elster's decision and the Nazi court's subsequent sentence proved to be a bone of contention between the general and his fellow high-ranking prisoners when he arrived in the United States. Despite being interrogated by CSDIC at Wilton Park along with Generals Ramcke and von Heyking and Admiral Weber, Elster did not accompany his colleagues to Trent Park. Rather, after two days, he was transferred to Camp Clinton, Mississippi, by American request.[76]

Elster did not go alone. A week after his capture, on September 23, 1944, ten of the generals from Trent Park departed for the United States. Three of these officers—von Sponeck, von Liebenstein, and Krause—had long been residents of the English camp. The other seven—Vierow, Spang, Menny, Badinski, Sattler, Schramm, and Stolberg—had only briefly been at Camp No. 11. A month later, on October 25, the British transferred nine more senior officers from Trent Park to America. This group included Generals Seyffardt, Rauch, von Wülfingen, Gutknecht, and von der Mosel and Admirals Schirmer, Kähler, von Tresckow, and Weber.[77]

A photograph of German prisoner-of-war generals at Trent Park, November 1944. *Front row, left to right:* Generalleutnant Rüdiger von Heyking, Generalleutnant Karl Wilhelm von Schlieben, and Generalleutnant Wilhelm Daser. *Back row, left to right:* General der Infanterie Dietrich von Choltitz, Oberst Gerhard Wilck, General der Fallschirmtruppe Bernhard-Hermann Ramcke, Generalmajor Knut Eberding, and Oberst Eberhard Wildermuth. (German Federal Archive [Bundesarchiv], Bild 146-2005-1036 / Photographer: Unknown)

There do not appear to have been any special Allied criteria for choosing which senior officers to transfer to the United States. These two groups constituted a mix of cooperative "anti-Nazis" and uncooperative "Nazis," as well as others who had been in England for some time and many who had only recently arrived. It appears most likely that the British chose to send those prisoners from whom they had already gathered as much information as they thought possible as well as those in whom the Americans expressed particular interest.

November 1944 saw the addition of only a few new faces at Trent Park, including Brigadier General Knut Eberding and Major General Wilhelm Daser, commanding the Sixty-Fourth and Seventieth Infantry Divisions, respectively. The Allies captured both in the Battle of the Scheldt Estuary. The Germans doggedly defended this coastal area of Belgium to prevent the

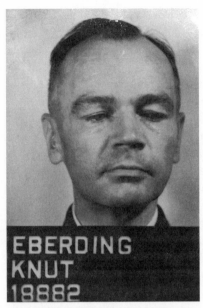 

Generalmajor Knut Eberding (Courtesy of the Mississippi Armed Forces Museum)

SS-Brigadeführer Anton Dunckern (Courtesy of the Mississippi Armed Forces Museum)

Allies from capturing Antwerp, the port that was essential for supplying an Allied advance into German territory. Eberding was an "efficient, ruthless officer" who chose to fight the Canadian Second Corps rather than surrender, inflicting significant casualties and considerably delaying the Canadian advance to Antwerp, although he destroyed his own division in the process.[78] Daser serves as an interesting contrast to Eberding. Defending the same area, both received the same orders from their superiors: "Negotiations quite out of the question; fight until the last; in case of desertion relatives [will be] made responsible." Yet Daser chose to surrender, citing potentially high civilian casualties, while Eberding adhered to his orders despite the destruction of his unit and the deaths of hundreds of his men. Eberding even later admitted into British microphones that he had issued an order that "the next of kin of all deserters would be called to account at home."[79]

Two weeks later and 250 miles away, members of the American Tenth Regiment, Fifth Division, captured SS Brigadeführer and Generalmajor der Polizei (Brigadier General) Anton Dunckern, commanding Gestapo officer for Alsace-Lorraine, in the city of Metz, France. The Americans did not realize at first that Dunckern was such an important catch, as he "crawled out from behind a beer barrel" in a saloon where he had been hiding. Dunckern had been sent to Metz to organize the city's defense after many of the German soldiers garrisoned there had abandoned it. He had apparently established himself as a small-time dictator in the city, regularly having people sent off to Germany, or threatening to do so if they did not cooperate. Indeed, using such threats, Dunckern appears to have both enlarged his personal art collection and indulged his taste for French women.[80]

American soldiers reported that Dunckern was arrogant and rude upon his surrender and that he immediately began to complain about having to stand outside in the rain. As he then began walking to a nearby shelter without a word to anyone, American GI Leonard O'Reilly remembered, "We told him to stand still and he kept going, so we just slapped our rifles on him and he stopped." American lieutenant Harry Colburn stated that "[Dunckern] looked like he could spit at me. We had to push him into line because he didn't want to go with the other prisoners. He acted like he was insulted being taken by a bunch of guys as ratty-looking as us." Finally, after Dunckern entered the prisoner-of-war enclosure, American major Edward Marsh realized whom the Americans had captured and asked for Dunckern's pay book to confirm it. Upon establishing Dunckern's identity and rank, one of the American officers chastised him by asking if Gestapo officers were allowed to surrender. Dunckern retorted that he surrendered only because he had had a gun in his back. The American officer sarcastically suggested that "maybe [he] should have resisted them" and given the Americans an excuse to shoot him.[81]

Dunckern's die-hard attitude did not soften once he arrived at Trent Park. The British officers respected him as "an officer of first class ability" with "exceptional powers of observation" and "a prodigious memory for detail." But they stated that Dunckern "met his interrogators with steady recalcitrance and evasiveness which he sustained with a skill and determination fully in keeping with his experience and abilities." Despite the difficulty in gathering information from the Gestapo general, he proved useful. Perhaps inadvertently—British records are not clear in this regard—he supplied the Allies with information about the command structure and personnel of both the Sicherheitspolizei and Sicherheitsdienst (SD) units under his command, as well as the specific duties and organization of the units in the Alsace-Lorraine region.[82]

The final group of German general officers who would later find themselves in American custody arrived in England in December 1944, having been captured in the latter part of November.[83] Two days after the capture of

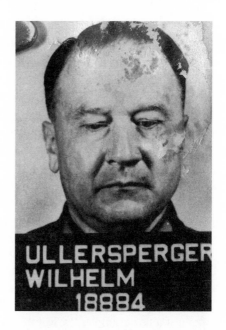

Generalmajor Wilhelm Ullersperger
(Courtesy of the Mississippi Armed
Forces Museum)

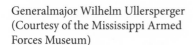

Dunckern, when the Americans completed the sweep of Metz, they also captured Major General Heinrich Kittel, commander of the 462nd Volksgrenadier Division and commandant of the city.[84] On the same day that Kittel fell into American hands in Metz, November 22, 1944, the Allies also captured Brigadier General Hans Bruhn, who commanded the 553rd Volksgrenadier Division, when he surrendered in Saverne, a French city located about a hundred miles southeast of Metz, near Strasbourg.[85] On November 23, 1944, the French captured Brigadier General Wilhelm Ullersperger, commanding officer of fortress engineers in Vosges, France, a city about eighty miles west of Strasbourg. Finally, the Allies captured Brigadier General Franz Vaterrodt. General Vaterrodt had originally been assigned as commandant of Strasbourg in March 1941 because of ill health, but he remained in this position until his capture on November 25, 1944.[86]

Hundreds of additional Wehrmacht general officers arrived in England as prisoners of war before and after the German surrender in May 1945. And a number of generals captured prior to the end of November 1944 were eventually transferred to American custody—the last group departed in May 1945. Yet all the senior officer prisoners eventually transferred from Britain to the United States arrived in England prior to January 1945.

Because of the continual turnover of prisoners between June 1944 and the end of the war in May 1945, the environment at Trent Park became somewhat of a carousel. Despite this obstacle, CSDIC and Mother continued their interrogations and eavesdropping on the senior Wehrmacht officers in their custody. In many respects, the same conflicts that the British observed among their prisoners prior to D-Day reemerged, albeit with different casts of characters. The first and most obvious of these was the animosity between those generals who continued to express their support for the Hitler regime and those who ostensibly now opposed it.

Despite the political animosity and recurrent confrontations among the prisoners, the British gleaned a large volume of intelligence from the generals by continuing to eavesdrop on their private conversations. Obtaining information that could have a positive impact on the outcome of the war remained Britain's primary intelligence goal in regard to the monitoring of its German generals. Between D-Day and the German surrender in May 1945, CSDIC gathered information about the German order of battle in the Balkans, German fortifications on the Eastern Front, strategic reserves in France, the staff and defense of Fortress Cherbourg, delayed-action mines in Cherbourg harbor, and the morale of German troops in various regions, to offer just a few examples.[87] Given the amount of resources devoted to gathering this information and the fact that CSDIC consistently maintained its eavesdropping efforts at Trent Park from the arrival of its first prisoner in August 1942 until Germany's surrender in May 1945, the British must have obtained some valuable intelligence.

In spite of Britain's interest in the generals' conversations, particularly those involving discussions of war crimes, by April 1945 CSDIC could no longer house all of its general officer prisoners at Trent Park. London initially sent two more small groups of generals to the United States, including von Choltitz, Ullersperger, Eberding, Ramcke, and Dunckern in early April and von Heyking, Daser, Vaterrodt, Bruhn, and Kittel in May.[88] The departure of these last five generals, coupled with the German surrender in early May, marked the end of British transfers to the United States. Instead, London began sending the German generals to other locations in Britain, including Camp No. 1, Grizedale Hall in Lancashire, where noted British military historian Basil Liddell Hart forged an amicable professional relationship with some of these men.

The volume of prisoners arriving in England forced the British to choose these alternative accommodations. Of the 302 German generals held in Britain at some point during or immediately after the Second World War, 248 arrived after April 1945. Furthermore, the British lost interest in most of these men once the war in Europe had concluded. Within five months of the

German surrender, CSDIC had ceased to monitor any of the German general officers in Britain. Its supplemental homes soon closed, Latimer House in August and Wilton Park in November, and CSDIC transferred all of the generals out of Trent Park and closed that camp on October 19, 1945. Many of the generals remained prisoners of war in Britain for almost three more years. Special Camp No. 11 at Bridgend in Wales became the home for German general officers on January 9, 1946, but since CSDIC did not operate this particular camp there were no interrogations or eavesdropping on the men who resided there.[89]

With the war in Europe coming to a close, the British focus quickly shifted to simply gathering information about war crimes. The London District Cage became the official War Crimes Interrogation Unit and most senior German officers endured at least a few days of interrogation there for this purpose.[90] This change in focus and the abrupt loss of interest in the German generals when the war ended suggests that the primary purpose of Britain's accommodation of senior Wehrmacht officer POWs had been to gain operational and tactical intelligence that could aid Allied victory in the war. Once Germany had been defeated, the generals were no longer of much value and were set aside until such time as they could be safely repatriated.

Yet British intelligence did not lose interest in Wehrmacht generals entirely. The British and their American allies developed a different relationship with dozens of these officers after the war. By this time, however, the Anglo-American relationship itself had changed. The Americans now took the lead in fostering the Western Allied partnership with the German generals and the British appeared content to play a secondary role. Britain had achieved its all-important wartime goal and now let the Americans take center stage in the early years of the Cold War. It is to the evolution of U.S. policy regarding its general officer prisoners, driven by changing American national security interests, that we now turn.

2

Hitler's Generals
Come to America

While the British hosted their *Afrikaner* generals at stately Trent Park, American authorities originally embarked on a similar process with the four generals sent to the United States in June 1943. Using what they had learned from the combined Anglo-American intelligence efforts in North Africa, U.S. officials initially attempted to emulate British practices. They placed the generals in a lavish environment enhanced with secret microphones and set about gathering information from the newly arrived prisoners.

The first parcel of Wehrmacht generals to arrive in the United States consisted of Generals Gustav von Vaerst, Karl Bülowius, Willibald Borowietz, and Carl Peter Bernard Köchy. Colonel August Viktor von Quast accompanied General von Vaerst as his chief of staff. At the time of his capture, von Quast had notified both the British and American authorities that he was awaiting promotion to brigadier general. Indeed, within less than three months—on August 1, 1943—Berlin promoted von Quast to *Generalmajor* (brigadier general). However, due to the German military's attempts to promote large numbers of its enlisted soldiers to noncommissioned officers (NCOs) both immediately prior to capture and during the course of their internment as prisoners of war in an effort to take advantage of the Geneva Convention's prohibition against forcing NCOs to work, the U.S. War Department balked at most prisoners' claims of last-minute promotion. These circumstances eventually resulted in the War Department's issuance of Prisoner of War Circular No. 11 in December 1943, which stated that "no evidence of promotion of a prisoner which is received by the War Department after the prisoner has come into the custody of the United States or previous

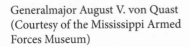

Generalmajor August V. von Quast
(Courtesy of the Mississippi Armed
Forces Museum)

Allied detaining power, will be recognized by the United States as accomplishing the promotion of the prisoner of war." Thus, while the German generals at Clinton repeatedly requested American recognition of "General" von Quast's promotion and treated him as one of their own, American authorities did not consider him a general.[1]

Upon notifying the Americans of their intent to transfer these men to American custody, British authorities emphasized that in their experience the prisoners took "time to settle down" and that interrogation did not produce optimum results until "full realization of captivity and incipient boredom settle in." The British also expressed their delight that British and American authorities saw "eye-to-eye on all these interrogation matters," indicating that the Americans either intended to follow the British model of treatment for German prisoner-of-war generals or had at least led British authorities to believe that they did.[2]

Understandably, given the status of these high-ranking prisoners, American authorities utilized one of their top interrogators, Major Duncan Spencer, to supervise the exchange of prisoners and to assist in the initial formulation of American procedure in accommodating and interrogating these men. Spencer had been attached to MI19, the branch of British military intelligence responsible for prisoners of war, since March 1943. He was familiar with both the British "operational plan" and the prisoners' "individual characteristics," and the British lauded his "efficiency" and "thorough grip of interrogation organization."[3]

Besides utilizing their top personnel, U.S. officials also sought an appropriate location to place the generals once they arrived in America. In mid-1942 American authorities had anticipated the need for secluded locations to interrogate prisoners of war of special importance, such as U-boat officers and enlisted men with special technical skills. Ideally, they sought two locations, one on each coast. Washington decided to house the most important German military personnel at Fort Hunt, Virginia, a former Civilian Conservation Corps facility located near Mount Vernon in the Washington, D.C., area. Particularly valuable Japanese prisoners would be sent to a renovated resort hotel at Byron Hot Springs, California, about fifty miles from San Francisco near the small town of Tracy. Because of Japanese cultural taboos against surrendering, however, the Allies captured a much smaller number of Japanese soldiers. Consequently, Byron Hot Springs had few occupants in the early stages of American involvement in the war. So the U.S. War Department quickly opted to use this facility to interrogate German POWs as well, including this first parcel of Wehrmacht general officers.[4]

Byron Hot Springs had been a popular playground for Hollywood celebrities in the years before the Second World War. Having served as a regular getaway for actors like Clark Gable, the opulent resort was tailor-made for a high-security, secret operation. The elite hotel complex could not be seen from the passing road and the 210-acre property's relatively flat terrain allowed for easy construction of fencing and clear fields of fire for guards should any prisoners attempt to escape. The grounds also included a five-acre palm tree park, cement walkways connecting all the buildings, and a tennis court. Its finest feature, of course, was the hot springs. Byron Hot Springs had developed a reputation similar to that of a hot springs resort in Carlsbad, Germany, something that American authorities believed might be helpful in getting German prisoners to let down their guard and speak more freely.[5]

In addition to its amenities and secluded location, the resort also came at the right price. The War Department originally estimated that it would cost over $300,000 to acquire and adequately renovate any potential interrogation center property. Mrs. Mae Reed, the owner of Byron Hot Springs in 1942, donated the resort complex to the U.S. Army for the duration of the war as a patriotic act in honor of her son, a medical corps officer who had been killed in the First World War. Consequently, the cost of renovating the resort, which included the construction of fences and guard towers as well as the installation of important technical equipment, totaled only $173,000.[6]

The Byron Hot Springs interrogation center had been in operation for only five months at the time of the generals' arrival in June 1943. The U.S. government had acquired the hotel and surrounding property from Mrs. Reed in June 1942 and then took six months preparing the complex to accommodate prisoners of war. For security reasons, the site's official address was simply "Post Office Box 651, Tracy, California," and its existence was kept from the American public until well after the end of the war. Camp authorities established the hotel manor as the center of operations, with prisoners' quarters located on the third floor of the former resort. American officers' quarters and interrogation rooms occupied the building's lower stories, and the other buildings in the complex housed additional officers and military police, a dental clinic, laundry, barber shop, recreation room, and other necessities. The facilities accommodated 173 German and 71 Japanese POWs during 1943, but during the month of June the American staff devoted their sole attention to von Vaerst, Bülowius, Borowietz, Köchy, and von Quast. Indeed, the interrogation of German prisoners from U-203 had to be expedited to meet the War Department requirement that all other prisoners of war be removed before the generals arrived.[7]

The generals first arrived in the United States at Fort George Meade, Maryland, on June 3, 1943, and almost immediately departed for Byron Hot Springs in a plush Pullman car. During their long train ride west, as well as throughout their internment in American prisoner-of-war camps, they rigidly adhered to their military precedent and traditions. For instance, during meals, all the officers sat at the tables in order of rank. In the evenings the four generals routinely shared a bottle or two of scotch whiskey, occasionally including the colonel and other lower-ranking officers in their social gatherings. Each general had his own valet who had accompanied him since capture. One of the generals' orderlies, Sergeant Albert Lauser, confided that "most of the generals [were] partial to their liquid refreshment." He noted that most of the German generals under whom he had served were heavy drinkers, although they usually drank discreetly, typically in the late evening, and that the generals' drinking was "often apparent the next morning in the savage humor with which they rise to meet the cares and responsibilities of a new day."[8]

Part of the preparation for the arrival of prisoners of war at Byron Hot Springs included the installation of twenty-five recording devices and one hundred microphones in the prisoners' quarters, something the Americans had likely learned from their British allies.[9] As with their fellow prisoners in England, it seems likely that the four general officers in California must have realized that their conversations were being recorded by microphones in their rooms. And again, the nature of the information the generals revealed in "private" raises questions about the generals' motivations for sharing such information if they knew it was for American consumption.

Curiously, the generals in American custody did not express the same optimism about the war that their counterparts in England did. For example, as Generals von Vaerst and Borowietz finished listening to a news broadcast one evening, both expressed pessimism about Germany's chances in the war. Von Vaerst remarked that "[Germany needs] everything, everything is needed. It is going very badly for us—very badly." The two men discussed the Allied bombings of Hamburg, Bremen, Lübeck, and other German cities and speculated that the number of bombers that the United States could supply for the effort would only increase. Interestingly, when Major von Meyer entered the room, the pessimistic conversation between his two superior officers quickly changed.[10] Clearly the generals thought it important to conceal their pessimistic views of the war from subordinates, either in an effort to sustain morale or because they feared that these types of statements might be reported to authorities in Berlin. Had these two men remained in England, these types of "defeatist" comments would have landed them in the "anti-Nazi" clique at Trent Park.

American authorities also obtained information from the generals through direct interrogation. In fact, the Americans, in contrast to their British counterparts, seemed to rely a great deal more on direct interrogation of the generals for information than they did on the microphones they had surreptitiously placed in the generals' rooms. Notably, these interrogations seemed to have always taken place with two or more of the generals present, rather than isolating the officers. But like their British allies, American authorities also attempted to construct character sketches of the generals in their custody along the way.

The Americans regarded von Vaerst and Köchy, in particular, as the most intelligent and experienced of the four generals at Byron Hot Springs. Von Vaerst, being the highest-ranking of the generals then in American custody, was the recognized leader among the German prisoners. He and his colleague General Bülowius both indicated their "astonishment" that with so many Germans in the United States, the two countries should be at war. They insisted that the Germans had "no feeling against [the United States]"— Germany's declaration of war on December 11, 1941, apparently notwithstanding—and they looked forward to a time when Germany and the United States could be allied.[11]

Von Vaerst reserved his hatred and suspicion for the Russians, indicating his surprise that the British and the Americans could be allied with the Russians in any fashion. He noted his belief that the German command's biggest mistake was invading Russia in June 1941, stating that "only after it was too late" did the Germans realize the size of the Russian army. He later indicated that the severity of the Russian winter was "the only thing that had saved the Russians thus far." Von Vaerst and all his colleagues consistently portrayed the Russians as "little better than beasts" and emphasized "the peril of the Russians to western civilization." Von Vaerst ended his last interrogation at Byron Hot Springs by noting that "even though we cannot make any further invasion of Russia, we can and must hold the Russians away from Germany."[12]

These comments bred suspicion among the American interrogators that the generals were attempting to justify German brutality against the Russians, both soldiers and civilians, on the Eastern Front. Yet it seems equally likely that the generals at Byron Hot Springs intended their comments to engender some kind of kindred spirit between Germany and the Western Allies. By this point in the war, the Germans had good reason to fear Russian reprisals and appear to have been desperately trying to dismiss German-American differences in the hope that the Western Allies would come to see the Soviets as the graver threat to Western civilization.

The former German air field regional commander in Tunisia, Brigadier General Carl Peter Bernard Köchy, like his colleague von Vaerst, impressed American authorities as "a very intelligent man" and one of "imagination and thoughtful character." Indeed, Köchy was a prize catch, having served in both the German Army and Navy before transferring to the air force. With regard to the German war with Russia, Köchy did not believe that defeat was inevitable, although he felt it to be likely, and he did not share von Vaerst's conviction that the Germans could continue to hold the territory they then possessed in western Russia. Like von Vaerst, however, Köchy saw the Eastern Front as the crucial theater of the war for Germany, characterizing the German hatred for the Russians as unparalleled in history.[13]

Köchy possessed a fairly realistic view of the international scene at the time, stating that "no matter the outcome of the war," Britain "had long ceased to be the dominating influence in the world" and that the United States would "fall heir to that world-wide influence." He felt that if defeat became inevitable, Germany would surrender to Britain and the United States unconditionally, if necessary, noting that "if Germany's wagon became small and broken, her only hope would be to hitch it to a star."[14]

Like von Vaerst, Köchy seemed to be attempting to foster some sort of

German alliance with the Western Allies to save Germany from Soviet occupation. Moreover, his comment about Germany potentially surrendering "unconditionally, if necessary" may have been an allusion to the conclusion of the First World War, in which the Germans signed an armistice but did not unconditionally surrender. Perhaps Köchy, and likely numerous other German general officers, realized by this point that the war could not be won but maintained hope that Germany could possibly extricate itself without entirely capitulating. As both his and von Vaerst's comments attest, their biggest concern by June 1943 was not winning the war but keeping the Soviets out of Germany.

In contrast to Generals von Vaerst and Köchy, American authorities viewed General Borowietz as a man of "limited outlook," characterizing him as having "had neither the time nor the inclination to think," and as one whose "statements and opinions on world affairs are therefore of very small importance compared with those of General Köchy."[15] Curiously, American officials appeared even less interested in General Bülowius. While they interrogated him along with his fellow generals, they offered no discussion of his personal beliefs and experiences or any assessment of his intelligence or character. Perhaps American interrogators took less interest in Bülowius because he had commanded the Manteuffel Division for only a short time before surrendering and because he had been criticized for performing poorly in his previous position as commander of the Afrika Korps. Perhaps Bülowius simply offered very little of interest to his interrogators. American records provide no explanation for their lack of interest in the general.

In addition to seeking technical information and the generals' perspectives on the war, the Americans, like their British counterparts, also attempted to gauge each general's political views—at least von Vaerst, Borowietz, and Köchy. No evaluation of Bülowius can be found in the American records. Remarkably, General von Vaerst stated that he and his colleagues were Nazis and "strong believers in Hitler," although adding that "it took the [Nazis] a considerable time to convince them that the ideals, plans, and aims of the Party would be the only thing that would restore a united and strong Germany." Conversely, Köchy appeared quite critical of the Nazi regime, noting that he felt strongly that "the present Nazi hierarchy is to a great extent composed of men unfitted for the position, and unworthy of their tasks, and that they are there almost solely because of having shared Hitler's early struggles." He noted his strong disapproval of the concentration camps and "gangster methods" that he believed were responsible for arousing worldwide hatred of Germany and that would likely lead to Germany's defeat in the war. Borowietz did not seem concerned with "political or ideological conditions," reportedly not mentioning Hitler or the Nazi regime at all.[16]

It is important to note that the generals made these comments directly to the Byron Hot Springs interrogators, not into American microphones. This adds a potentially new dimension to assessing the prisoners' motivations for making such statements. One wonders if von Vaerst's stated loyalty to the Nazi regime accurately reflected his personal convictions. Maybe von Vaerst indeed shared Hitler's vision for a greater Germany, or, as the highest-ranking German officer at Byron Hot Springs, perhaps he sought to set a proper example of loyalty to the German state for his subordinates. Given the threats by Nazi stalwarts of reporting prisoner disloyalty to authorities in Berlin, perhaps von Vaerst feared expressing his genuine political views for fear of reprisals against his family in Germany. Like von Arnim at Trent Park, von Vaerst's position of leadership among the prisoners in California and his sometimes contradictory statements made his political views difficult to adequately ascertain. That the Americans later chose him as a candidate for reeducation, however, suggests that he changed his stated views while in captivity, initially masked some fairly strong anti-Nazi sentiments, or deceived the Americans into thinking that he had. Considering that the American staff at Byron Hot Springs held von Vaerst in high regard from the beginning suggests that they did not take his early pro-Nazi statements too seriously.

General Köchy may be even more of an enigma. The Americans regarded Köchy quite highly, perhaps because he initially appeared to be the most openly anti-Nazi of the general officer prisoners at Byron Hot Springs. Curiously, however, the general later fell under a great deal of suspicion from Allied officials in postwar Germany. His name appeared on several Allied lists of suspected "militarists" to be watched by occupation authorities after his repatriation. It seems puzzling that a prisoner like Köchy, initially held in such high regard, would eventually find himself the object of such suspicion. Perhaps Köchy secretly harbored pro-Nazi sentiments throughout his incarceration in the United States that reemerged in Europe following the war. Notably, the Allies distinguished between potential militarists and Nazi sympathizers during the postwar occupation of Germany despite the fact that they seemed to view these two as one and the same during the prisoners' wartime captivity. In this light, perhaps Köchy sincerely condemned the National Socialist leadership and their "gangster methods." Yet, as the British came to suspect about many of their general officer prisoners at Trent Park, perhaps Köchy despised Hitler and the Nazis not because they attempted to place Germany in a dominant position in Europe but because they failed to do so.

Ultimately, the Americans did not reach the same kind of concrete con-clusions about the political persuasions of their German generals that the British did at Trent Park. American authorities stamped the files of all of these German generals, as well as those of their accompanying subordinates, "Nazi sympathies undetermined."[17] The Americans made no further attempts to determine any of their captive generals' political views until well after the success of the Allied invasion of Normandy. At that time, the emergence of American concerns about the postwar reconstruction of Germany made these types of concerns more relevant. American emulation of British treat-ment of general officer prisoners abruptly ended as well. Camp authorities at Byron Hot Springs notified the Provost Marshal General's Office on June 29, 1943, that the prisoners should be transferred to a suitable internment camp and all interrogations ceased.

Notably, Washington had already decided before the generals had been transferred to California that their stay at Byron Hot Springs would be brief. On the very day the generals first arrived in the United States—June 3, 1943—the U.S. Provost Marshal General's Office had authorized the con-struction of a compound at the existing prisoner-of-war camp in Clinton, Mississippi, specifically for the long-term internment of German general of-ficer prisoners. While the "generals' camp" was not scheduled to be complet-ed until early fall, American authorities could not wait that long. Presumably, the American interrogators believed little further information of any value could be obtained from these prisoners and it was no longer worth the ex-pense to keep them at Byron Hot Springs. Furthermore, because American military intelligence operated only two interrogation facilities, it needed to make room at Byron Hot Springs for other prisoners possessing potentially valuable information.

Consequently, the generals and their aides were temporarily transferred to Camp Mexia, Texas, to await the completion of their designated home in Mississippi. The use of elegant accommodations like those in California for general officer prisoners obviously represented the exception rather than the rule. In fact, aside from the three weeks when von Vaerst and his colleagues occupied Byron Hot Springs, the elite interrogation center almost exclusively housed enlisted men and noncommissioned officers. None of the other Ger-man generals who were later transferred to the United States ever came to this facility. Unlike in Britain, America's finest prisoner-of-war accommoda-tions were barely seen by its highest-ranking prisoners.

Aside from the brevity of the endeavor, the approach taken by U.S. in-terrogators toward their captive German generals also calls into question the seriousness of the American effort. The British interrogation team that sent these generals to the United States informed the Americans that prisoners took "time to settle down" and that optimum interrogation results occurred only after "full realization of captivity and incipient boredom settle in." Yet American authorities held the generals at Byron Hot Springs for only a little over three weeks before transferring them to a regular internment camp. Furthermore, American interrogators speculated midway through the internment and interrogation process that "pessimism is not expressed when more than two [of the generals] are present."[18] Since the Americans clearly suspected that these men would not reveal their real feelings about the war in the presence of their colleagues, and certainly not in the presence of subordinate officers, it would be reasonable to assume that they would have interviewed each one individually. There is no evidence that they did; in fact, the generals were almost always paired for interrogations and frequently interviewed in groups of three or more.

Perhaps the Americans felt the information they received was not worth their time and expense. Indeed, most of the information appears to have been less than vital to the Allied war effort. Nevertheless, the nature of information received from a prisoner is in part a function of the questions and approach of the interrogators. Despite the initial oversight provided by Major Spencer, an American officer who was highly regarded by the British and experienced in CSDIC interrogation procedures, it appears that the Americans did not see eye to eye with the British on all these interrogation matters after all. With the first group of generals revealing little useful information and the British supplying American military intelligence with information on the generals in England, Washington saw no need to continue the operation.

Unfortunately for the generals in the United States, not only did the two Allies' respective policies regarding interrogation diverge, but significant discrepancies in the manner in which the two nations accommodated their captured German generals emerged as well. Where the British continued to host their "guests" in a stately mansion at Trent Park, the Americans began providing their general officer prisoners with poorly insulated bungalows that barely met the minimum requirements of the Geneva Convention. And where British intelligence maintained its interrogation efforts and surveillance of the generals' conversations throughout the war, American authorities abandoned the process entirely and made no further attempts to gather intelligence from their captive generals. For all intents and purposes, the Americans viewed these men as they did any other prisoners of war.

After their transfer to Texas in July 1943, the generals in the United States angrily complained about the accommodations provided for them at Camp Mexia, a far cry from the opulence to which they had quickly become accustomed at Byron Hot Springs. Their complaints, however, fell on deaf ears. More German general officers arrived in the United States in 1943 and 1944, but American authorities took little interest in them. Camp Mexia's accommodations, spartan by the generals' standards, provided a foretaste of much of the rest of the time these prisoners would spend in the United States.

On July 2, 1943, the four German generals and Colonel von Quast departed California by train. They arrived in Mexia, Texas, on July 8, the first day of hundred-plus-degree temperatures in the summer of 1943. A little over two weeks later, on July 24, Mexia experienced a record high temperature of 105 degrees. This trend continued through August, with a new record high of 107 degrees established on August 16. In late August, when morning temperatures finally dipped into the mid-seventies, the *Mexia Weekly Herald* exuberantly noted that "Hope Springs in Hearts of Heat Weary Sufferers."[19] The temperatures of northern California must have instantly become a fond memory for men plunged into the sweltering humidity of a hot Texas summer, particularly in an era predating the widespread availability of air conditioning.

Camp Mexia was a typical large prisoner-of-war camp in the United States during the Second World War. It was built on land already owned by the federal government about three miles outside of Mexia, a small Texas town east of Waco and about eighty miles south of Dallas. The Provost Marshal General's Office commonly chose small towns like Mexia because any prisoners who managed to escape would have a difficult time sabotaging industry in places where little existed. The town's relatively close proximity to a major city like Dallas, however, offered easy access to necessary supplies, equipment, and personnel. Moreover, placing POW camps in the American South was relatively cheap because it relieved the U.S. Army Corps of Engineers of having to insulate the numerous barracks necessary to accommodate all of America's prisoners of war.

The prisoner-of-war camp at Mexia contained two sections: one large enclosure comprising four compounds, each capable of accommodating up to sixteen hundred enlisted prisoners, and a smaller enclosure built to house up to one thousand officer prisoners. Eventually, Camp Mexia would become the largest POW camp in the state of Texas when it reached its full capacity of over six thousand prisoners. When the generals arrived in July 1943, however, the camp had been occupied for only about a month and there were fewer than four thousand prisoners residing there.[20]

An area several hundred yards wide divided the officers' enclosure from that of the enlisted men. The American guard companies' quarters were located in this open space. The two sections were connected by a barbed-wire corridor through which select enlisted prisoners were allowed to enter the officers' enclosure to fulfill their responsibilities as orderlies for the senior officers. American army doctors, with the aid of German doctors who were themselves prisoners, provided medical care to the POWs and American personnel alike at the camp hospital, a modern facility with x-ray equipment and operating rooms. The enlisted prisoners prepared food for the entire camp and did laundry for the officers. Furthermore, because the camp had only recently been built, other enlisted prisoners busied themselves constructing sidewalks and gardens within the officers' compound as well as around the camp administration barracks.[21]

Fortunately for the generals and the other officer prisoners, they had better-quality barracks than did the enlisted prisoners of war at Camp Mexia. The officers' apartments were constructed using sheetrock, rather than the tar-paper walls the enlisted POWs were forced to endure, and while the officers shared quarters, there were only two officers assigned to an apartment and each man had his own bedroom. The generals were also regularly allowed to take strolls outside of the camp accompanied by an American officer, but only after giving their word of honor not to escape. Unfortunately for the generals, there was not much to look at outside the fence. According to Rudolf Fischer, a representative of the Swiss government who inspected the camp in September 1943, Camp Mexia "leaves much to be desired in the way of beautification. It has not been possible to get grass to take root and in high winds the camp is very dusty."[22]

Despite the swirling dust and the oppressive heat and humidity of Camp Mexia, American commanding officer Colonel Thomas Bays fostered a very "cordial" relationship with his prisoners, including the newly arrived generals. Indeed, General von Vaerst applauded Colonel Bays's gentlemanly approach, stating that the camp commandant was "always correct" in his manners. A camp inspector from the International Committee of the Red Cross who visited Camp Mexia in August 1943 also commended Colonel Bays's leadership, noting that overall the prisoners' morale was "excellent."[23]

Colonel Bays strove to provide adequate recreation areas and facilities for the prisoners, including overseeing the construction of several tennis courts and the remodeling of some existing buildings into theaters equipped with raised stages and sloping seats; he even obtained a 35-mm movie projector and some radios for prisoner use. Bays also encouraged the development of a prisoner educational program that included plans for courses in architecture, political science, physics, chemistry, medicine, botany, and law, among others. Unfortunately, book shortages and censorship rules hindered attempts to get the school system up and running during the prisoners' first few months at Camp Mexia. While these early obstacles were eventually overcome, the generals were transferred to Mississippi before they could take advantage of this program.[24]

In spite of Colonel Bays's efforts to provide adequate facilities for the prisoners at Mexia, the generals, in particular, were dissatisfied. Admittedly, two main problems existed, the first being that no amount of minor remodeling could make Camp Mexia into a resort like Byron Hot Springs or an estate like Trent Park. The generals, miserable from the sweltering heat and comparatively unattractive surroundings, quickly compared their previous camps in England and California with their new, if temporary, home in Texas and found American treatment sadly wanting.

In Camp Mexia's defense, it had not been intended as a long-term stay for the generals. Facilities specifically designed for these men had been under construction at Camp Clinton, Mississippi, since the generals had first arrived in America. Unfortunately, construction delays postponed the transfer of the generals to Clinton. The generals' camp was originally slated to open on September 1, 1943, but that was delayed until the first week of October. But even had the generals been transferred as originally planned, the damage to American prestige, in the generals' eyes, would already have been done. In fact, by the end of July, when the generals had yet to spend a full month in Mexia, the headquarters for the Eighth Service Command (which included Camp Mexia) sent the following telegram to the provost marshal general in Washington, D.C.: "German General Officers at Prisoner of War Camp Mexia, Texas, Protesting Present Accommodations. Recommend Transfer at Earliest Practical Date to Clinton, Mississippi." All that Camp Mexia personnel could do was to assure the generals that accommodations more appropriate to their rank were being prepared for them.[25]

The subpar housing, the scorching sun of midsummer in Texas, and the dusty wind of Camp Mexia caused the generals a great deal of consternation. Yet the second main problem at Mexia and what may have galled the senior prisoners the most was the insolence, as they saw it, with which many of the American officers treated them. General von Vaerst, according to Rudolf Fischer of the Swiss legation, was "considerably perturbed by the treatment which he has received in the United States." Von Vaerst claimed that the British treated general officer prisoners "more appropriately" than did the

Americans. He complained to the Swiss legation that, with the exception of Colonel Bays, "he had not been treated with the chivalry and civility which he believed he had a right to expect." The general was offended that "many American officers had not exhibited confidence in his word as a German officer and that the treatment accorded him was similar to that accorded to a criminal."[26]

American treatment of von Vaerst and his fellow generals, as well as the rest of the German prisoner population in America, was founded almost entirely upon the dictates of international law in the form of the 1929 International Convention Relative to the Treatment of Prisoners of War, otherwise known as the Geneva Convention. The United States strictly adhered to the 1929 Geneva Convention in the hope that this would compel Nazi Germany to treat American soldiers held in German prisoner-of-war camps accordingly. The treaty required that POW camps be constructed to the same standards as military installations for the home nation's own soldiers. In other words, the POW camps in America were required to offer German prisoners of war the same conditions as did American base camps for U.S. military personnel. American observance of the law went to such extremes that in some camps where not enough barrack space existed to house both prisoners and American guards, both had to live in tents and the barracks sat empty until more could be built and the problem rectified.[27]

This was certainly not the case with Camp Mexia, or any camp in the United States that housed German generals. General officer prisoners enjoyed their own furnished apartments, aides de camp and batmen to service their immediate needs, and forty dollars per month in salary without being required to work.[28] They lived in enclosures segregated from the enlisted and noncommissioned officer compounds, and while the Geneva Convention required that they salute American officers, this requirement applied only to U.S. officers of equal or higher rank. Since few American generals ever wandered through U.S. prisoner-of-war camps and most American POW camp commanding officers were not general officers, the German prisoner-of-war generals rarely had to do anything except enjoy a life of leisure, however boring, while engaging in artistic pursuits and recreational activities or simply complaining about their living conditions.[29]

There is a difference, however, between providing a safe, comfortable environment with life's basic necessities as required by international law and accommodating gentlemen in a manner to which they are accustomed to living. The German generals were aghast to discover that U.S. military installations offered American generals accommodations similar to theirs and that

Camp Mexia met the basic housing requirements of the Geneva Convention. Furthermore, considering the lack of respect for aristocratic institutions that many of the American officers and guard personnel at Mexia apparently exhibited, the German generals likely felt more at home in an English prisoner-of-war camp than they did in the United States. Fortunately for them, their stay in Texas was brief. Unfortunately, they soon found an equally poor environment in Mississippi.

On June 3, 1943, U.S. Army Service Forces Headquarters authorized the construction of "General officer prisoner of war compounds at Clinton, Mississippi, and Monticello, Arkansas." Washington designated Clinton for German general officers and Monticello for Italians. The directive called for each compound to hold up to thirty-one generals and as many as thirty-two lower-ranking officers who could serve as aides-de-camp. It also called for future expansion to accommodate a total of fifty-one generals and fifty-six aides of the appropriate nationality in each location.[30]

American authorities initially strove to provide what they believed to be superior accommodations for their general officer prisoners. Like the officers' compound at Camp Mexia, the generals' compound at Clinton offered more amenities than did the enlisted men's quarters. During construction in July 1943 the initial camp commandant, Colonel Charles C. Loughlin, arranged to have the total area of the generals' compound enlarged by moving the north fence line about one hundred yards farther out. This allowed the compound to include "a small brook and grove of trees which would add to the beautification of this area." Once completed, the generals' compound consisted of eighteen residential buildings. The ranking general officer enjoyed his own small house, composed of a living room and dining room, two bedrooms, a kitchen, and a bath. Fifteen other houses, built in a fashion similar to the ranking officer's home, each accommodated two lower-ranking generals who shared quarters. The two additional barracks in the compound housed the generals' aides-de-camp.[31]

The generals' homes were well furnished. The living room of each house contained a polished wooden desk, two wooden chairs, and a matching settee, all of which were upholstered in red leather. A table and other smaller furnishings were also provided to complement the living rooms. The Provost Marshal General's Office also allowed German prisoner-of-war officers to have radios and newspapers, provided they met the approval of U.S. government censors. The YMCA and the International Committee of the Red Cross provided additional books, recreational equipment, and supplies for hobbies and artistic endeavors. One of the earliest German generals to arrive at Camp

Clinton was reported to have been a talented artist who adorned the walls of his living room with his own watercolor creations.[32]

The generals' compound also included an officers' club and a canteen where all of the officers could purchase toiletries and food items in addition to eating the daily meals provided by the camp. The generals, like all German POWs in American camps, were allowed to purchase two bottles of beer per day and the meals provided for the generals consisted of the same quantity of field rations as those provided for American officers and enlisted men. For help with domestic chores, Clinton's stockade commander, Major Harry Miller, assigned each general his own orderly, chosen from among the camp's enlisted prisoner population. These prisoners tended to the generals' daily needs, doing tasks such as laundry, cleaning, and fetching supplies, leaving the officers who served as the generals' aides to deal with weightier tasks. In case these facilities and services were unsatisfactory, the generals could send official messages or complaints to the camp's commanding officer by placing written statements in a mailbox located in the compound. These messages were then routinely carried by one of the camp guards to the commandant's office.[33]

The first generals to arrive at Camp Clinton were Gotthard Frantz and Ernst Schnarrenberger. They boarded a train at Ft. George Meade, Maryland, the typical point of arrival for German prisoners of war coming to the United States from England, and arrived in Clinton, Mississippi, on October 7, 1943. They were quickly joined by the senior officers from California, whose transfer by train from Camp Mexia had finally been authorized on October 5. These generals arrived a few days after Frantz and Schnarrenberger, likely owing to delays in preparing the men for transfer and the travel time required to traverse the four hundred miles from north Texas to central Mississippi by rail. These seven prisoners, six generals and one colonel, and their lower-ranking aides would be the sole occupants of Camp Clinton's officers' compound for over eight months, until the British began sending other generals from Trent Park to Mississippi in the spring and summer of 1944.[34]

The transfers of these senior prisoners and their initial adjustment to life at Camp Clinton appear to have been effected fairly easily. This may be due, in part, to the quality of the guards initially assigned to the camp. An inspection report issued by the Provost Marshal General's Office, dated July 18–19, 1943, praised the "excellency [sic]" of the 458th and 459th Military Police Escort Guard (MPEG) Companies stationed at the camp. These American military police had been stationed there since July 4, 1943, in preparation for the arrival of the first enlisted prisoners near the end of the month. The 487th

MPEG Company arrived in September to help prepare the camp to open the newly completed officers' compound. All of these guard units had been specially trained to handle German general officer prisoners before their arrival in October.[35]

Despite American preparation and training, the first problem arose only a few days after the generals arrived. Gustav von Vaerst, as the highest-ranking general, became the camp spokesman for the officers' compound. In this capacity, he notified the U.S. War Department in a letter dated October 13, 1943, that the aides of two of the "generals," Carl Köchy and August von Quast, had not been transferred with them. Von Vaerst's letter, sent through Camp Clinton's new commanding officer, Colonel James L. McIlhenny, requested that the two aides, Captain Albert Giesecke and Lieutenant Gerhard Runge, be immediately transferred to Clinton from Camp Mexia, Texas. The dispute centered on von Quast's rank. While von Vaerst referred in his letter to "Colonel in General von Quast," American officials still insisted that von Quast was simply a colonel. Consequently, the War Department responded to von Vaerst's letter almost three weeks later by declaring that von Quast was "a colonel and not a general officer, and, therefore, is not entitled to an aide." Their reply explained that von Quast himself had been sent to Camp Clinton only because he served as an aide to von Vaerst and not because of any impending promotion.[36] The War Department eventually acquiesced in the transfers of Giesecke and Runge, but not until July 1944.[37]

Other problems between the generals and their captors in Mississippi soon followed. Like their colleagues in England, the generals at Camp Clinton requested permission to take walks outside of the camp. While British authorities at Camp No. 11 required the generals to sign "paroles," written oaths not to escape once outside the fence, American authorities initially objected to allowing the generals out of the camp at all. Major General G. V. Strong, director of military intelligence for the War Department, stated that "due to the numerous cases of brutality toward American prisoners by the Germans" he did "not feel that a relaxation of treatment on our part [was] warranted." General Strong did not specify the cases of brutality to which he was referring, but his objection to offering the generals parole was obviously intended as a punitive measure.[38]

The American general and his colleagues quickly had a change of heart, however, and offered the German general officers at Camp Clinton an opportunity for parole similar to that offered by the British. The Americans demanded that certain conditions be met, however, including the requirements that each general must sign his own individual parole form, "all paroles must be for a specified period of time" and include the written consent of the senior German officer, the paroled generals must be "accompanied by an American officer," and the generals could not travel farther than five miles from the camp or enter any populated areas.[39]

Surprisingly, after finally receiving permission from the U.S. War Department to walk outside the confines of Camp Clinton, the generals refused to sign any parole forms promising not to escape. Consequently, while their aides took weekly walks with American officers in the Mississippi countryside, those who would not sign the forms remained in the camp. Seven months later, in May 1944, a camp inspector reported that the generals were still requesting permission to walk outside the camp without having to sign the parole form and these requests were still being denied.[40]

Other routine misunderstandings or simple oversights occurred. Yet, alarmingly, a series of reports filed by camp inspectors from the Swiss legation and the U.S. War and State Departments revealed the development of much more serious concerns, which had arisen by early 1944. Dr. Edward Feer of the Swiss legation, the protecting power charged with ensuring that American officials followed all of the provisions of the Geneva Convention, visited Camp Clinton for three days in February 1944. He was accompanied by Bernard Gufler, chief of the Internees Section of the U.S. State Department's Special War Problems Division. Whereas the War Department acted as the custodian of prisoners in the United States, the State Department took responsibility for the foreign relations aspects of the operation. Gufler and the Internees Section oversaw this task.[41]

The two men filed a damning report of American treatment of the prisoner-of-war generals, insisting that "immediate attention" to this issue by American authorities was "imperative." Feer and Gufler first called attention to the generals' lack of sufficient clothing. During the winter of 1943–1944, the prisoners had only their thin khaki Afrika Korps uniforms, designed to be worn in hot, desert service. They had not even been issued more appropriate underwear. The only garments Clinton authorities provided "were of abnormally large size and fitted only the tallest" of the generals. Furthermore, the shoes provided for the generals by the camp administration were "in such a worn out and dirty condition that their acceptance was refused [by the generals] as inconsistent with the high rank of the prisoners."[42]

Similar complaints were issued about the bedding. The cotton comforters provided for the officers had been previously used and were dirty and torn. The Swiss inspector stated that "on cold and windy days the officers [were] literally freezing." Making matters worse, when the officers attempted to alleviate their discomfort by ordering desired items from American mail order firms, a privilege allowed the prisoners as long as they could pay for the items from their monthly salaries, the orders were processed extremely slowly by camp personnel. Indeed, the inspection report claimed that "only ten per cent of all the orders placed during the last four to five months [had] been carried out." The Swiss inspector concluded in regard to the clothing situation that "the German generals at Camp Clinton and the accompanying officers [were] worse off than the enlisted men in any American P.O.W. camp visited so far."[43]

Poor assessments of the clothing and bedding were only the beginning. Feer and Gufler continued their litany of criticisms, contending that the generals also suffered due to the poorly insulated flooring that made their houses unnecessarily cold in the winter. After fighting in the North African desert, even a comparatively mild winter in Mississippi would not have been comfortable for men sitting idle in poorly insulated homes and without proper attire and blankets.[44]

In addition to being cold, the generals apparently also suffered from boredom. Feer and Gufler observed that the officers lacked a sufficient quantity of books and recreation equipment. Where American POW camps typically provided common libraries for enlisted prisoners, the general officers were allowed to obtain their own individual books. The officers would then often share their collections with each other to augment the amount of reading material available. According to the inspectors, however, von Vaerst, who was the senior general and who had been in the United States for over seven months, had been able to acquire only three books. The generals had turned to wood carving, painting, and gardening due to the dearth of reading material and because these were apparently the only activities for which they could obtain adequate supplies. But even some of these activities had met with frustration, as the American guards in the generals' compound had "carelessly trampled the gardens" during their daily patrols.[45]

Yet what most troubled the Swiss inspector and his State Department counterpart was a visible discrepancy between the treatment provided for the generals and that provided the enlisted prisoners in the adjacent compounds. The two inspectors lauded "the atmosphere of the enlisted men's stockade" and the "excellent administration" and "relationship between the commanding officer and his staff with the enlisted men held prisoner." Astonishingly, the inspectors stated that the generals' compound "makes an impression so sharply in contrast to the impression made by the enlisted men's stockade as to be startling." They were convinced that "the generals [had] been placed at a long distance from the camp administration and forgotten."[46]

This obvious discrepancy in accommodations and amenities between the compounds, something the generals could easily observe through the barbed wire, stirred a great deal of resentment among them. They expressed their belief to the Swiss representative that "the Camp Commander had probably been ordered by Washington to isolate them in their 'village' and humiliate them by systematic neglect." They felt "abandoned." They further bemoaned the fact that on the rare occasion when an American officer visited them, he almost always began by mentioning how busy he was, giving the "impression that it would be inadvisable for them to take up anything with him except the most extremely vital matters."[47]

The Swiss representative made special note of the complaints of General Frantz, who was "particularly bitter" about the treatment he had received while in American custody. Frantz had worked for an American company for many years before the war and deplored his current conditions, particularly when contrasted with the lavish treatment he received while on earlier business trips to Detroit. Moreover, Feer reported that all the general officers felt "abandoned to the care of privates and non-commissioned officers, many of whom [had] apparently handled them in an exceedingly rude and ill-considered manner."[48]

This kind of behavior contrasted sharply with the "most flattering attention" that had been paid to these officers by the British. Generals Frantz and Schnarrenberger, who had been transferred directly to Clinton from Trent Park, claimed that "considerate treatment [had] stopped abruptly when they were handed over to the American military authorities in England." The other generals fondly recalled the American Major Spencer, who had "handled them with tact and consideration," and the lavish accommodations they had enjoyed at Byron Hot Springs. But there was a striking contrast between the treatment they had previously received from the British and from American personnel in California and the treatment they subsequently received. This discrepancy convinced the generals that "their present state [was] the result not of neglect but of a deliberate desire on the part of the War Department to humiliate them."[49]

Making matters worse, the Swiss representative feared the generals' suspicions might be correct. He was "greatly upset by the manner in which the Generals were being treated." Both Feer and Gufler questioned how well America could understand European problems if they treated "Europeans of rank and culture" in this manner. "A good many tricks have been missed in the handling of the German Generals," Gufler stated, noting his impression that "the United States is decidedly not putting a good foot forward in its treatment of them." The inspectors recommended providing more reading material, clothing, and recreational equipment. Most importantly, they advised Clinton authorities to appoint some American officer personnel "to pay more attention to this side of the camp's activities," referring to the need to build some kind of relationship between the American camp personnel and the general officer prisoners. Feer and Gufler suggested that "some attention paid to the Generals might in the future bear valuable fruit to the United States."[50]

Feer and Gufler's condemnation of Camp Clinton's officer compound was only the first in a long series of complaints, by both camp inspectors and the generals themselves, about American treatment of these men. The strongest indictment of the treatment of the German generals at Camp Clinton came three months later, in May 1944. After a follow-up inspection by Bernard Gufler, this time accompanied by Lieutenant Colonel M. C. Bernays of the U.S. War Department's Personnel Division, the two men condemned American treatment of these senior prisoners, singling out Clinton commanding officer James McIlhenny for criticism. The two inspectors characterized Camp Clinton as "superficially attractive but otherwise [leaving] a good deal to be desired." They laid the blame for Clinton's shortcomings squarely at the feet of McIlhenny and his staff by noting that "the prisoners have a number of complaints not heard in other camps, most of which could probably be straightened out if someone in authority in camp administration would show more energy and imagination than hitherto has been displayed by this camp administration."[51]

Regarding the general officer prisoners, Gufler and Bernays issued a now-familiar list of complaints, noting that many were requests that the generals had already made when Gufler visited the camp three months prior. These requests included the assignment of orderlies for Köchy and von Quast, American recognition of von Quast's promotion to brigadier general, the generals' petition to take walks outside the camp without signing formal parole forms, the "necessity of insulating their houses, especially the floors," and the prisoners' wish for tennis courts and possibly a swimming pool. The generals also wanted to send pictures of themselves and their bungalows, as well as some portraits of the camp painted by Schnarrenberger and Borowietz, to their families and friends in Germany.[52]

With the exception of insulating the generals' quarters, the two inspectors recognized that some of these complaints were minor. Their overall assessment of the camp, however, remained highly critical. As representatives of the American government, Gufler and Bernays expressed their impression that "we [the United States] still continue to miss tricks at every turn in our handling of these high officers. They [the generals] still speak highly of their excellent treatment by the British and of the excellent treatment some of them had in the United States prior to their arrival at Camp Clinton. [The generals] still appear to feel neglected and ignored and apparently are in truth neglected and ignored." The inspectors observed that the camp failed to provide "many little things" that the generals desired to purchase with their own money, despite the fact that these items could easily be obtained in Jackson, a short drive away.[53]

Significantly, especially for two Americans inspecting one of their own nation's prisoner-of-war camps, Gufler and Bernays suggested that their government might be ill-suited for the job of handling high-ranking prisoners of war. They concluded that "unless we can learn to play a cleverer game with these general officers it might appear advisable to turn them back to the British who know how to play the game." The two inspectors recommended transferring the generals to Camp Crossville, Tennessee, "unless some arrangements can be made to manage matters better from a point of view of our long term interest at Camp Clinton." They believed it would be worth the cost and trouble of relocating these prisoners because they felt Crossville's commanding officer, Colonel Harry E. Dudley, would be "capable and willing to handle the problems presented by those general officers much more to the credit and profit of the United States than it is being handled at Clinton."[54]

A large part of the problem stemmed from the War Department's choice of commanding officers. Considering the American need for qualified officers overseas, a significant portion of prisoner-of-war camp commandants consisted of U.S. Army officers who were either brought out of retirement, close to retirement, or unqualified in some fashion for other positions. Furthermore, these commanding officers exercised a great deal of autonomy in the running of their respective camps. Thus, the atmosphere of an American POW camp largely reflected the character and ability of its commanding officer, who had almost certainly been chosen more for convenience than qualifications.

Unfortunately for the generals at Camp Clinton, the U.S. War Department had entrusted the care of these prisoners to a commanding officer, Colonel McIlhenny, whom the American camp inspectors found unimaginative, lacking in energy, and negligent. Moreover, the colonel did not appear particularly concerned about addressing any of the issues raised by the various inspectors who had visited Camp Clinton. McIlhenny kept the inspectors waiting, delayed appointments, and generally displayed a strong disregard for what these men were trying to accomplish.

Further complicating the problem of poor leadership, the needs of American combat forces overseas required the services of the crack military police guard companies that had originally been stationed at Clinton. Beginning in the spring of 1944, the inability to find men suitable to serve as camp guards became a common problem at the prisoner-of-war camps in the United States. A memorandum prepared by the U.S. State Department in December 1944 summed up the situation by observing that "most camp commanders [were] handicapped by the assignment of soldiers as guard personnel who have certain handicaps, mostly of a mental nature." Almost all of the young men physically and mentally fit for combat duty were sent to Europe or the Pacific, leaving only those deemed unfit in some fashion with responsibility for the POW camps.[55]

The problem became so acute that it spurred a U.S. War Department investigation into the "status of training and physical condition of men assigned to Clinton, Mississippi," in August 1944. Following the investigation, Director of Military Training John P. Clegg concluded in regard to Clinton's guard personnel that "these men seem to have had sufficient training to do functional duty here if they have properly assimilated it. In some instances this is doubtful." Indeed, the investigators assessed each of the 262 guards then assigned to Camp Clinton and produced a report titled "Partial List of Enlisted Men Suffering from Mental Disturbances Employed by Prisoner of War Camp [Clinton] during Month of August 1944." This list included 69 men assigned to guard duty at Clinton who had averaged almost three transfers each before assuming their positions in Mississippi. Some of these men had been previously transferred as many as eight or ten times, suggesting that these guards had been reassigned to Camp Clinton due to prior poor performance at other camps.[56]

Furthermore, from the total list of 262 American guards at Clinton, 34 were diagnosed with "psychoneurosis," 7 with "hysteria," 9 with "anxiety," and 7 as being in a "constitutional psychopathic state." Other common diagnoses included "inadequate personality," "mental deficiency," "emotional immaturity," "emotional instability," "low mentality," "alcoholism," and "moron." The report identified one private as suffering from "borderline mental deficiency with mild antisocial tendencies, mild psychopathic trends and mild neurotic tendencies." The list goes on.[57]

No aspect of the accommodation of the German prisoner-of-war generals better epitomizes the differences between the American and British treatment of these men than the quality of the respective camp guard personnel after the summer of 1944. The highly qualified and well-trained men of the

first three MPEG companies had been replaced by limited-duty soldiers possessing far less ability, and in many cases severe weaknesses. Generals Frantz
and Schnarrenberger had arrived in the United States after a summer at Trent
Park where they regularly interacted with British officers, including the aristocratic Lord Aberfeldy, who displayed exemplary military courtesy. Generals von Vaerst, Borowietz, Bülowius, and Köchy and Colonel von Quast
arrived from Camp Mexia expecting treatment that American authorities
had promised would be more suitable to their rank. Upon arriving in Mississippi, these generals found drunkenness, idiocy, and incompetence among
the American personnel with whom they would have the most daily contact.

British authorities reserved the finest men available to serve as officers
and guards on the estates housing their general officer prisoners, while the
guards at American camps seem to have been some of the worst lot available.
Throughout the generals' stay at Camp Clinton, a number of other problems and complaints would arise, but none of these exceeded the absurdity
of placing America's highest-ranking prisoners of war in the hands of some
of the U.S. military's least qualified personnel. Moreover, this problem last-
ed throughout the war. Regardless of the changes that the War Department
would eventually make in its treatment of the German generals, these prisoners continued to find that a significant portion of their guard personnel were
not fit to serve in this capacity.

The criticisms that Gufler and Bernays leveled at the American treatment
of German general officers demonstrated that the problems largely resulted
from the dictates of an uncooperative camp commandant and the behavior
of his largely unqualified personnel rather than systemic War Department
policies intended to isolate or humiliate the generals. It is understandable
that American combat forces required the best personnel available, even at
the expense of the overall quality of personnel at installations in the United
States. However, one questions why the War Department did not take greater care to provide for its senior officer prisoners by finding a more suitable
camp administrator and staff for at least this one camp. That it did not do so
and that, in fact, the provost marshal general allowed Colonel McIlhenny
to remain in his post for months after the inspectors indicted his leadership
suggests American disregard for the importance of these prisoners. U.S. War
and State Department officials eventually reconsidered the value of the general officers in their custody and made policy changes accordingly, but not
until compelled to do so by the success of the Normandy campaign and the
consequent emergence of American concerns regarding the postwar reconstruction of Europe.

3

The Seeds of the American Transformation

Following the successful Allied invasion of northwest France in June 1944, Washington finally initiated a relationship with its senior German officer prisoners. Driven by a burgeoning sense of imminent victory, American policy makers began thinking ahead to the postwar reconstruction of Europe and what role, if any, the men in their custody might play in that process. Change began slowly.

Less than two weeks after D-Day, the British realized the need to free space at Trent Park for the many Wehrmacht generals who would likely be captured in the coming months and began transferring some of the generals to American custody. CSDIC started by sending three of its biggest troublemakers. Generals Ludwig Crüwell and Hans Jürgen von Arnim, along with their aides-de-camp, departed for the United States on June 17, 1944. One week later, after a transatlantic flight and rail passage from Fort George Meade, Maryland, the two senior officers arrived at Camp Clinton. Within a few more weeks, Heinrich von Hülsen joined his "pro-Nazi" colleagues as a prisoner of the Americans at the Mississippi camp.[1]

A little over two months later, after a flood of German general officers surrendered to the Allies in southern and western France, three more generals arrived in Clinton, Mississippi. These three officers, Ludwig Bieringer, Ferdinand Neuling, and Hans Schuberth, were the first generals to arrive on American soil who had not first been prisoners of the British. Rather than allowing CSDIC to take the lead in interrogating these three generals as it had in the past, the two Allies collaborated on the effort through a joint operation in France labeled "CSDIC West." American interrogator Lieutenant Colonel

Generalmajor Heinrich-Hermann von Hülsen (Courtesy of the Mississippi Armed Forces Museum)

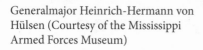

Gerald Duin, who would later play a prominent role in the American post-war relationship with Wehrmacht generals in the United States, interrogated these three generals as part of the combined operation and then immediately transferred them to Camp Clinton.[2] Considering that the British needed to make space at Trent Park and that the interrogations took place as part of a coordinated effort, the British almost certainly supported the direct transfer of these three prisoners to the United States. But this arrangement represented the seeds of independent American activity that would continue to grow until, by the end of the war, American military intelligence supplanted CSDIC's leadership in regard to the Anglo-American relationship with German general officer prisoners.

In addition to the three generals who arrived directly from France, other prisoners were transferred to Clinton by Trent Park authorities during the fall of 1944 as the Allied advance in Western Europe brought numerous new faces to the English camp. On September 19, 1944, Admiral Walter Hennecke arrived in the United States and quickly joined the growing number of senior officers in Mississippi. Hennecke was unique in that he was the first high-ranking German naval prisoner to arrive in American custody, creating some difficulties for American authorities. No facilities existed to accommodate high-ranking officers at any of the camps in the United States designated for German naval prisoners of war. Consequently, War Department officials, like their counterparts in the British War Office, chose to place Hennecke with army officers in order to keep him with men of similar rank. Therefore, the admiral found himself at Camp Clinton surrounded by German Army generals for several months before any fellow senior naval officers joined him in the United States.[3]

Hennecke's naval status also made it more difficult to assign him an aide. Clinton officials ordinarily assigned the general officers a suitable subordinate officer from among the camp's prisoner population. However, von Arnim, who became the senior officer and camp spokesman upon his arrival in June, requested that an officer prisoner from one of the German naval POW camps be transferred to Clinton to work with Hennecke. To the credit of the American commanding officer, Colonel McIlhenny, and his superiors in the Provost Marshal General's Office, they complied with Hennecke and von Arnim's request and sought a naval officer prisoner from Camp McCain, Mississippi, as a more suitable aide for the newly arrived admiral.[4]

Curiously, von Arnim also made a similar request on behalf of General Crüwell. In Crüwell's case, his aide was a year older than he was, and the general sought a more energetic, younger officer prisoner with whom he might have perhaps a less awkward relationship. Von Arnim specifically requested that the Provost Marshal General's Office transfer Major Anton Sinkel, who

Major Anton Sinkel (Courtesy of the
Mississippi Armed Forces Museum)

was then interned at Camp Alva, Oklahoma, to Clinton to serve as Crüwell's new aide. Again, Colonel McIlhenny and Washington officials approved the generals' request, perhaps indicating a slight change of heart from their past disregard for the generals' wishes.[5]

Yet the approval of Major Sinkel's transfer is also somewhat puzzling. Sinkel had previously been the designated spokesman for the prisoners at Camp Trinidad, Colorado, and had been sent to Camp Alva, a camp specifically designated for pro-Nazi agitators, because of his involvement in some Nazi activity in the Colorado camp.[6] Perhaps Sinkel's internment at Alva was purely coincidental, as not every prisoner there would have necessarily been a hard-core National Socialist. That Sinkel spoke proficient English and subsequently served as von Arnim's interpreter certainly made him an asset to the generals at Clinton. But von Arnim's increasingly vocal support for the Nazi regime during his stay in Mississippi, coupled with Sinkel's prior activity and residence at a "Nazi" camp, points to a potential connection between Sinkel and von Arnim and suggests the influence of ulterior motives in requesting the former's transfer to Camp Clinton.

Following the arrangement of aides for Hennecke and Crüwell, still more generals made their way to the United States. By the end of September 1944, a large mix of newly captured German generals and some old hands who had been in England for some time had crossed the Atlantic. On September 28 eleven new faces arrived at Clinton: Generals Erwin Vierow, Karl Spang, Curt Badinski, Theodor Graf von Sponeck, Erwin Menny, Fritz Krause, Kurt Freiherr von Liebenstein, Christoph Graf zu Stolberg-Stolberg, Robert Sattler, Hans-Georg Schramm, and Hubertus von Aulock.[7] This group more than doubled the number of generals at Camp Clinton.

The new arrivals barely had time to acclimate to their new surroundings before the Allies added even more generals to the mix. General Botho Elster and his large entourage of aides and orderlies arrived in early November, followed by six additional Wehrmacht senior officers by the end of the month. The last parcel included Generals Erwin Rauch, Paul Seyffardt, Alfred Gutknecht, Hans von der Mosel, Otto Richter, and Detlef Bock von Wülfingen. This brought the total population of Clinton's officer compound to thirty-two, including Colonel von Quast, who still awaited American recognition of his promotion but who was allowed to live in the enclosure because he served as an aide to General von Vaerst.[8] In the six months following D-Day, the number of general officers at Camp Clinton had quadrupled. This finally spurred American policy makers to take their relationship with these men more seriously.

It took a while for Washington's changing perceptions of the importance of its German general officer prisoners to translate into policy, and still longer for these policy changes to produce significant changes at the camp level. An inspection report filed in July 1944 by Werner Weingärtner of the Swiss legation and John Brown Mason of the U.S. State Department echoed familiar refrains. Weingärtner characterized the situation in the generals' compound as "deplorable," citing the lack of a number of items and the "attitude of the Camp Commander." Mason concurred, saying, "While promises and assurances in regard to certain needed improvements have been given repeatedly to the spokesman [von Arnim] by the American Army authorities since last winter, on the whole the promises have either not been kept at all or were fulfilled only just prior to the visit of the Swiss representative." He observed that the generals kept a written record of the exact dates of their requests and the camp administration's responses. For a month, camp officials had ignored the generals' request for garden furniture to be made by POW carpenters at Clinton. Finally, and inexplicably, the camp administration responded that the generals should simply order these items from Sears, Roebuck or Montgomery Ward. Unfortunately for the generals, these types of mail order requests also typically went unfulfilled for weeks on end. Repeated appeals for cigars had met with success only in early July, right before Weingärtner and Mason's visit.[9] However, the U.S. Provost Marshal General's Office did not consider these "deplorable" conditions.

The two camp inspectors also produced a list of now-typical prisoner requests, including American recognition of von Quast's promotion to brigadier general, the assignment of a German Protestant minister and a German Catholic priest to serve the officers' compound, insulation and double flooring for their quarters, a swimming pool, and tennis courts. Colonel McIlhenny had approved a tennis court for the generals' compound as early as December 1943 but, seven months later, construction had yet to begin. The generals also complained that their mess room and recreation building were too hot in the summer, suggesting that some awnings be added to provide shade over the doors and windows. And they bemoaned the fact that a carpenter shop, some American personnel offices, and toilets for the orderlies took up valuable space in their recreation hall.[10]

The inspectors viewed most of these contentions as minor, aside from the long-standing complaints about a lack of insulation and adequate flooring in the generals' quarters and some new allegations of gunshots near the generals' compound. Von Arnim expressed concern that a gun had been fired outside the generals' quarters the week before the inspectors visited the camp.

Apparently, one of the newly arrived and inexperienced camp guards had carelessly mishandled his machine gun. What caused even graver concern for the inspectors and the generals alike was that this was not the first time this had happened. Months earlier, a local squirrel hunter had fired a shot just outside the fence line. This certainly raised questions about why camp officials would allow hunting so close to the camp perimeter. Moreover, that gunshots had twice been fired in the vicinity of the generals' compound generated concerns about the prisoners' safety.[11]

Despite these concerns, one long-standing dispute between the prisoners and the camp administration actually brought the Swiss representative to the Americans' defense. The generals still refused to sign paroles giving their "word of honor" as German officers not to attempt to escape if they were allowed to walk outside the camp. The prisoners offered to "promise" not to escape but objected to being forced to provide a formal oath for simply "enjoying conveniences or pleasures." They sought to reserve their words of honor for extremely important occasions. In fact, one of the senior prisoners noted that he had not once been compelled to offer a formal oath in his thirty-five years in the German military. The Swiss inspector had surprisingly little sympathy for the general's argument and supported Colonel McIlhenny's decision to deny the generals parole until they followed the proper protocol.[12]

Also surprising, considering the number of complaints the generals voiced and the inspectors' condemnation of Clinton's accommodations, the prisoners expressed a clear preference for remaining at the camp. When the inspectors asked if the officers might like to transfer to a different camp they overwhelmingly stated that they preferred the "relative spaciousness, and the quite attractive, rustic atmosphere of their compound—dotted with many large trees—and its quiet atmosphere." They also appreciated that they could attend soccer games, theatrical productions, and concerts held in the enlisted prisoners' compound and that all of their quarters had been equipped with large new refrigerators.[13] Perhaps the generals had simply grown tired of transferring from one camp to another and were willing to settle for inadequate accommodations if it meant staying put for a while. All the inspectors' criticisms aside, it is also possible that the generals appreciated Camp Clinton more than they let on. Regardless, they expressed no interest in the possibility of seeking greener pastures.

Despite the generals' preference for remaining at Clinton, the camp inspectors still criticized the camp's overall accommodation of the German general officers. "The chief and basic difficulty at Camp Clinton, as far as the generals' compound [was] concerned," according to both the Swiss representative and the State Department official, was "the attitude of the camp commander." While they praised Colonel McIlhenny's administration of the enlisted prisoners' compound, they suggested that "running a camp for captured generals [was] a responsibility of a different character." The commander had inculcated his staff officers with his perspective that "an enemy is an enemy, and a POW a POW," insinuating that all prisoners should be treated the same, regardless of rank. Making matters worse, the colonel suffered from a heart condition that necessitated his leaving much of the daily interaction with the generals to his executive officer, Captain Winfred J. Tidwell. While the inspectors conceded that Tidwell was a "friendly and well-intentioned" soldier, they contended that "his background as a master sergeant for some twenty years who now holds a temporary commission" could "hardly be considered the best preparation for dealing with high-ranking generals."[14]

American Captain Walter Rapp spent several weeks at Clinton in the fall of 1944 and described McIlhenny and Tidwell in even harsher terms. According to Rapp, McIlhenny's illness affected his disposition and "neither his heart nor soul [were] in this matter at all." Rapp described McIlhenny as "very erratic" and he was astonished by the colonel's conviction that he was doing an excellent job. "He just does what he has to" and "works only about 4–5 hours per day," Rapp complained. "He detests improvements and only does things now because the PMGO order him to." Rapp's description of the executive officer was even more caustic. According to Rapp, Tidwell was "a lazy, ignorant 'yes man' who holds his position because he has no initiative and is the Colonel's mouthpiece." Rapp admitted that Tidwell was "a nice fellow, but uneducated and crude and lacks the poise, background and interest to deal with German general officers."[15]

Not surprisingly, these officers' attitudes influenced those of their personnel. The generals complained to the inspectors that American noncommissioned officers refused to salute them and, according to the prisoner spokesman for the German enlisted compound, the American NCOs frequently ridiculed the German enlisted prisoners for doing so. The Americans informed their captives that "the generals [were] only prisoners and they need not salute them," an almost verbatim reiteration of their commanding officer's attitude. Weingärtner intimated that the American NCOs at Clinton had "no manners" and blamed a lack of proper instruction from their superiors for this shortcoming.[16]

The camp commander and his subordinates displayed the same lack of regard in their relations with the inspectors. On the first day of their visit, Weingärtner asked to meet with Colonel McIlhenny early in the morning before he began his inspection, a common request from camp inspectors. Tidwell, the executive officer, informed the Swiss representative that McIlhenny usually did not arrive until nine or ten in the morning and would not be available that particular day until three in the afternoon because of a Kiwanis Club luncheon he wished to attend. Furthermore, once McIlhenny finally arrived and decided to meet with the inspectors, he insistently called them away from an ongoing meeting with the generals. He then advised the inspectors that they should keep their discussion brief because he wanted to leave early to attend a ball game. The executive officer also displayed little courtesy or regard for the inspectors. Instead of making himself available on the last evening of their visit, another customary courtesy, he "excused himself early in the evening to go to a movie in town."[17]

In part because of the commander's inconsiderate attitude, Weingärtner and Mason recommended that the provost marshal general replace McIlhenny as camp commandant. They observed that "the German generals are naturally much interested in the type of American officer they meet. [The United States] could make a favorable and lasting impression [on these prisoners] and more in the future, if we put in charge an American officer able to deal with them with tact, consideration and insight." Echoing the remarks of past inspectors, they concluded their report by stating that, "at the present time, the United States Government is missing a unique opportunity at Camp Clinton to influence in our favor [these] German generals who some day will return to a Germany that will ask them: 'What is America like?'"[18]

The inspectors based their belief that American officials could favorably influence the generals on the latter's expressed interest in numerous aspects of American history and culture. The Swiss representative asked the generals to prepare a list of topics of interest to them for possible books and lectures that might be supplied by American officials. The prisoners' list overwhelmingly featured American topics, including the "animals, plants and geography of the Americas, especially the United States," "history of the American Indians," American literature, American art, the U.S. Constitution, and biographies of famous Americans, like George Washington and Abraham Lincoln. General von Vaerst even requested works by Walter Lippmann, an American writer whom the Nazis had bitterly criticized. The inspectors saw these as positive signs that the generals might be open to the American message.[19]

This encouragement, coupled with the third highly critical assessment of Camp Clinton's treatment of the German general officers in six months, finally struck a chord with American policy makers now beginning to look to the future of postwar Germany. For starters, the U.S. Provost Marshal General's Office insisted that repairs and improvements be made to the generals' quarters. In doing so, however, it paid strict adherence to the provision of the Geneva Convention that required accommodations for POWs to match those provided U.S. soldiers of equal rank. The generals and three separate teams of camp inspectors had all complained about cracks in the walls of the generals' apartments and the lack of insulation and double flooring that exacerbated both the summer heat and the winter cold. The U.S. Army Corps of Engineers repaired the exterior siding of the generals' homes, caulked the cracks in the walls, and closed the holes in the floors by nailing batten underneath the flooring, which brought the buildings up to the same standards as those provided American general officers. According to U.S. War Department policy, however, Mississippi's southern location placed Camp Clinton in a temperature zone that did not require insulation for American officer housing. Consequently, War Department officials denied the generals' quarters any additional insulation because this would have exceeded the quality of physical accommodations provided to American generals. If American officers in southern climates were required to live without insulation, the German generals would have to do the same. Likewise, the War Department refused to install awnings for the generals' mess room and recreation hall because these items were not provided for American officers either.[20]

In addition to having basic repairs made to the generals' quarters, the PMGO sent Brigadier General Blackshear M. Bryan, the assistant provost marshal general, to personally meet with Colonel McIlhenny and explain to him the importance of "handling general officer prisoners in a fashion which will reflect credit on the United States and create among the prisoners a favorable attitude toward this country and its institutions." General Bryan informed McIlhenny that the colonel should "visit the Germans, ascertain the things they desired, inform them whether or not he could procure them, and above all, that he should make good his promises." Bryan further stressed the need to provide "small comfort items not provided for ordinary prisoners of war."[21]

Following his meeting with General Bryan, McIlhenny responded immediately. He notified his superiors that he would now have "more intimate contacts" with the German general officers, would "acquiesce to their requests wherever possible," and would "make a special point of obtaining small purchases for them within a reasonable length of time." He pledged to do so "at once with tact, consideration and insight."[22] He proved to be a man of his word.

A little over a week after McIlhenny vowed to make changes at Camp

Clinton, two inspectors from the PMGO's Prisoner of War Division visited the camp and noticed a significant difference already. First, McIlhenny had finally explained to the generals that some of their requests simply could not be fulfilled, for legitimate reasons. On three separate occasions, for instance, McIlhenny had requested in writing that the PMGO recognize von Quast's promotion to general officer. It was finally explained to the prisoners that this was not going to happen because of existing U.S. War Department regulations. The camp inspectors stated that "the generals understood." Moreover, the generals' requests for the construction of a swimming pool in their compound or access to one outside the camp would also not be possible. First, construction of a pool required "critical material," namely concrete, that was too vital to the American war effort to expend on prisoners of war or even American civilians. And allowing prisoners of war access to public recreation facilities like swimming pools in nearby towns was out of the question for reasons related to both American public opinion and the prisoners' safety. The inspectors again stated that the generals understood why these requests could not be fulfilled.[23] Surely, German career military officers appreciated the demands of wartime mobilization and the dictates of military regulations.

Had this reasoning been explained to the generals months earlier, a great deal of confusion and complaining might have been avoided. That McIlhenny took the time to do so in August 1944 demonstrated the commandant's interest in building a better relationship with his prisoners. But what most impressed the inspectors was not McIlhenny's explanations but his actions. True to his word, he was now doing his utmost to provide all he could for the generals. War Department officials had refused to provide awnings over the doors and windows of the generals' mess and recreation buildings because these items exceeded the accommodations provided for American general officers. McIlhenny circumvented this policy by placing scrap lumber and the necessary tools at the prisoners' disposal and permitting the generals' orderlies to construct and install the awnings themselves. This worked so well that awnings were added to the officers' quarters as well, which exceeded the generals' original request. And instead of denying the generals tennis courts because this too would have required cement, McIlhenny ordered construction of clay courts, one of which was nearly completed at the time of the inspectors' visit in August 1944 while another was added shortly thereafter.[24]

The camp commander now sought to address virtually all of the senior officers' concerns. He relocated the American personnel offices out of the prisoners' recreation hall and initiated plans to remodel the building to suit the generals' needs. The American guard who accidentally fired his weapon near the officers' compound received disciplinary punishment, and Mc-Ilhenny began allowing the generals regular walks outside the camp after Washington reached some compromise with the men over the wording of the parole forms they were required to sign. The commandant also promised to show films in the prisoners' compound and ordered a large number of books to supplement the POW camp library. Remarkably, for the first time in Mc-Ilhenny's administration at Camp Clinton, inspectors reported the existence of a "very congenial relationship" between the commanding officer and his general officer prisoners.[25]

McIlhenny's treatment of the German generals only improved. When Emil Greuter from the Swiss legation and Charles Eberhardt of the U.S. State Department inspected Clinton in January 1945, they found a very different camp from the one their organizations had condemned six months earlier. Of course, the most noticeable change from the prior visit was the considerably larger number of prisoners. Fifty-three prisoners inhabited the officers' compound at Clinton, twenty-nine of them listed as general officers.[26] Curiously, this number reflected the departure of three of the senior officers in the previous few months. Admiral Hennecke had been transferred to Camp Pryor, Oklahoma, where he joined other high-ranking German naval officers, and General von der Mosel had temporarily gone to the POW hospital at Camp Forrest, Tennessee, for unspecified health reasons. The third departure, that of Gotthard Frantz, was unique. Like von der Mosel, Frantz was beset by health problems. He had spent a month in a British hospital while a prisoner at Trent Park and his chronic ailments continued to plague him during his time in the United States. Consequently, American authorities opted to repatriate Frantz in early 1945 for health reasons. Unfortunately for Frantz, this American decision brought unintended consequences. He arrived in Germany on the first of February, only to be captured by the Soviet Army two months later, in April 1945. He then spent over four years as a prisoner of war in the Soviet Union before finally being allowed to again return to Germany, on November 2, 1949.[27]

Other transfers out of Camp Clinton occurred in the following months, most of these for health reasons. On the very day of Greuter and Eberhardt's visit in January, Clinton camp authorities began arrangements for the transfer of General Bülowius. He too was bound for the POW hospital at Camp Forrest, Tennessee, although unlike his colleague von der Mosel, Bülowius never returned to Clinton. Bülowius suffered from "involutional melancholia, manifested in depression and delusions of persecution." The general was convinced that he had been given a death sentence by an impromptu court-martial of his peers at Clinton. American investigations found these claims to be entirely unfounded. Nonetheless, these delusions drove Bülowius to attempt to take his own life by slashing his wrists. This first attempt proved unsuccessful, causing only superficial wounds. On March 26, 1945, however, the general wrote a suicide note to his friend and fellow prisoner, Willibald Borowietz. The following day, he removed the leather straps from his brief-case and hanged himself from the crossbars of the window in his room at the mental health ward of the Camp Forrest POW hospital. By the time the American medical staff found him, he was dead.[28]

Bülowius was not the only German prisoner-of-war general to take his own life. Ironically, Borowietz, the friend and fellow prisoner to whom Bülowius had addressed his suicide note, followed suit a little over three months later. The local newspaper, the *Clarion-Ledger* in Jackson, reported that Borowietz had "just dropped over dead" from a "cerebral hemorrhage" on July 1, 1945. Rumors quickly spread, almost certainly originating with American personnel who worked at the camp, that the general had commit-ted suicide, but camp officials refused to confirm these reports. Many years after the war ended and the camp closed, W. P. Taylor, a member of the Ameri-can guard personnel who had been stationed at Clinton in July 1945, vividly remembered that Borowietz "got in a bath tub filled with water and stuck his finger in a light socket. It was instant suicide." While the autopsy results do not appear to have been publicized, the official records of the U.S. Provost Marshal General's Office list Borowietz's cause of death as "electric shock," corroborat-ing Taylor's story of Borowietz's death being a suicide by electrocution.[29]

One other Clinton general also committed suicide, although not until he returned to Germany. Alfred Gutknecht displayed typical, albeit somewhat extreme characteristics of "barbed-wire psychosis"—the damage to a pris-oner's mental health after months of captivity. Clinton camp officials stated that by January 1945 Gutknecht "had reached the stage where, pacing the compound like a caged animal, continually crowding against the wire enclo-sure, he seemed in danger of being fired upon by some guard. He refused to accompany the other officers on their daily walks, saying that they 'walked too slowly.'" Clinton medical authorities transferred Gutknecht to Glennan General Hospital in Okmulgee, Oklahoma, which had recently been desig-nated as an asylum for mentally ill prisoners of war. Unlike his colleague Bülowius, who had been sent to Camp Forrest, Tennessee, Gutknecht re-covered enough to survive his ordeal as a prisoner of war and return to Ger-many. Yet, tragically, he took his own life in Berlin on November 12, 1946, shortly after he had returned home.[30]

Despite the temptation to assume "barbed-wire psychosis," it is almost impossible to determine why any of these men would have chosen to commit suicide. American officials conducted a study comparing the suicide rate among all prisoners of war in the United States with that among the American civilian population and found almost identical results. Thus it seems most likely that each of the three generals who committed suicide probably already suffered from some form of mental illness and the generals' status as prisoners of war simply exacerbated their condition.[31]

Aside from these suicides, only one other Wehrmacht general died while a prisoner of war in the United States. Hans Schuberth died from a brain tumor on April 4, 1945, in Kennedy Army General Hospital in Memphis, Tennessee, where he had been transferred a month earlier. Regardless of his service to the enemy or his status as a prisoner of war, American authorities allowed his fellow prisoners to pay their respects in proper military fashion. Eight days later he was buried in the cemetery at Camp Como, Mississippi, a short distance from Memphis. His body first laid in state in the camp's prisoner-of-war chapel, guarded by German prisoner-of-war officers from the camp. For his funeral, a Nazi flag bearing the swastika was draped across his casket, which was carried by the German officers through two lines of German prisoners solemnly offering a Nazi stiff-armed salute. Three drummers and a small band, all prisoners of war, led the procession to the cemetery, a mile away from the prisoner stockade, followed by the hearse bearing the deceased general and lines of unguarded prisoners. The procession returned to camp after two of the prisoners offered an oration and a eulogy in German and a squad of American soldiers fired three volleys over Schuberth's grave.[32]

These tragedies notwithstanding, Greuter and Eberhardt were also immediately struck by the greatly improved attitude of Camp Clinton's administration during their January 1945 inspection. Where Weingärtner and Mason had been largely disregarded during their two-day visit in July 1944, Tidwell met Greuter and Eberhardt early in the morning at the front gate and escorted them to the camp commander's office, where McIlhenny awaited their arrival. The two American officers showed the inspectors "every courtesy and attention," including McIlhenny joining the two men for dinner in the officers' mess both evenings of their visit.[33]

Not only were the American personnel noticeably more professional, but the generals' living conditions also showed "marked improvement." In fact, the inspectors' January 1945 description of the camp illustrates that the American administration had addressed almost every previous complaint. The generals had been enjoying the new clay tennis court, completed four months earlier in September 1944, a German minister and priest now conducted services in the officers' compound, and camp personnel permitted the generals outside of the camp several times each week. Usually the generals took regular two-hour walks escorted by an American officer along the roads surrounding Clinton, and two days each week the officers were allowed unescorted visits to the Mississippi River Basin Model being constructed by the enlisted prisoners adjacent to the camp.[34]

Even more remarkable, Greuter and Eberhardt commended the "good job" McIlhenny had done in repairing the building in the officers' compound. Denied sufficient lumber, the commandant secured the use of a type of "tar paper linoleum" for the floors in the generals' quarters and had the interior walls in the apartments, mess hall, recreation hall, and chapel repainted. Furthermore, McIlhenny had partitions built between the toilets in the building used for showers and bathrooms despite the fact that the generals' prior requests to this effect had been denied by the U.S. War Department.[35] Camp Clinton's commanding officer obviously took seriously his superiors' admonition to acquiesce to the generals' requests wherever possible.

Yet Greuter and Eberhardt continued to criticize McIlhenny's administration of Camp Clinton, despite their admission that the generals "had no complaints, only wishes or requests" and that these requests largely involved articles that were restricted for prisoners of war. The Swiss inspectors seemed to be caught in a maze of their own creation. Eberhardt conceded that "nothing should be allowed to detract from the really commendable work of Colonel McIlhenny," but the two inspectors pressed for further improvements nonetheless. They believed that "a camp commander [who was] not too-rules-and-regulations-bound, and with some initiative and imagination, could and might well have closer and more frequent contacts with these generals, and also make certain concessions and possibly waivers of strict application of regulations to permit the generals to be supplied with various articles for their personal use even though such articles may at the moment be on the restricted list."[36] Thus the inspectors charged that McIlhenny lacked the proper initiative for the position of commandant at an important post like Clinton in large measure because he refused to exceed or circumvent existing U.S. War Department regulations in his relations with the German general officers.

American expectations had clearly risen. One year earlier, condemnations of the generals' compound at Camp Clinton by the Swiss legation and the U.S. Department of State garnered little attention. By January 1945, seven months after the successful Allied invasion of northwest France and at a point in the war when Allied officials believed victory to be imminent, camp inspectors now criticized the very same camp administration for failing to circumvent War Department regulations. American beliefs that these generals might be of use after the war now compelled Washington to demand that the generals in its custody receive treatment that paralleled that accorded to the generals in Britain.

The International Committee of the Red Cross agreed. On the first of February 1945, Paul Schnyder and Dr. Max Zehnder of the Red Cross arrived at Camp Clinton. These visitors reiterated the criticisms of Clinton's treatment of the generals made the month prior by Greuter and Eberhardt. Their inspection report stated that McIlhenny "was informed of the desire of the officers to buy pajamas with their own money, but the colonel refused, pursuant to instructions contained in [U.S. War Department prisoner-of-war] circular no. 50, which forbids such purchases." Schnyder and Zehnder continued by observing that McIlhenny refused to authorize the generals to purchase the reading glasses that several of them apparently needed, and the generals' requests for cigars and chests for the safekeeping of their personal effects had apparently gone unfulfilled. The Red Cross inspectors concluded that "this camp makes a rather good impression, although it appears a little neglected by the authorities."[37] That a lack of pajamas and cigars qualified the camp to be characterized as "a little neglected" illustrates the high international expectations for the treatment of general officer prisoners.

As early as August 1944, officials in the U.S. State Department had begun to reexamine American treatment of the German generals at Camp Clinton, likely in response to the series of critical camp inspections during the spring and summer of 1944. Noting the high "social standing and general prestige" of general officers in Germany, John Brown Mason of the State Department argued that, upon repatriation, "several or all of [the German generals at Clinton were] likely to exercise considerable influence on Germany's life regardless of the type of German government which may then be in existence." Mason observed that approximately thirty German generals were already in Soviet custody and that these prisoners were likely to "return to Germany deeply impressed with their experiences against and inside Russia" and "with memories of special courtesies and opportunities extended to at least half of them." He stressed that it would be in the best interest of the United States if "there should be among the returned German prisoner of war officers a strong contingent of generals who have strong and favorable impressions of *this* country."[38]

With this end in mind, Mason proposed a nine-point "Course of Action."

His plan started with treating the generals in a fashion that would impress them with the "knowledge that they were treated as generals and gentlemen [in the United States], more in line with the way they [had] been treated in Great Britain and in contrast with the reception given them at Clinton." Mason suggested that the generals have the opportunity to become better acquainted with the "enormous economic strength and industrial power of the United States" as well as "certain aspects of American history, political life, education and cultural activities." To this end, films, books, lectures, and even visits to places like shipyards and ordnance depots or museums, historic sites, and universities should be employed.[39]

Mason "strongly recommended that the post of camp commander at [Camp Clinton] be assigned to a retired American general, preferably a graduate of West Point or other military school," and that this officer "possess a strong sense of military tradition and courtesy." He believed the commandant of the generals' camp should be widely traveled and well educated so as to "present an intelligent American attitude" to the generals in U.S. custody. Mason also recommended the appointment of a camp educational officer of similar mindset, albeit not necessarily of the same high rank, and with the ability to speak German to assist the camp commander. He suggested that a POW officer be assigned to teach the generals the English language and that each general be given the opportunity to purchase his own radio so that any extremists among them could not prevent their fellow prisoners from listening to American news broadcasts. Moreover, he suggested that the generals should be furnished with copies of the Nazi newspapers *Völkischer Beobachter* and *Der Angriff* as well as the leading Swiss newspaper, *Neue Zürcher Zeitung.* The Swiss paper, printed in German and obviously not of Allied origin, was popular with anti-Nazi Germans because of its "reputation for truthfulness" and its informative articles by "outstanding contributors." Mason believed the "obvious contrast" between the Swiss paper and the Nazi papers would have "a much stronger educational value than even the best newspaper published in the United States." Mason also stressed the importance of selecting an appropriate German priest and German minister to serve the generals' religious needs. He stated that religious guidance "by its very nature [was] anti-Nazi, without any need for 'political' sermons," and he thought that most of the generals were religious men who were "generally respectful to the Christian Churches."[40]

Mason's recommended course of action for the general officer prisoners came at a time when the U.S. War Department was implementing an "intellectual diversion" or reeducation program for all of the German prisoners of war in the United States. The newly created Prisoner of War Special Projects Division of the Provost Marshal General's Office, led by Lieutenant Colonel Edward Davison, initiated the operation on September 6, 1944. The goals of the program included correcting "misinformation and prejudices surviving Nazi conditioning" and convincing the prisoners to "understand and believe historical and ethical truth as generally conceived by Western civilization." If the agency accomplished these goals, the German POWs "might come to respect the American people and their ideological values" and "form the nucleus of a new German ideology which will reject militarism and totalitarian controls and will advocate a democratic system of government" for postwar Germany. American camp authorities now sought to achieve these goals by enlarging POW camp libraries, showing films, and providing prominent lecturers for the prisoners and subscriptions to American newspapers and magazines, all with an emphasis on detailing American culture and democratic values. In effect, a propaganda offensive had begun. "Assistant executive officers" were assigned to each of the major POW camps in the United States with the sole purpose of implementing and supervising the reeducation program.[41]

Mason's proposals regarding the German generals, especially his reliance on educational materials, newspapers, and film, most likely sprang from the State and War Department discussions of the reeducation program that had taken place during the spring and summer of 1944. Mason based his recommendations, however, on the assumption that the general officer prisoners would play key roles in postwar German government and society. Curiously, Lieutenant Colonel Davison and Major General Wilhelm D. Styer, the chief of staff for the Army Service Forces, had other ideas.

Styer wrote to Davison in late September 1944, concerned about Mason's lack of understanding of both the enemy generals and Allied war aims, and he offered his own recommendations for the generals' "re-education" program. Styer's primary concern was Mason's assumption that the general officers would play influential roles in postwar Germany. Styer stated that this was "contrary to official policy towards Germany" and declared that this could not "be made a basis for the policy of [the Special Projects Division] in regard to German generals in our custody." Rather, he insisted, "no Junker general will ever be able to exercise any influence whatsoever in the future of Germany. That, to put it mildly, is one of the essential war aims of the Allies expressed in many speeches by Allied leaders, and in accordance with the wishes of the majority of the American people." Styer did not oppose organizing a reeducation program for the generals. But he advocated one based on the assumption that any American use of German generals after the war would only be in isolated cases where the circumstances had been properly evaluated.[42]

Styer did not believe that the British harbored any designs for using the generals in postwar Germany either. In fact, he seemed perturbed by the numerous inspection reports from Camp Clinton that took for granted the German generals' contentions that the British had treated them much better than the Americans did. Based on information he had received from American personnel who had at some point been attached to CSDIC in England, Styer contended that "the British [had] no doubt about the true nature of a Junker general." If the British granted their captive generals any privileges that exceeded American treatment of these men, they did so "for psychological warfare reasons only and not to 'preserve them and their influence' in Germany."[43]

Styer also took issue with Mason's characterization of religious guidance for the prisoners as being inherently anti-Nazi and his belief that most of the generals respected Christianity. Indeed, Styer questioned the need to provide the generals with a German priest and minister at all, stating that German Army chaplains were not Christians in the American sense. "They indoctrinate the German soldier with Wotanism," according to Styer, "and close each service with a prayer for final victory and Hitler." If the Provost Marshal General's Office wanted to provide religious guidance to the generals, Styer cautioned that it should at least be highly judicious in selecting German personnel.[44]

Styer's comments highlight a fundamental issue regarding American treatment of German general officer prisoners. The British based their policy toward POW generals largely on their immediate interest in winning the war. Whether this involved surreptitiously gathering military intelligence or attempting to use the generals for psychological warfare, the focus remained on defeating Nazi Germany. Once this task had been accomplished, the British quickly lost interest in Wehrmacht general officers. Conversely, American policy regarding the United States's captive generals lacked direction until late in the war. Washington was not motivated to gather intelligence from the generals, in part because the British graciously shared the fruits of their efforts with the War Department. John Brown Mason and the State Department recommended using generals to rebuild postwar Germany, but this advice was at odds with existing war aims, including the elimination of German militarism. American treatment of Wehrmacht prisoner-of-war generals proceeded haphazardly because Washington lacked a clear idea of what it wanted from these men.

In spite of his objections regarding the basis for Mason's proposal, Styer concurred that some form of reorientation program was needed for the POW generals. He advocated the immediate assignment of a German officer prisoner to provide English-language instruction for the generals and the provision of subscriptions to Swiss newspapers and one copy each of the *New York Times* and *Life* for each captive general. Styer agreed that each general should be permitted to purchase his own radio and that special lectures and tours of industrial and historical sites should be provided. Styer concluded by observing that it was common knowledge that "the American personnel at Camp Clinton [were] not tops." However, he believed that the appointment of a well-qualified assistant executive officer for the camp could compensate for much of the existing discrepancy.[45]

Styer supported the idea of a reeducation program for the generals on the basis that they might be used to influence the outcome of the war but not in order to allow them any role in postwar Germany. After the War and State Departments weighed the proposals of both Mason and Styer, Washington finally seemed to reach some consensus on a reeducation policy for the German general officer prisoners. The first steps included "an affirmative program to indoctrinate the general officer prisoners at Camp Clinton with a favorable attitude toward this country and its institutions, and, if possible, to utilize them for psychological warfare purposes and for the purpose of favorably influencing other German prisoners in United States custody." The War Department left "psychological warfare purposes" undefined. In light of references to Soviet efforts in this regard, it is quite likely that American officials envisioned asking the generals to offer public statements critical of the Nazi regime that might undermine morale among both German troops fighting in Western Europe and German civilians suffering on the home front.[46] But, again, this was not clearly defined.

In regard to indoctrinating the generals with a favorable attitude toward the United States, the reeducation program incorporated many of the tactics suggested by Mason and Styer. Authorities at Clinton and their War Department superiors increased the library holdings in the generals' compound to over two thousand volumes, all approved by American censors. The collection largely consisted of books on American history, literature, and culture, as well as other important works dealing with democratic values and Western civilization. Most of these were in English, although Washington attempted to provide as many German-language volumes as possible. In addition to the expanded library, the generals received subscriptions to *Time, Newsweek, Life, Collier's, Reader's Digest,* and the *Saturday Evening Post,* among others, and several daily copies of the *New York Times*. Clinton officials also purchased a 16-mm film projector for the generals' recreation building, where motion pictures, particularly those emphasizing the familiar themes of American culture and democratic values, were shown twice a week. Washington made arrangements with Harvard University to send a professor "to confer with the German general officer prisoners of war on educational topics of interest to them" and created a special fund to pay for incidentals that the generals desired, such as the pajamas and slippers that the prisoners had repeatedly requested in the past.[47]

While putting this program together, Washington officials also entertained the possibility of offering the generals a change of scenery to complement their new intellectual diversions. Because of the myriad criticisms of Colonel McIlhenny, whom some in the Provost Marshal General's Office referred to as "the impossible camp commander at Clinton," discussions began within the War Department in the fall of 1944 about the possibility of transferring the general officer prisoners to Camp Pryor, Oklahoma. While Pryor later housed officer prisoners, American authorities decided not to use it for the German generals. Instead, they directed their attention to a former Japanese American relocation center in Jerome, Arkansas. The Japanese Americans had been evacuated from Jerome in June 1944 and the camp had been appropriated by the War Department and reactivated as a prisoner-of-war camp a few months later. Washington initially seemed quite interested in improving accommodations for the general officer prisoners and believed Jerome had "quarters which [compared] favorably with the buildings occupied by the German generals in England."[48] For undetermined reasons, the idea of transferring all of the generals to Arkansas was abandoned. Certainly, the War Department quickly discovered that Jerome did not compare as favorably with Trent Park as it had initially suspected. Moreover, the camp would not be ready to receive high-ranking occupants for quite some time. Whether because of these reasons or because the officers at Clinton did not wish to relocate, Washington gave up the idea of moving the generals to a different camp and kept them at Clinton for the duration of the war.

Along with favorably impressing the generals by introducing them to American history and culture, American authorities also needed to assign to Clinton an officer with special qualifications who could insinuate himself into the prisoners' confidence and secretly ascertain the suitability and willingness of any of the generals to collaborate with American officials for the purposes of psychological warfare. The PMGO's Special Projects Division planned to provide a permanent assistant executive officer to Camp Clinton to supervise the intellectual diversion program of the entire camp. But a special officer was immediately sent for temporary duty to carry out the psychological warfare mission.

For this special assignment, the provost marshal general chose Captain Walter Hans Rapp. Born in Germany, albeit to American parents, Rapp spoke German fluently. He also showed "a good understanding of German soldier mentality." He had graduated from Stanford Law School and from the U.S. Army's Command and General Staff College at Fort Leavenworth, Kansas. His military career thus far had provided him with "considerable experience in the Mediterranean Theater as [a] military intelligence officer, especially in the interrogation of prisoners."[49]

Rapp arrived at Camp Clinton in mid-November 1944. At the time of his arrival, Captain Tidwell, Clinton's executive officer, was away on a special teaching assignment at Fort Sam Houston, Texas. This allowed Colonel McIlhenny to introduce Rapp to the prisoners and American personnel as Tidwell's temporary replacement, which explained his short, four-week stay in the camp. Taking over Tidwell's responsibilities as the American liaison with the general officer prisoners, including accompanying them on their daily walks, provided Rapp with a great opportunity for significant daily interaction with the generals. Moreover, McIlhenny informed the prisoners that Rapp had been "exclusively assigned to take care of their desires and requests." This announcement, coupled with Rapp's ability to converse with the generals in their own language, delighted the prisoners, particularly von Arnim, who felt that American authorities were finally making a special effort to address the generals' requests and concerns.[50]

Captain Rapp's primary "mission," as the Provost Marshal General's Office referred to his assignment, was the first attempt by American officials to evaluate the political orientation of individual officers since the first small parcel of generals had been interned at Byron Hot Springs seventeen months earlier in June 1943. Obstacles arose immediately. First, Rapp criticized the placement of general officer prisoners at a camp that also housed German enlisted POWs. The generals' orderlies and kitchen personnel went back and forth between the two compounds every day, allowing the enlisted prisoners to keep constant tabs on the generals' activities and amenities, as well as to overhear a great deal of their conversations. This arrangement, according to Rapp, presented two problems. First, the enlisted men came to resent the generals for receiving better treatment than they did. The enlisted POWs understood that certain privileges accompanied higher rank but were angry because they believed these circumstances had already been abused in the German Army prior to their capture.[51]

Second, and more important to the mission, many of the generals were unwilling to speak openly about any potential anti-Nazi sentiments, according to Rapp, due to the social environment of the camp. Many of the generals' aides and orderlies operated "a kind of espionage system," using it to eavesdrop on the generals' conversations and report these comments to their own NCOs or camp spokesmen, who in turn circulated this information back to von Arnim in the generals' compound.[52] Considering von Arnim's threats about postwar Nazi retribution against pessimists and defeatists and the real fear that family members in Germany might suffer if these kinds of accusations made it back to Germany during the war, it is not surprising that many of the senior officers wished to stay out of political discussions.

Aside from these legitimate fears, Rapp also revealed a division among the general officers themselves. Much like the prisoners at Trent Park, the generals divided politically according to when they were captured, Rapp believed. One group of generals had all been captured in North Africa in the spring of 1943, and consequently their comrades referred to them as *Afrikaner,* or Africans. The other group, labeled *Franzosen,* or Frenchmen, had all been captured during or after the Allied invasion of Normandy beginning in June 1944.[53]

Rapp described the *Afrikaner* as the "least susceptible to [American] ways of life and thought" and as men who "still [believed] in Hitler and his ability to win this war." He attributed this to the fact that these prisoners, who at this point had been in captivity for over eighteen months, did not have firsthand knowledge of the Allied air assault on Germany or the successful Soviet offensive on the Eastern Front. The letters they received from their families made little mention of the hardships on the German home front, likely in an effort to keep from exacerbating the prisoners' fears and anxiety about their families when there was virtually nothing they could do to help. Because of this ignorance about the state of the war, Rapp believed, the *Afrikaner* generals simply dismissed reports from American newspapers and radio broadcasts as propaganda and steadfastly held unrealistic hopes that new secret weapons or a great military leader, perhaps even another Rommel, would emerge to save the day for the German Fatherland.[54]

The *Franzosen* generals, by contrast, held more realistic views of the war, according to Rapp. Unlike their *Afrikaner* counterparts, some of these men had been in Germany within the previous few months. They had "personally felt the shortage of food, the rule of the Gestapo and the destruction [of

Germany] through air power." A few of these men had even seen their homes destroyed or had lost their families, and "such horrible experience[s] [had] made a lasting and profound impression upon them as far as the ultimate outcome of this war [was] concerned." Rapp reported that if the *Französen* generals dared to even describe the prevalent conditions in Germany in the fall of 1944, their *Afrikaner* counterparts would castigate their pessimism, defeatism, and "lies." Because of these circumstances, Rapp recommended that American officials segregate the general officer prisoners by date of capture as soon as possible. This, he believed, would easily separate the potentially "anti-Nazi" officers from the stalwart "Nazis" without tainting the individual reputations of the men with whom the Americans sought to collaborate.[55]

While Washington tried to determine exactly what to do with the "anti-Nazi" prisoners, Rapp continued his daily interaction with the generals. The most important part of his mission involved speaking to the officers individually, where possible, and assessing each man's relative willingness to collaborate with American authorities. Given Rapp's short stay at Clinton, he admittedly had little time to properly evaluate the individual generals. In fact, his reports to the PMGO in Washington provide assessments of only nineteen of the thirty-one general officer prisoners then interned in Mississippi. Yet Rapp's evaluations are important because they provided the basis for American decisions about which generals would later be transferred to the soon-to-be-established reeducation camp in Arkansas. Rapp's reports are also notable because they illustrate some differences with earlier British characterizations of some of these men and because they sometimes undermine Rapp's own facile categorizations of the *Afrikaner* and the *Französen* generals.

Rapp expressed pleasant surprise at how quickly he made connections with "four or five generals who [were] willing to throw in their fortune" with American authorities, although he stressed the need to provide these prisoners "complete security, treatment compatible with their honor as soldiers, and certain recommended privileges." The most promising among these anti-Nazi prisoners, according to Rapp, were Botho Elster and Ludwig Bieringer. Elster immediately informed Rapp that he realized the purpose of the American captain's mission and that Washington "could count on him one hundred percent." The general pointed to his decision to surrender twenty thousand men as evidence of his German, as opposed to Nazi, patriotism, which he claimed prevented him from supporting Hitler's "government of hoodlums." Elster assured Rapp that a significant number of the generals at Clinton believed as he did and that if the Americans showed patience and did not pressure them these men would eventually come forward as well.

Elster quickly introduced Rapp to a handful of other anti-Nazi generals and arranged to provide the American captain with "inside information" from the officers' compound.[56] It appeared that Rapp's mission was going to pay dividends sooner than expected.

Rapp described Bieringer as "the most intelligent and most cultured individual of all the generals contacted thus far" and as "one of the most outspoken anti-Hitler men in this camp." Like Elster, Bieringer felt "ashamed sometimes to belong to a nation who had managed to put gangsters into a government seat." With understandable skepticism, Rapp asked the general why he and his colleagues had not done anything to resist the Hitler regime in Germany if they had long held this attitude in regard to the Nazi government. Bieringer resorted to the now-familiar refrain that "as a professional soldier it was against rules and etiquette to delve into politics" and that the German generals had not awoken to the dangers presented by the Nazi regime until it was too late. While Rapp did not find Bieringer's response entirely satisfactory, he did recommend this general as a strong candidate for collaborative activity with American authorities.[57]

Rapp also suggested the possibility of working with Admiral Hennecke and Generals Seyffardt, Badinski, and von Liebenstein. Rapp saw Hennecke as "an impressive individual" with "a rather broad outlook on life and a fairly good cultural background." Hennecke convinced Rapp that he was adamantly opposed to Hitler's government but echoed Bieringer in regard to the Wehrmacht officer corps's lack of opposition to National Socialism, stating that "as a soldier one obeys and does not criticize." Rapp thought Hennecke might be useful in influencing German naval prisoners in the United States and played an instrumental role in effecting Hennecke's transfer so the admiral could join other high-ranking naval officers.[58]

The "congenial and happy go lucky" Seyffardt also favorably impressed the American captain. While he too openly expressed profoundly anti-Nazi sentiments, Seyffardt emphasized how impressed he was by the American prosecution of the war and the considerate manner in which he had been treated at Camp Clinton. Like Seyffardt, the "loudmouthed and unpolished" Badinski showed a great deal of respect for "such an excellent foe" as the U.S. military and openly spoke of his anti-Hitler views. Rapp saw Badinski as less of a prospect for assistance with psychological warfare, however, both because of his lack of education and because he demonstrated no interest in involving himself in politics, Camp Clinton's or otherwise.[59]

For the Americans, one of the most intriguing of the anti-Nazi general prospects was von Liebenstein. Rapp's basic characterization of the general as a cultured and educated man of the arts coincided with that given by the general's British captors at Trent Park. However, where CSDIC saw von Liebenstein as second only to von Thoma in terms of his explicit opposition to Nazism and his willingness to collaborate with Allied authorities, Rapp found his political expressions somewhat more subdued. In fact, Rapp described von Liebenstein as a "very cautious man" and only "moderately anti-Nazi." Perhaps the environment of Camp Clinton was less accepting of anti-Nazi sentiments and that attitude made von Liebenstein less comfortable expressing his political views. Perhaps, like a political chameleon, von Liebenstein attempted to blend into his environment. Regardless, Lieutenant Colonel Davison, Rapp's superior officer in the PMGO's Special Projects Division, had suggested that Rapp solicit information from CSDIC regarding those generals, like von Liebenstein and most of the others at Clinton, who had previously been in British custody.[60] It appears that Rapp followed this advice and, after doing so, attributed von Liebenstein's cautiousness to insecurity rather than seeing it as an indication of the level of his anti-Nazi political views. That von Liebenstein later emerged as an American favorite suggests that the general must have begun expressing anti-Nazi sentiments more adamantly.

A large part of the reason that Camp Clinton may not have been as hospitable toward the expression of anti-Nazi sentiments as Trent Park has to do with the Mississippi camp's composition. First, by late 1944, Clinton held over thirty general officer prisoners, as compared to the thirteen men at Trent Park during the majority of von Liebenstein's time there. This may well have affected the willingness of individual prisoners to speak out. Perhaps of more significance, however, was the way senior officer and camp leader von Arnim exercised "a very severe command over the rest of the officers" at Clinton.[61] At Trent Park, the pro-Nazi views of von Arnim and his sycophant Crüwell had been largely opposed by the majority of their peers, with the Nazi stalwarts including only about four of the thirteen generals interned in the camp. At Clinton, von Arnim wielded a great deal more influence. First, among the eighteen generals that Rapp had occasion to evaluate during his month at Clinton, the American captain found only six of them willing to openly express opposition to the Hitler regime, whereas eight of them were openly pro-Nazi or at least staunch defenders of the German government, regardless of who was in charge. Five were unwilling to commit themselves. This decidedly different prisoner environment, coupled with von Arnim's espionage network and threats of retaliation or court-martial after the war, may have hushed a number of otherwise vocal Nazi opponents.

Consequently, the Americans viewed von Arnim as being considerably more sinister than did the British, who had largely seen him as pathetic. Rapp described von Arnim as "very much pro-Nazi" and possessing "a rather genuine dislike for everything the United States stands for." Rapp did not find von Arnim to be particularly intelligent or well educated and concluded that he would never have reached such a high rank in the Wehrmacht if he had not been such "a good Nazi and only took command after everything was lost in Tunisia." General von Sponeck concurred with Rapp's assessment. In his memoirs, he ridiculed von Arnim's support of the Hitler regime and claimed that he never understood why von Arnim had been chosen to succeed Rommel in North Africa. "I disliked [von Arnim] from the beginning," wrote von Sponeck. Apparently, von Sponeck was not alone. Despite von Arnim's control of the officers' compound, there appears to have been some internal resistance to his authority. Rapp reported that "the instigations of many officers personally opposed to General von Arnim" succeeded in having him replaced as camp spokesman by General Neuling in late November 1944. The aging, perhaps somewhat senile Neuling, while declaring no political affiliations whatsoever, was at least extremely well liked by his fellow generals. He immediately improved relations with the American camp administration by cutting down on the number of petty requests made to McIlhenny and his staff.[62]

This change in camp leadership, however, appears to have been an isolated incident. The majority of the prisoners either remained committed National Socialists or kept their political persuasions to themselves. One prisoner, von Aulock, feigned a lack of interest in politics in order to keep a low profile. Some of his fellow prisoners informed Rapp that von Aulock had only recently been an *SS-Obergruppenführer* (the SS equivalent to a three-star general) but had been "transferred 'in grade' to the Army to avoid possible detection and punishment." Unfortunately, Rapp's informants did not make clear what von Aulock may have done to warrant possible punishment after the war.[63]

Two of the generals continued to puzzle Allied observers. Carl Köchy had been the most vocal opponent of the Nazi regime among the general officer prisoners questioned by American interrogators at Byron Hot Springs in June 1943. At Camp Clinton in late 1944, Köchy was still "very dignified and polished" and appeared to "choose his friends from amongst the 'pro United States' generals." Yet Rapp contended that the German airman had "lost contact with reality" during the year and a half in which he had been a prisoner of war and that Köchy had become reluctant to share his true political opinions, if he had any at all.[64]

Generalmajor Hubertus von Aulock (Courtesy of the Mississippi Armed Forces Museum)

Generalleutnant Carl Köchy (Courtesy of the Mississippi Armed Forces Museum)

Ludwig Crüwell remained the greatest mystery. The CSDIC operatives who evaluated him at Trent Park held him in extremely low regard, on one occasion even using the term "moron" to describe him. They saw him as a rabid supporter of the Nazi regime and one of the British camp's biggest troublemakers. Curiously, Rapp's assessment of Crüwell was quite different. Like the British, Rapp noted that Crüwell suffered from "barbed wire disease." But Rapp portrayed Crüwell as "very well read" and "very interested in English and American literature." In contrast to allegations that Crüwell was a "snake-in-the-grass" instigator at Trent Park, Rapp found the general to be a "cautious and careful man" who refused to openly proclaim his political views. And where the British continually remarked on Crüwell's pro-Nazi stance and his sycophantic relationship with von Arnim, Rapp wondered if Crüwell might actually harbor some anti-Nazi sentiments and thought the general was "certainly worth watching" for potential willingness to collaborate with the American authorities.[65]

Following the conclusion of Rapp's secret mission at Camp Clinton, U.S. War Department officials articulated a new program for the German prisoner-of-war generals in February 1945. Washington now found it imperative to segregate the potentially cooperative generals from those deemed uncooperative or even hostile to American ideals. Indeed, Major General Archer L. Lerch, the provost marshal general, argued that the cooperative prisoners needed to be transferred to an entirely different camp in order for the program to be successful. While a number of possible locations for this special camp were considered, including Logan Field Camp, located on the harbor in Baltimore, Maryland, the PMGO ultimately chose the newly commissioned Camp Dermott, Arkansas, in part because it believed the camp's accommodations could easily be made to exceed those provided at Camp Clinton.⁶⁶

The next order of business involved selecting the "cooperative" prisoners to be transferred. Washington based its general perspectives of each of the senior officer prisoners on Captain Rapp's earlier evaluations. Yet, considering Rapp's short stay at Clinton and his inability to properly assess all of the compound's occupants, the PMGO needed further information in order to make appropriate choices. Ludwig Bieringer must have continued to impress American authorities after Rapp's departure. Not only was Bieringer included in the group to be transferred to Arkansas, but Washington officials heavily relied on his opinion in choosing which of his fellow prisoners of war would accompany him. Ultimately, five general officer prisoners from Camp Clinton were chosen for transfer to Camp Dermott: Bieringer, Elster, von Liebenstein, von Sponeck, and von Vaerst.⁶⁷

Considering Rapp's high opinion of Bieringer and Elster, their selection was not surprising. Rapp found these two men to be the most cooperative generals at Camp Clinton and the most vocal opponents of National Socialism. Rapp found von Liebenstein to be cautious but likely to be cooperative as well. So the addition of his name to the list should be no surprise either, especially considering that he was a favorite at Trent Park and Rapp consulted his British counterparts at some point in the selection process. The selection of von Sponeck and von Vaerst is a bit more surprising, perhaps because neither man had been evaluated by Rapp. Von Sponeck had shown some opposition to Nazism while at Trent Park, although he had largely restricted his comments to his closest confidants, whereas von Vaerst had declared himself a Nazi while at Byron Hot Springs. The only evidence to suggest that von Vaerst might have harbored anti-Nazi sympathies was his earlier request for books by Walter Lippmann. The selection of these five men also undermines Rapp's conclusions about *Afrikaner* generals being Nazi sympathizers and *Französen* generals being defeatists. Of these five, two were *Französen* and three were *Afrikaner*.

The final aspects of the program for the generals involved the use of "specially selected media," including newspapers, magazines, books, and films, to politically reorient the generals remaining at Camp Clinton. The program also involved university lecturers, a carefully chosen prisoner-of-war chaplain, and a suitable officer prisoner to conduct English courses in the generals' compound. Curiously, as late as March 1945, the proposal to replace Colonel McIlhenny as Clinton's commanding officer with a more qualified American general officer was still circulating, but it never came to fruition.[68]

The Allied victories in Normandy had brought significantly more general officer prisoners to Camp Clinton. The quadrupling of the camp's population had in turn prompted Washington to reconsider its relationship with these men. Could they be useful in ending the war more expeditiously through psychological warfare? Would they be influential in turning the thousands of lower-ranking German POWs in the United States away from National Socialism? American officials initially thought so. They finally addressed the many criticisms of Camp Clinton and sought to make a more favorable impression on the German generals in their custody. Washington even carefully selected a handful of these men for special reeducation purposes. Yet, while the American relationship with Wehrmacht general officers would continue to expand as the war came to an end, it would not be along the lines laid out by Washington officials in February 1945. Instead, new faces would arrive that would push the collaborative efforts of American captors and German captives in a new direction.

4

Reeducating Hitler's Generals?

With the prospect of Germany's defeat on the horizon, Washington finally decided to put its captive enemy generals to use. Generals Gustav von Vaerst, Ludwig Bieringer, Botho Elster, Theodore Graf von Sponeck, and Kurt Freiherr von Liebenstein departed Camp Clinton on March 28, 1945. American personnel drove the prisoners almost 150 miles from the generals' compound in Mississippi to the newly established officers' camp outside Dermott, Arkansas.[1] Despite the intention of the Provost Marshal General's Office to accommodate the most cooperative German generals in a camp that rivaled Britain's Trent Park, these prisoners found life in Arkansas worse in some respects than their life in Mississippi.

The transfer of these five men constituted the first step in American plans to use German general officers for psychological warfare and for the purpose of influencing lower-ranking German POWs in American custody. The U.S. War Department specifically chose Camp Dermott, a former relocation center for Japanese Americans in the custody of the War Relocation Authority, because it "provided an opportunity to better the internment conditions of these general officers without excessive expenditure." In fact, Washington initially believed that accommodations at Dermott compared "favorably with the buildings occupied by the German generals in England."[2]

In the fall of 1944, officials from the PMGO met with War Relocation Authority personnel to develop a plan to convert the existing facilities into a functioning prisoner-of-war camp. Camp Dermott was built on almost a thousand acres of relatively flat land a few miles south of Dermott, a town of a few thousand people in southeast Arkansas. The PMGO designated thirteen buildings, with four apartments each, "for possible future occupancy by German prisoner of war general officers." Each apartment consisted of one or two bedrooms, a living room, kitchen, bathroom with a shower, and both a front and a back door and had hardwood floors. In light of the contentions over the condition of the generals' quarters at Camp Clinton, it was especially significant that the walls and ceilings of all of the apartments at Dermott were completely insulated. Given the camp's layout and specifications, Dermott could easily house dozens of general officer prisoners with their aides and orderlies in adjoining quarters. This feature appeared especially appealing considering the trouble at Clinton related to the generals' aides moving between the compounds and sharing information with the rest of the camp.[3]

Despite these features, American authorities quickly discovered that Camp Dermott's accommodations were not as impressive as they originally believed. The land surrounding the buildings was unattractive, most of it having been overtaken by weeds, and most of the wooden walkways connecting the buildings had fallen apart. The biggest problem was that the War Relocation Authority had stripped the camp of most of its material and equipment when the relocation center, previously designated "Camp Jerome," had closed a few months earlier. A November inspection by PMGO officials declared that, in its present state, Camp Dermott did not compare favorably with Camp Clinton, much less Trent Park, and estimated that it would take at least three months to bring facilities up to an acceptable level for housing general officer prisoners.[4]

Authorities in Washington were undeterred. War Department officials believed that Camp Dermott would make an excellent site for the cooperative general officer prisoners and simply delayed their plans to relocate these men until the buildings and grounds in Arkansas could be renovated. Yet, because of the number of POWs coming to the United States in the months following the invasion of Normandy in June, the PMGO activated Camp Dermott immediately and placed almost two thousand lower-ranking officer prisoners there by mid-November 1944.[5]

Initially, Camp Dermott was a different kind of POW camp. American officials sought to foster a more democratic environment, not only through prescribed intellectual diversions for the prisoners but also in the way the camp was constructed. Frank Stoltzfus of the Y.M.C.A., who inspected the camp in mid-December 1944, praised Dermott's open atmosphere, saying that one could move "over a wide area within the wire fence without the annoying additional blocked-off areas of barbed wire enclosures." The officers' camp was divided into four compounds "but one would not know of it," claimed Stoltzfus, "because there [were] no fences to block passage from one to another, and the movement everywhere [was] free and easy for one and all."[6]

The Y.M.C.A. inspector was also impressed by Dermott's commanding officer, Colonel Victor W. B. Wales. Stoltzfus described Wales as "a person of broad sympathies and deep understanding" and claimed that he had rarely seen prisoners of war "express such wholehearted admiration for their camp commander." Wales, a graduate of the U.S. Military Academy, had apparently won the respect of the German officers in his custody by attending the funeral of one of their fellow prisoners and greeting the prisoner population of over two thousand men "face to face." Stoltzfus was so impressed by Wales that he arranged to have the Y.M.C.A. temporarily loan Camp Dermott money for the purchase of some necessary supplies. Wales had cited funding problems as the main reason that he had not done more for the prisoners by December 1944 and Stoltzfus chose to help because of his trust in Wales's personal character, saying that "it [was] very fortunate indeed that the conduct of this German 'officers' camp [was] entrusted to such a person" as Colonel Wales.[7]

The appointment of a commanding officer of Wales's caliber was certainly influenced by lessons the PMGO had learned from dealing with Camp Clinton's commandant, James McIlhenny. Numerous critics of McIlhenny had suggested replacing him with an American general officer, preferably a graduate of the military academy, who was cultured, well traveled, and could deal with the German general officer prisoners as an equal. Placing Wales, a high-ranking, academy-educated American officer with sympathetic views of the prisoners, in charge of the operation at Dermott addressed these long-standing concerns about McIlhenny. Despite Wales's not being a general officer, in all other respects he epitomized the type of commandant that many in the War Department thought most appropriate for dealing with the German generals.

The camp's open physical arrangement, on the other hand, reflected the mission of the American "re-education" program at Camp Dermott. One of the stated goals of the War Department's new relationship with the Wehrmacht general officer prisoners was using these men to influence lower-ranking prisoners in the United States in favor of American democratic ideals. Undoubtedly, allowing the prisoner population of Dermott's four prisoner compounds to freely mix without barbed-wire restrictions would allow the generals to have direct contact with and presumably a strong influence on their subordinate officers in the camp. This arrangement also promoted American lessons about democracy by removing one of the authoritarian aspects of the camp.

Unfortunately for both American officials and sympathetic German prisoners, this arrangement had unintended consequences. In late February

1945, Captain William F. Raugust evaluated Camp Dermott for the PMGO's Special Projects Division, which was responsible for the reeducation program. Raugust found the social and intellectual environment at the Arkansas camp somewhat paradoxical. On one hand, since the chief goal of the reeducation program was to instill in the prisoners an appreciation for democratic ideals and western civilization, Camp Dermott was a model for its intellectual diversions. The camp's library already held an impressive sixty-five hundred volumes at the time of Raugust's visit and the assistant executive officer in charge of the program had ordered another $25,000 worth of books to add to this collection. Moreover, a large theater had been constructed that showed two motion pictures each week. But the most impressive aspect of the camp and the focal point of the American operation was "Dermott Camp University." Astoundingly, camp officials dedicated fourteen buildings to an educational program that offered six hundred different courses on two hundred subjects and featured 150 professors. Of the 3,156 prisoners living at Camp Dermott, approximately 2,000, or close to two-thirds of the prisoners, had enrolled in at least one class.[8]

Yet, in spite of the high level of prisoner participation in the educational program, the open and accessible nature of the camp aggravated an ongoing political divide among the prisoners. Captain Raugust stated that there was "every indication that an underground movement [was] in the process of being formed in both the officers' and enlisted men's compound." Camp officials believed that Nazi sympathizers were using so-called honor courts, in which they tried and punished their political opponents, to establish control of the camp's population, and violence had broken out among the enlisted prisoners. Indeed, American authorities tried seventeen German enlisted men for assaulting fellow prisoners. In one such incident, the perpetrators brazenly held two American guards in the corner of the barracks so they could not interfere with the beating of another prisoner.[9]

To make matters worse, the PMGO soon planned to transfer an additional six hundred officer prisoners to Dermott from Camp Alva, Oklahoma. The War Department had designated Alva as an American camp for Nazi agitators, and SS prisoners constituted a sizable portion of the camp's population. Raugust feared that the transfer of these six hundred potentially troublesome prisoners would only exacerbate the circumstances at Camp Dermott. Two prisoners at Dermott, Colonel Wilhelm Ludwig and Lieutenant Hans-Joachim Wolf, who had previously been interned at Camp Alva, claimed to have been "subjected to considerable political pressure from Gestapo and Schutzstaffel members" there. According to these prisoners, "super-Nazis virtually controlled the actions" of the other men at Camp Alva "by threatening violence to the less fanatical prisoners and to their families in Germany." Moreover, these Nazi thugs at Alva had organized an underground movement to encourage escapes, conduct sabotage, and carry on active resistance once the German military collapsed.[10]

The testimony regarding Nazi activity at Camp Alva and the planned transfer of hundreds of prisoners from that camp to Dermott raise questions about American motivations. It seems puzzling that the War Department would introduce large numbers of prisoners from a "Nazi" camp into the population of a reeducation camp specifically established for cooperative officers. Most likely, a shortage of housing for the flood of prisoners coming to the United States in late 1944 and early 1945 compelled Washington to take advantage of Dermott's potential to house up to ten thousand prisoners and forced U.S. officials to send German officers to Arkansas regardless of their political persuasions.

Remarkably, American officials do not appear to have anticipated the danger of placing hard-core "Nazis" in the same camp with cooperative prisoners. A special report on the "morale status of war prisoners" in February 1945 estimated that Nazi "super-fanatics" already made up about 10 percent of Camp Dermott's prisoner population. But the camp's assistant executive officer dismissed this dangerous minority as "a relatively small number to control effectively the remaining 90 percent to the point where either resistance or information would not be provided by the many other groups present."[11] Washington must have believed that the prisoners soon to arrive from Alva, as well as the Nazi malcontents already housed at Dermott, would be positively influenced by the educational program and the majority population of openly anti-Nazi prisoners.

This disregard for the potential danger of mixing pro- and anti-Nazi prisoner elements is especially remarkable considering the time and attention paid to carefully selecting the right general officer prisoners to be transferred from Clinton to Dermott in March 1945. Walter Rapp devoted over a month at Clinton to evaluating the generals and chose what he believed to be the five most cooperative senior officers. The War Department then took the extra step of sending furniture and accumulated items with the generals in covered trucks to make their new quarters as comfortable for them as possible.[12] This significant effort by American officials to carefully choose and transfer general officers would seem to be undermined by placing these men in a camp environment that was considerably more contentious than the one they left.

Given the influx of bad elements coming to Dermott in the spring of

1945, it is not surprising that the camp environment deteriorated further. Captain Raugust returned to Camp Dermott in mid-April 1945, only a few weeks after the five generals arrived, to follow up on the problems he first observed two months earlier. By the time of his second visit, Dermott's political environment had changed significantly for the worse. During the previous two months, seventeen hundred additional prisoners had been transferred to Camp Dermott. Half of these new arrivals had come from Camp Alva, as originally planned, and the other half from Camp Mexia, Texas. Astonishingly, War Department officials had chosen the worst of the lot from both camps for transfer to Dermott. Raugust described the approximately 850 transfers from Mexia as "Afrika Korps men who would not permit any of their number to either read American newspapers or listen to American news broadcasts." The American inspector believed these men were hard-core German patriots who were "utterly unaware of the changed conditions in Germany since their capture two years ago."[13]

The new arrivals from Alva were even worse. Raugust reported that many in this group were high-ranking officers who were "members of the Gestapo, SS men, and young fanatics. These men and the Mexia prisoners of war formed secret societies such as the Werewolves," according to Raugust, and "their aim was to maintain discipline and terrorize every prisoner of war in the camp." The Alva and Mexia prisoners "attempted rigid censorship of all reading material" and plotted to assassinate some of their fellow prisoners at Camp Dermott. One of the men on their hit list was General Elster. Elster had been chastised by some of his fellow generals at Camp Clinton, von Arnim in particular, for having surrendered twenty thousand men to a much-smaller American force in France. His new campmates sought to eliminate him as punishment for this "treason." Dermott officials had to take special precautions to protect Elster as well as other prisoners who had been threatened, including the camp spokesman and other high-ranking officers.[14]

The War Department had moved the most cooperative German generals to a far more dangerous environment and undermined the effectiveness of the reorientation program. Part of the Special Projects Division's overall re-education plan involved the circulation of a special news magazine, *Der Ruf* (The Call), in German POW camps throughout the United States. The magazine was prepared entirely by carefully selected anti-Nazi prisoners at a special camp in Rhode Island called "the Idea Factory." It offered realistic reports on the progress of the war and the state of the German home front and an introduction to American culture and democratic values. Raugust observed that the "terrorists" at Camp Dermott had discouraged the sale of *Der Ruf* "to the point where it was unsafe for a prisoner of war to be seen buying or reading that magazine." Furthermore, Raugust stated that "organized plots [had] been made against American personnel, including plans to take over the camp," and Colonel Wales "did not feel that he could quell the anticipated disturbances by prisoners of war on V-E Day with his present personnel." He requested that one hundred well-trained soldiers be sent to Camp Dermott immediately and that a battalion of troops at nearby Camp Robinson be prepared to arrive in case of emergency. The existing camp guard personnel had been on alert for several weeks prior to Raugust's visit.[15]

Apparently, whereas the Y.M.C.A. inspector had previously lauded the open atmosphere of the camp, Raugust now found at least one enclosure separated by barbed wire. As part of the plan to protect General Elster and others as well as to restore some order to the camp, Wales and his staff segregated almost two hundred "ringleaders" into a separate compound. They hoped that by removing these "Nazi" instigators, the plotting and threats against other prisoners would cease. Indeed, this seemed to ameliorate some of the harshest aspects of Nazi intimidation, but Dermott camp officials stated that a "fanatical Nazi element in this camp" remained "significantly influential" as late as September 1945, five months after Raugust's report.[16]

It is unclear why the War Department transferred some of the worst Nazi troublemakers in the United States to what was initially intended to be a reorientation camp for cooperative prisoners. Certainly, American officials could not have believed that the cooperative German officers, including the five generals, at Dermott would be a positive influence on the "terrorists" from Alva and Mexia. Indeed, it seems much more likely that authorities in Washington changed their minds about what to do with Camp Dermott and the general officer prisoners or perhaps had never really made up their minds in the first place.

As late as mid-January 1945, officers in the Special Projects Division still had no clearly defined policy regarding how they might use the German generals. In a memorandum dated January 15, 1945, Captain Rapp recommended to Lieutenant Colonel Davison that "immediate steps be taken to outline clearly the future utilization of German general prisoners of war." Rapp questioned what the War Department meant when it used the term "psychological warfare" in this context and what its ultimate goals might be in this regard. Furthermore, he recognized that a large number of enlisted POWs in the United States were "seriously concerned about our possible utilization of German generals for immediate or postwar use" and suggested that some of this apprehension might be relieved if American officials could offer a clearer picture of their intentions.[17] Curiously, Washington still seemed to be struggling to decide.

The War Department had established Camp Dermott as a reeducation camp for cooperative officer prisoners in the fall of 1944. At the same time, department officials had also planned the careful selection and transfer of the most cooperative general officer prisoners to join this group in Arkansas. Because of the need to renovate Dermott, however, the generals could not be transferred until the spring of 1945. Curiously, during this three- to four-month delay, the Special Projects Division solicited the opinions of the officer and enlisted prisoners interned at the Idea Factory in Rhode Island regarding potential American use of German generals in a variety of roles. The prisoners at the Rhode Island camp had been watched for several months before their selection for transfer to the Idea Factory, and American authorities deemed these men to be the most strongly anti-Nazi as well as some of the most intelligent and educated prisoners in American custody. Washington found their opinions revealing.

The prisoners at the Idea Factory argued against the use of German generals in almost any capacity. Lieutenant Dr. L. F. Mueller reminded his American captors that "only those military personalities were promoted by Hitler who justified the highest claims of political trustworthiness, indeed of energy, in a national-socialistic sense" and that this was particularly true of those appointed general officers. Mueller also argued that the generals would "find neither listeners nor a following in any degree among the German people after the war and defeat." He claimed that stalwart Nazis would be skeptical of any collaborative general's motives and likely brand him "a contracted traitor for the enemy." The German civilian population, on the other hand, would shun them, according to Mueller, because the Germans were likely to blame the generals for the enormous sacrifices that Germany had been forced to make during the war and for those that would continue after its end. He found "no positive or valued ability or practical knowledge among the persons of the German generals that one could not also find among trustworthy and irreproachable circles of the German people." Mueller concluded by emphatically declaring "the use of German generals by the Allies for any sort of task whatsoever contrary to the aims of this war, furthermore as dangerous, unsuitable and unnecessary."[18]

An anonymous group of officers, an individual officer named Lieutenant Birkhauser, and a group of enlisted men, all prisoners at the Idea Factory, also offered separate statements regarding the German generals. All of these statements echoed Mueller's sentiments opposing American use of German generals for reeducating other prisoners of war or the reconstruction of post-war German society. All three of the statements cited the impossibility of divesting German general officers of their militaristic beliefs. The officers contended that among Americans "the wrong conceptions about German generals [had] been created" and that "the exposition of generals in connection with postwar Germany and re-education of prisoners of war [was] a dangerous undertaking." They concluded that the previous twelve years under Nazi rule in Germany had "definitely and unequivocally shown how difficult it [was] to direct the steps of high ranking German military personalities towards non-aggressive political tendencies and for international cooperation and democratic ideas." In a similar refrain, Birkhauser added his belief that a German general would always remain "a man who finds the core of his life in the development and fulfillment of military power." Citing historical precedent, the enlisted men offered what may have been the most cogent argument against German generals taking a role in any kind of antimilitaristic reconstruction or reeducation plan. They observed that "after the collapse of the Bismarck Reich in 1918, the attempt was made to build a state which would serve the interests of the masses. It is noteworthy that generals did not make any positive contribution to this rebuilding." In fact, they pointed out, the generals quickly "began to support the organized powers which were aimed against the young republic."[19]

These statements also revealed skepticism about the sincerity of any of the generals' professions of opposition to National Socialism. The officers at the Idea Factory observed that "a German general who declares himself in the U.S.A. as anti-Nazi combines with such a position a definite political aim, and he will from time to time attempt to gain a position similar to that of General von Seydlitz in Russia." Lieutenant Birkhauser and the enlisted men both insisted that any high-ranking officers opposed to Nazism had already been removed by the Hitler regime prior to the war. They determined that while the general officers "may now loathe Hitler and despise the Nazi Party," it was "not because [Hitler] wanted to make the Reich a world-dominating power, but because [he] failed to do so."[20]

The anti-Nazi prisoners at the Idea Factory closed by asserting that the general officers had lost the respect of their men because of their dogged allegiance to Hitler's policies. They opined that "millions of German soldiers [had] experienced in this war . . . how German generals have foolishly sacrificed their men in order to execute the orders and plans for conquest of the 'Führer.'" This betrayal, they continued, had been "burned deeply in the hearts of German soldiers." And they stated that in this regard there was "no difference of opinion between anti-Nazis and other prisoners." The Idea Factory prisoners concluded by suggesting that "the only possibility to make use of a prisoner of war German general would be to use him for influencing nationalistic minded German officers in Allied prisoner of war camps," something the Americans were apparently attempting to do at Camp Dermott.[21]

In addition to soliciting the opinions of the most trusted German prisoners of war in American custody, the War Department also sought the opinion of Colonel Truman Smith. Smith had spent a number of years living in Berlin in the late 1930s, serving as the American military attaché to Germany. While he appeared less critical of the character of German generals than did the prisoners at the Idea Factory, Smith was equally pessimistic about the program's potential for success. Citing the "lack of a national policy on the ultimate disposition and future of Germany as a nation," Smith argued that American authorities were "not in a position to offer anything to these German general officers at this time." Therefore, he concluded that any long-term reorientation of the generals in the United States would be unsuccessful. He did recommend, however, "the creation of a relationship with these officers that would permit [the United States] to achieve maximum benefits from their services once a national policy [was] established." To foster this relationship, Smith reiterated others' suggestion of the appointment of an American general as commanding officer at Camp Clinton and recommended that other American generals make formal courtesy calls to visit the German generals interned there. Curiously, Smith opposed the plan to segregate some of the generals by transferring them to a different camp, like Dermott.[22]

By February 1945, a month before the five generals were slated to be transferred to Dermott from Camp Clinton, the War Department had been advised against using even the most collaborative Wehrmacht general officer prisoners for any special purposes. Perhaps as a consequence of these revelations, Washington never bothered to clearly define what it meant by "psychological warfare," and the idea of using the generals for this purpose was dropped altogether. Similarly, War Department officials made no plans to include any of the generals in the postwar reconstruction of Germany and no further discussion ensued about how the generals might influence their subordinate prisoners at Dermott or anywhere else. Indeed, it appears that Washington simply changed its mind about what to do with the five generals being sent to Arkansas. Obviously, the transfer of the generals to Dermott continued, as the plan had been set in motion months earlier. But the idea of engaging these men in a collaborative relationship with American authorities petered out. Instead, the War Department took advantage of Camp Dermott's unusually large supply of housing suitable for officer prisoners, and reorientation took a backseat to logistical demands.

In addition to assessing the potential reeducation program, Truman Smith's comments also highlighted the underlying problem with American policy toward German general officers in the United States as a whole: Washington had not figured out what it wanted to do with Germany after the war. President Franklin Roosevelt had done more to obscure American policy regarding occupied Germany than to provide any kind of unified direction. He expressed his views in a cable to Secretary of State Cordell Hull in October 1944, writing, "It is all very well for us to make all kinds of preparations for the treatment of Germany, but there are some matters in regard to such treatment that lead me to believe that speed on these matters is not an essential at the present moment. It may be in a week, or it may be in a month, or it may be several months hence. I dislike making detailed plans for a country which we do not yet occupy."[23]

What policy existed had emerged from the internal workings of the War Department, the creation of the Civil Affairs Division in particular. War Department officials had initially begun considering the potential occupation of Germany with the creation of a small military government division within the Provost Marshal General's Office in July 1942. The division created the Military Government School, located on the campus of the University of Virginia, to train American officers for the coming occupation duties. In March 1943 the War Department's newly created Civil Affairs Division (CAD), led by Major General John Hilldring, assumed the responsibility for training military government officers as well as a number of other duties.[24]

CAD organized a similar training program at Fort Custer, Michigan, which recruited hundreds of surplus officers from various army units. CAD also recruited civilian applicants, largely from professional positions, who earned officer commissions. All of these men received a month's training at Fort Custer before departing for Civil Affairs Training Schools at various American university campuses. They then received more training at the Civil Affairs Center in Shrivenham, England, before being sent to Germany to begin their assignments.[25]

Despite training hundreds of officers for military occupation duties, CAD suffered from the same overall lack of direction regarding American goals for postwar Germany. Historian Edward Peterson contends that CAD "emphasized the combat functions of military government and how to help the advancing armies" but "relatively little attention was paid to the job of military government after hostilities ceased." Moreover, CAD officials in

Washington resented State Department involvement, often refusing to meet with State Department officials regarding military occupation policy matters. Ultimately, CAD simply relayed messages from American commanders in Germany to higher War Department officials, allowing U.S. occupation policy to be largely determined by the American military governor, Lieutenant General Lucius D. Clay, and his subordinates in the field.[26]

Even during the first years after the war, authorities in Washington failed to devise clear American objectives for the reconstruction of Germany aside from the need for denazification and demilitarization. Had overall goals for Germany been determined earlier, the Provost Marshal General's Office could have better formulated plans for Germany's senior officer prisoners in America. But lacking a unified policy from Washington, the nature of the American relationship with Wehrmacht generals continued to be determined on a mostly ad hoc basis, as it had been from its inception.

Even in regard to the stated American objectives of denazification and demilitarization, Washington struggled to provide a coherent policy, at least when it came to its prisoners of war. The environment at Camp Dermott epitomizes this struggle. Even while promoting their new reorientation program, American authorities in Washington and Arkansas stood by and watched Nazi enthusiasts intimidate any German prisoners who attempted to ally themselves with American ideals. This raises serious questions about American priorities. If the progress of the war in the spring of 1945 had convinced American authorities that victory was imminent, which it surely must have, then what kept the U.S. military from cracking down on the minority of Nazi sympathizers among its prisoner-of-war population at Camp Dermott and other POW camps in the United States? Would the democratic ideals that the American reorientation program sought to inculcate not have been better illustrated by protecting the prisoners' freedom to explore and express them?

Apparently, American authorities prioritized order and discipline within their prisoner-of-war camps more highly than they did any attempts to denazify or demilitarize the prisoners. American camp authorities usually found that leaving the existing German military hierarchy intact, Nazi intimidation notwithstanding, meant that their POW camps functioned efficiently. Thus, when given the choice between a well-disciplined, Nazi-led prisoner-of-war camp on the one hand or a potentially open-minded but less cohesive prisoner population on the other, American officials often chose the former. The need for order—and for POW labor in camps that housed enlisted prisoners—ranked first among American priorities.

Despite this lack of national policy and continued Nazi intimidation,

Camp Dermott's assistant executive officer, Captain Alfred Baldwin, continued praising the political stance of the generals in his custody and promoting the educational program at the camp. He was most impressed by Elster, von Liebenstein, and von Sponeck. Baldwin described Elster as "markedly anti-Nazi," "very intelligent," and "thoroughly trustworthy," although, given his lack of popularity with the pro-Nazi elements at both Clinton and Dermott, he may not have had much choice. But the American officer also characterized both von Liebenstein and von Sponeck as intelligent and trustworthy anti-Nazi officers who had been "cooperative with U.S. authorities."[27]

Dermott's educational program also continued to receive rave reviews from camp inspectors. Y.M.C.A. representative Olle Axberg visited the camp in June 1945 and simply described the program as "astonishing," the expansive curriculum in particular. Dermott offered 439 courses taught by 286 teachers and featured a "vivarium" that included "a hundred animal, bird and insect specimens." Baldwin and his staff had recently spent $54,000 on educational materials that included three hundred subscriptions to the *New York Times,* two hundred copies of the *Chicago Tribune,* and one thousand issues of *Time.* Axberg also stated that "one hundred percent of the prisoners of war" attended the two films shown weekly in the camp theater.[28]

Axberg's observations portray a camp with the overwhelming majority of the prisoners involved in the intellectual diversions provided by the American reeducation program. Yet it is important to note that in the courses taken by prisoners at Camp Dermott, half of the students and almost two-thirds of the instructors were engaged in study of the English language. Captain Alexander Lakes, a field service officer from the Special Projects Division, assessed Dermott's program in August 1945, the month following Axberg's visit. Lakes criticized the lack of courses in American history, geography, and civics, topics that were intended to be the focal point of the reorientation program, and expressed skepticism about the overabundance of chemistry and science courses taken by the prisoners. Moreover, he stated his suspicions that the curriculum of a course in jurisprudence, taught by one of the prisoners, involved the teaching of Nazi ideology.[29]

Lakes also questioned the absence of a camp newspaper at Dermott, another staple of the American reeducation program. These camp newspapers, written and edited by trusted anti-Nazi prisoners, were intended to serve as a complement to the circulation of *Der Ruf* by offering a local prisoner perspective. Camp officials asserted that no POW newspaper existed at Dermott because the officer prisoners at the camp were "of a higher than average intellectual caliber" and had "gained the most personally from the success of the Nazi Party." This, the officials contended, explained why "the fanatical Nazi element in this camp, though weaker than prior to V-E Day, [remained] significantly influential." Dermott authorities believed that books and articles by renowned British and American writers would appeal more to the German officer prisoners in the camp than would essays by their anti-Nazi colleagues. Camp officials conceded that only one true "re-education" course, a 250-prisoner class on the U.S. Constitution, had been prepared. They cited "the necessity for the utmost care in their preparation and for the appointment of a reliable teaching and supervisory staff" as the reason for such a dearth of courses dealing with American culture and values.[30]

The incongruity of the prisoner-of-war camp being highly involved in a reeducation program, albeit one overwhelmingly focused on English and science courses, while also being heavily influenced by a "Nazi element" continued for the remainder of the prisoners' stay in Arkansas. When Olle Axberg returned to Camp Dermott in October 1945, along with Louis Phillipp of the U.S. Department of State, the two men reported that camp officials had spent a total of almost $200,000 on books for the large camp library, which now held over eighty-seven hundred volumes. The inspectors complimented the camp's music and art programs. Dermott possessed over two hundred musical instruments valued at over $30,000 and boasted the first play written and presented by prisoners of war in an American camp, a historical production titled *Christopher Columbus*. Yet Axberg and Phillipp also reported that the camp now had segregated compounds where an open camp environment had once existed. Their report also indicated that the "Nazi" Colonel Rudolf Otto continued to serve as prisoner spokesman and that most of Dermott's prisoners had come from Camp Alva, Oklahoma.[31]

Complaints surfaced as well, particularly in regard to the reduction of food rations for the prisoners during the spring and summer of 1945. The Allied liberation of their own, underfed prisoners of war from German camps beginning in early 1945, along with the discovery of the horrors of the Nazi concentration camps, caused an adverse reaction toward German POWs by the American public. This reaction, coupled with the War Department's need to prepare for the invasion of Japan, prompted Washington to significantly reduce food rations allotted to German prisoners of war in camps across the United States and to replace some items with less desirable substitutes. American authorities abandoned this policy by the fall of 1945 due to the need for healthy POW labor and a realization that the tenets of the American reorientation program were less likely to be absorbed by men with empty stomachs. Yet some damage to the prisoners' confidence in American democratic values had been done. Many of the prisoners viewed this brief episode as an act of American vengeance on a defeated enemy and it set back the reeducation program accordingly.

Admiral Paul Meixner, who had been transferred to Dermott in the summer of 1945, put his English skills to immediate use serving as a translator for the camp's ranking general, Gustav von Vaerst. His first responsibility, as it turned out, was to relay von Vaerst's complaints to Axberg and Phillipp in October 1945 about the treatment of the prisoners at Dermott. Meixner boldly stated that "the future of the world and of Germany [rested] upon collaboration between the Western powers and Germany." He believed that "the Germans were ready for such collaboration and they had full confidence in the United States." Meixner pointed out, however, that "the treatment which the prisoners of war had received since V-E Day was bad," especially the reduction in prisoner rations, and that it had shaken their positive perceptions of American ideals. Considering that food allotments had been partially restored a few weeks before Axberg and Phillipp's visit, the generals' complaints became a moot point. Indeed, the inspectors declared that the prisoners received "fair and honorable treatment," despite "their repeated complaints over the size of the ration."[32]

In addition to the reduction in the amount and quality of available food, a number of other changes had occurred at Camp Dermott since Axberg's previous visit. For instance, the well-respected Colonel Wales had been replaced by Colonel James H. Kuttner as camp commanding officer. Kuttner was not the West Point graduate that camp inspectors had requested and appears to have been transferred to Dermott from a post in the Louisiana National Guard. More importantly, the camp had assumed additional roles in regard to housing senior officer prisoners. No longer was Dermott designated only for cooperative general officers. By the fall of 1945 it had become home to numerous naval prisoners. In addition to Meixner, Walter Hennecke, previously at Camp Clinton, and fellow admirals Alfred Schirmer, Hans von Tresckow, and Carl Weber had all arrived at the Arkansas camp. Furthermore, Generals Heinrich Aschenbrenner, Walter Vierow, Curt Gallenkamp, and Hermann Pollert had come to Dermott in the fall of 1945 after spending a few months being observed and interrogated by American personnel at Fort Hunt, Virginia.[33]

These changes illustrate Washington's abandonment of the idea of reeducating and collaborating with the German general officers at Camp Dermott. War Department officials such as Colonel Truman Smith and numerous inspectors of both Camps Clinton and Dermott had suggested the assignment of a high-ranking graduate of the U.S. Military Academy as commanding officer of any camp housing German general officers. Yet the well-respected Colonel Wales, who largely met these criteria, was replaced by an officer of lesser qualifications. Moreover, some of the new transfers represented the type of senior officers whom American authorities least desired to include in any plans for postwar Germany. Both Curt Gallenkamp and Walter Vierow were later convicted of war crimes. Gallenkamp had commanded the German Eightieth Corps in France in September 1944 when it captured thirty-two paratroopers from the British First Special Air Service Regiment. After first sending these prisoners of war to Poitiers prison for interrogation by the Sicherheitspolizei (German security police), Gallenkamp ordered that all the men be shot. Two days later, a German unit drove the British prisoners outside Poitiers, executed them "on the orders of Hitler," and subsequently reported to the International Red Cross that they had all been killed in action. A British military court convicted Gallenkamp of the murder of these prisoners in March 1947 and sentenced him to death. His sentence, however, was commuted to life imprisonment and he was released in February 1952. Similarly, Vierow was later convicted of war crimes by a Yugoslavian court and sentenced to twenty years in prison. He too received an early release, in 1953.[34]

Remarkably, an "open" camp originally conceived as a haven for anti-Nazi officer prisoners had become a nest of Nazi extremists and war criminals. Indeed, Camp Dermott had been supplanted as the "anti-Nazi" camp by Camp Ruston, Louisiana. As early as the spring of 1944, well before the conception of American plans to segregate cooperative general officers, Ruston had been "designated for the internment of German Army officers and enlisted men, POWs, who [had] been classified as Anti-Nazi by the Office of Assistant Chief of Staff, G-2" of the War Department. By the spring of 1945, the Louisiana camp's one thousand prisoners consisted of a mix of officers, NCOs, and enlisted men as well as a blend of army and navy prisoners, almost all of whom had been classified as "anti-Nazi." William Raugust examined the reeducation program at Ruston two weeks prior to his first visit to Dermott in February 1945. He observed that the prisoners were requesting lectures on American history and American government and that three films were shown weekly to all of the prisoners. Significantly, Raugust reported the absence of any type of Nazi underground at the camp.[35]

Like Raugust from the Special Projects Division, Olle Axberg from the Y.M.C.A. also visited Ruston a few weeks prior to his first visit to Dermott. In May 1945 Axberg noticed that Camp Ruston possessed some unique characteristics. First, both the prisoner spokesman in the officers' compound and the American assistant executive officer in charge of the reeducation program were former university professors. Perhaps because of these impressive educational credentials, the camp offered an array of courses for the prisoners, including not only English-language instruction but also French, Russian, Spanish, and Portuguese. European, German, and Austrian history, the history of art, American literature, meteorology, electrical engineering, and "monetary politics," among other topics, were included in the list of ongoing classes at the time of Axberg's visit. Moreover, some interesting topics appeared on the list of weekly roundtable discussions conducted by the prisoners. Small groups of prisoners, ranging from ten to thirty men, discussed theology, law, and the "sense and purpose in gymnastics," and a remarkable seventy-five regularly discoursed on "traffic and commercial life in West Africa." Most notably, one hundred prisoners met to pore over the proposals for a United Nations organization emanating from the Dumbarton Oaks Conference. Axberg concluded his report by observing the presence of eleven professional painters and sculptors among the prisoners at Camp Ruston.[36]

Ruston appears to have been everything that Dermott was not. American officials and camp inspectors feared a growing Nazi underground at Dermott as early as February 1945, a month prior to the arrival of the five general officers from Clinton, when reports proclaimed that none existed at Ruston. In regard to the reorientation program, the fractious political divide and Nazi intimidation at Dermott stood in contrast to Ruston's intellectual environment, replete with professional artists and university professors. And by late summer 1945, when a "fanatical Nazi element" remained "significantly influential" in the Arkansas camp, inspectors from the PMGO reported that the "officers and enlisted prisoner compounds [at Ruston] were found to be in an unusually neat and orderly condition" and they rated the military courtesy displayed by the prisoners as "excellent." And this assessment came after the Louisiana camp's prisoner population had grown to almost three thousand men.[37]

The puzzlement derives not from the fact that Washington eventually sent newly arriving "anti-Nazi" generals to Ruston rather than Dermott, but that it had not done so sooner. It is curious that the War Department expended considerable time and resources choosing general officers to be transferred to Dermott and endured a months-long delay in preparing that camp for their arrival when it could have easily sent these prisoners to a highly regarded, existing anti-Nazi camp at Ruston that was located even closer to Clinton than Dermott was. That Washington officials chose to send the generals to Dermott in the spring of 1945 instead of to Ruston suggests that the War Department initially harbored some ideas about working with the generals in some capacity at the Arkansas camp, likely using them to influence nationalistic-minded prisoners. Washington abandoned this idea and transferred an overwhelming number of Nazi stalwarts to Dermott during the spring and summer of 1945. Yet it remains puzzling why the most cooperative generals—Elster, Bieringer, von Liebenstein, and von Sponeck in particular—were not subsequently transferred to Ruston, once the War Department determined that they would not be used in the Arkansas camp.

Von Sponeck wrote a memoir about his experiences in the Second World War and devoted a significant portion of the work to his time in Allied prisoner-of-war camps. Notably, the general made no mention of any political strife or Nazi intimidation among the prisoners at Camp Dermott. Von Sponeck stated that the generals and their aides-de-camp dined in their own barracks and had little contact with the rest of the prisoner population.[38] Apparently, segregated, barbed-wire enclosures had been constructed at Dermott by the time of the generals' arrival in late March 1945. While this suggests that the generals were in no particular danger or in uncomfortable circumstances in Arkansas, it also establishes that the generals did not engage in any kind of attempts to influence the other prisoners in the camp. If Washington had chosen not to use them, why not transfer these anti-Nazi generals to a real anti-Nazi camp?

Inspector Olle Axberg returned to Camp Ruston in the fall of 1945. By this time, the War Department had transferred to other locations almost all of the prisoners who had been interned there during the Y.M.C.A. representative's first visit. The Louisiana camp had come to hold not only a mixture of officers and enlisted men, as before, but a blend of nationalities as well, including German and Italian prisoners as well as over one hundred Russians who had been conscripted by German forces in northern France and were subsequently captured by the Allies. Despite these changes, Axberg again praised the commanding officer, Colonel Thomas A. Bay, and his staff for displaying the "greatest hospitality" and stated that they simply had "a grand time together." Moreover, he characterized the library facilities and services as "excellent" and observed that the educational program included courses in English, American history, and American civics, which accorded exactly with the tenets of the American POW reorientation program.[39]

By September 1945, following the conclusion of the war, Washington began sending senior anti-Nazi officer prisoners to Camp Ruston. Curiously, when Military Intelligence Service interrogators finished with General Walter

Vierow and sent him to Camp Dermott, they sent his Fort Hunt roommates, Captain Karl Gebhardt, Major Reinhold Koenning, and Colonel Werner von Tippelskirch, to Ruston. This may best highlight the different War Department perspectives on the two camps. The war criminal Vierow joined the Nazi-influenced crowd in Arkansas while his Fort Hunt colleagues, obviously believed to be of different political stripes, were transported to the anti-Nazi environs of Ruston, Louisiana. Other luminaries soon followed. Brigadier General Hans Gaul arrived at Ruston in mid-October 1945 and Brigadier General Rudolf Herrmann came one week later. Both prisoners had been "classified as anti-Nazi" and the War Department wanted them interned "with the other anti-Nazi German prisoners of war" at Camp Ruston.[40]

In spite of Washington's decision after the war ended to send anti-Nazi officer prisoners to Camp Ruston rather than to Camp Dermott, there is no evidence that any kind of special reorientation program was initiated in the Louisiana camp. In fact, it appears that Hans Gaul and Rudolf Herrmann were the only two German general officers sent to Ruston. Most likely, the War Department sent these two prisoners to Louisiana because they were openly anti-Nazi and had already provided American authorities with any valuable information they possessed. Since they had been cooperative and, by the time of their arrival in the United States, the reorientation program at Camp Dermott had not developed, the friendly atmosphere awaiting them at Ruston seemed like the logical choice.

While Washington devoted a great deal of attention to Camps Dermott and Ruston, some of the most intriguing developments occurred among the generals who remained at Camp Clinton. Shortly after the departure of von Vaerst, Elster, Bieringer, von Sponeck, and von Liebenstein in late March 1945, five more generals had taken their place in the generals' compound in Mississippi. British authorities at Trent Park, in a move to make room for yet another influx of German general officer prisoners, had transferred these five men to American custody. Upon their arrival at National Airport in Washington, D.C., on April 12, 1945, the PMGO transferred Generals Dietrich von Choltitz, Hermann Ramcke, Wilhelm Ullersperger, and Knut Eberding, along with SS General Anton Dunckern, to Camp Clinton.[41]

These men quickly became involved in a significant upheaval among the prisoners at Clinton. Following the end of hostilities in Germany, Clinton's general officer prisoners split into two groups, one doggedly retaining their pro-Nazi sympathies despite the collapse of the Hitler regime and the other openly denouncing Nazism. The break was precipitated by a change in

American rules. Shortly after Germany's surrender, Clinton camp authorities issued a directive to the prisoners "prohibiting the possession or displaying of any Nazi insignia except those worn on the uniform." Spurred by this directive, one faction of the generals completely removed all swastika insignias from their uniforms, angering the pro-Nazi clique, who saw this as an act of treason. The divide became so extensive that the two groups refused to associate, sitting on opposite sides of the mess hall during meals and refusing to speak to one another in the barracks. At one point the disagreement became so heated that it erupted into a fistfight between two of the generals. To quell the disturbance and prevent future confrontations, the housing situation had to be rearranged so that only generals with similar political beliefs shared quarters.[42]

This type of political divide among the generals at Clinton had occurred previously, after the so-called *Französen* had arrived in the summer and fall of 1944 and found themselves at odds with the *Afrikaner*. The curious aspect of the factions in the spring of 1945, however, was both their composition and leadership. The prisoners split almost in half, with fourteen "anti-Nazis" and thirteen "Nazis." Remarkably, the supposed *Afrikaner*, the generals alleged to be the most virulent Nazis, were evenly split between the two factions. Four of the *Afrikaner* joined one group and four the other, and curiously, the unspoken leader of both factions was an *Afrikaner*. It is no surprise that ranking general and long-time German patriot von Arnim continued to head up the pro-Nazi faction after the war concluded, although by this time he had perhaps become even more adamant in his views. Remarkably, however, the new leader of the anti-Nazi faction was none other than Ludwig Crüwell.[43]

British observers had once referred to Crüwell as a "nitwit" and a "moron" and viewed him as a Nazi stalwart. They considered him one of the biggest troublemakers among the generals at Trent Park because of his continual complaining, instigation of confrontations between his fellow prisoners, and vocal support for Hitler. Curiously, Crüwell did not create the same impression among American camp authorities after being transferred across the Atlantic in June 1944, although the Americans did not closely observe or eavesdrop on their general officer prisoners like the British did. Regardless, after the fall of the Hitler regime, Crüwell emerged as an openly defiant anti-Nazi leader among the generals in American custody, raising questions about his motivations.

Hermann Ramcke wrote about the political divide among the generals at Camp Clinton in his memoir, *Fallschirmjäger: Damals und Danach*. While he did not mention Ludwig Crüwell specifically, Ramcke condemned those senior officers like Crüwell who claimed after the war ended that they had always secretly opposed Hitler's leadership. Ramcke alleged that these prisoners were opportunists who sought early repatriation and the potential of obtaining a good position in postwar Germany by "loudly supporting democratic re-education" in American prisoner-of-war camps. He charged these men with engaging in "all kinds of ridiculous acts" to win favor with the Americans, including removing the swastika insignias from their uniforms.[44]

Considering Ramcke's firm support for Hitler and the Nazi regime, even after the end of the war in Europe, his view of Crüwell and other prisoners who showed some willingness to collaborate with the Americans is not surprising. Moreover, there were certainly a number of Wehrmacht generals who suddenly converted to anti-Nazism when the war ended though they had previously not opposed Hitler; in some cases they had even supported him. Yet some generals may have had legitimate reasons for their change of heart other than simple opportunism. Crüwell may serve as the best example. As previously stated, he had four children living in Germany during the war. Following the death of his wife, they had been cared for temporarily by Frau Emmy Göring, the wife of one of the most prominent leaders in the Nazi regime. The Nazis frequently targeted the families of those they believed had betrayed them and could easily have done so in this case, having firsthand knowledge of the identity and whereabouts of Crüwell's children. Perhaps his highly vocal support for Hitler was a ruse intended to protect his children. Had he expressed opposition to National Socialism in a British or American prisoner-of-war camp prior to Germany's collapse, and had news of this reached the Nazi leadership, his children might have been in grave danger. Von Choltitz supported the idea that Crüwell's pro-Nazi views were solely intended to protect his children. He expressed complete surprise upon hearing of Crüwell's pro-Nazi activities at Trent Park because, according to von Choltitz, when the Nazis had first risen to power in Germany and it was still possible to vocalize opposition to the regime, Crüwell had been a "wild and open anti-Nazi."[45]

Both Crüwell and Ramcke maintained the positions they staked out at Camp Clinton in the summer of 1945. Following the resumption of his life in postwar Germany, Crüwell enjoyed a prosperous postwar career and remained an active collaborator with Western Allied interests in the Federal Republic of Germany. Whether this meant that he finally felt safe revealing his genuine democratic sympathies or opportunistically saw the handwriting on the wall will likely never be determined. Ramcke, on the other hand, became one of the West's most vocal German critics. No one doubted his sincerity when he labeled Allied soldiers "war criminals" in a speech before a reunion of SS veterans in October 1952.[46]

The rift between the generals at Clinton continued for the remaining ten months they would spend in Mississippi before returning to Europe in March 1946. Camp officials accepted it as a permanent fixture in the camp and learned to work around it. In August 1945, for instance, Lieutenant Louis B. Wishar, who took responsibility for Camp Clinton's reeducation program in the spring of 1945, arranged for a series of lectures on American history to be presented to the generals in German. Each of these lectures was given twice, once for the "anti-Nazi" group of general officers and once for the "Nazis." The ongoing English-language instruction was organized in the same fashion. Two parallel courses were offered at each level, "less advanced" and "more advanced," so as to accommodate the wishes of the prisoners that the two cliques remain separated.[47]

Curiously, considering the animosity that existed between the two groups of generals, two International Red Cross inspectors who visited Camp Clinton in November 1945, together with Charles Eberhardt of the U.S. Department of State, found "no complaints worthy of mention." By this date the generals seemed most anxious about their impending repatriation, especially those whose homes were now located in the Russian-occupied zone of Germany. They were much less concerned with the kinds of routine matters, like a lack of pajamas or slippers, that had occupied their attention in the past. Surprisingly, the inspectors stated that there were no complaints about the food rations, which, as in all other German POW camps in America, had been reduced following the end of the war and the news of Nazi atrocities. Eberhardt and the Red Cross representatives reported that, by November 1945, the prisoners received thirty-four hundred calories per day, with more for the enlisted prisoners working on the Mississippi River Model Project, and found the generals satisfied with this allotment.[48]

Apparently, not all of the generals were quite so content. Ramcke blasted American authorities in his memoirs. He criticized the "unreasonable propaganda" against the German people that had appeared in the American press, the "unbearable reduction of rations" after May 1945 that, he claimed, violated international law, and the complete withdrawal of tobacco and other luxuries. Ramcke argued that this treatment of prisoners of war by the American government undermined the ongoing reeducation program, contending that courses in American democracy would be ineffectual if American officials refused to model democratic behavior themselves.[49]

Ramcke penned letters of complaint to Bryon Price, the director of the

U.S. Office of Censorship, and U.S. Senator James O. Eastland, Democrat of Mississippi. Ramcke suspected that the letters would never reach these men if sent through normal camp channels, which included review by U.S. Army censors, or if he asked one of the American camp employees to mail the letters for him. Astonishingly, he decided to leave the camp and mail them himself. Ramcke found a slight depression on the north side of the camp that led to a large drainage pipe, an area where American personnel had a limited view from the guard towers. He improvised a wire cutter and a handsaw that he used to cut through both the camp fence and the iron grate blocking the entrance to the drainage pipe. Feigning sickness during morning roll call on New Year's Day 1946, Ramcke slipped out of the camp and managed to catch a ride to Jackson from an unsuspecting driver on the nearby highway.[50]

To disguise his lack of English-language skills, Ramcke claimed, he practiced some basic American slang phrases and pretended to be hard of hearing. He used a dollar bill that an American officer had given him as a memento to purchase stamps at a local drugstore and enjoyed a hearty breakfast of ham, eggs, pancakes, and his first real cup of coffee in months. Because he needed to return to the camp under the cover of darkness, Ramcke had to kill time until sunset. After venturing to the post office to mail his letters, he spent the afternoon reading the newspaper, smoking a cigar, and watching members of Jackson's high society celebrate the New Year at the regal Heidelberg Hotel. The German general finally sneaked into the woods across from the POW camp in the late afternoon and slipped back through the wire fence undetected after nightfall.[51]

It was just a matter of time before camp authorities caught wind of Ramcke's stunt. Because he had signed his full name to both of the letters he mailed, Washington officials had a relatively easy time figuring out the origin of the letters. Upon being confronted at Camp Clinton in mid-February 1946 by Colonel McIlhenny, who happened to be holding a copy of Ramcke's letter to Byron Price, the general confessed that he had mailed it himself but refused to provide any details as to how he had accomplished this feat. McIlhenny sent Ramcke to Camp Shelby, Mississippi, where he was placed in solitary confinement and restricted to a diet of bread and water. After four days of this treatment, Ramcke finally agreed to talk, but he told camp authorities that he had escaped by digging under the camp fence.[52] Most likely, he wanted to keep his real escape route open in case he felt the need to exploit it a second time. It is doubtful that American authorities believed his story, especially considering that there would have been no trace of digging along the fence line, but they also likely saw no point in continuing the restricted diet and solitary confinement. The German generals were scheduled to be returned to Europe the following month and Camp Clinton was slated to be closed. Further punishing Ramcke to prevent any future escapes would have been unnecessary.[53]

Amazingly, Ramcke's escape did not mark the first time that residents of Jackson, Mississippi, had seen a German general walking the streets. In fact, American authorities periodically allowed the generals to go into Jackson accompanied by an armed American guard, which may explain why Ramcke did not seem to arouse any suspicion despite his poor English skills. Sergeant R. B. Howard served as a guard at Camp Clinton from mid-1945 until the camp closed in March 1946. He recalled that the generals were allowed daily walks outside the camp. One of them—Howard did not provide the general's name—rose early one morning, "dressed himself in his finest Nazi uniform, had his aide polish his boots to a mirror finish, and started walking." The generals frequently walked outside the camp for several hours at a time, so it did not cause much alarm when this particular prisoner did not return for quite some time. He eventually reemerged later in the day bearing a receipt for breakfast at the Walgreens drugstore in downtown Jackson. The general proudly proclaimed that he had paid for breakfast with a dollar bill he had hidden in his shoe. Howard and his fellow guards had no idea how he got to town or "how Jacksonians had allowed a German officer, in full uniform, to stroll through the streets and visit a downtown store unmolested."[54]

It is possible that Howard's story refers to Ramcke's "escape." The details about a hidden dollar bill and breakfast at a downtown Jackson drugstore in the two stories are quite similar. Perhaps Ramcke took advantage of the opportunity provided by a daily walk to hitchhike into town and mail his letters. He may not have wanted to admit this to camp authorities for fear that they would curtail the generals' daily excursions.

The American Lieutenant Frank Venturini served at Clinton until early 1945. In regard to Ramcke's visit to Jackson, he stated that "earlier in the war, when things were a lot tighter, he would not have gotten away with that." But by 1945, Americans were beginning to view German military personnel, high-ranking officers in particular, in a different light.[55] Remarkably, Harold Fonger, a member of the American 459th Military Police Escort Guard Company stationed at Camp Clinton until mid-summer 1944, related another such incident. According to Fonger, General von Arnim requested to see a movie in Jackson on one occasion, and Fonger was instructed to take von Arnim into town. "I was provided with a staff car and a pistol," recalled Fonger, and "the general was in full-dress uniform, swastika and all." Fonger described how nervous he felt as he escorted von Arnim to Jackson and parked the car several blocks from the theater. Would he be able to properly protect von Arnim, wondered Fonger, should local residents be angered by this Nazi general's presence in town and attempt to confront or even assault him? Much to Fonger's relief, the two men went to the movie, even followed it up with a cup of coffee and a piece of pie at Walgreens, and returned to Clinton without incident. Astonishingly, "no one noticed," remarked Fonger. "No one even looked."[56]

Apparently, Americans had grown so accustomed to German prisoners of war in the United States by the fall of 1945 that some even invited them to public functions. An American couple, Mr. and Mrs. W. K. von Uhlenhorst-Ziechmann, wrote the War Department in October 1945 requesting that American officials temporarily parole General von Choltitz so he could visit them in Shaker Heights, Ohio. Mrs. Uhlenhorst-Ziechmann was the niece of von Choltitz's wife and, because of this relationship, she wanted the general to "stand as sponsor" at the baptism of the couple's son. Colonel A. M. Tollefson, director of the PMGO's Prisoner of War Operations Division, politely informed the Uhlenhorst-Ziechmanns that it was "the policy of the War Department that no prisoner of war held in the United States may be paroled or released into the custody of a relative or friend for a visit, or for any other purpose." Thus their request was denied.[57]

Following the end of the war in Europe on May 8, 1945, the general officers at Clinton remained in the United States as prisoners of war for almost another year, waiting for various administrative matters to be settled. The War Department, however, reduced Camp Clinton's status to that of a branch camp subordinate to Camp Shelby, Mississippi, in August 1945. Along with this change came a new commanding officer, Captain Laurence O. Cherbonnier. Despite having a significantly lower rank than that of his predecessor, Colonel McIlhenny, Cherbonnier was well received by both the camp inspectors and the prisoner-of-war generals alike. In fact, the International Red Cross inspectors who visited Clinton in November 1945 "expressed their pleasure at finding the camp so well administered" and "paid Captain Cherbonnier the unusual compliment of congratulating him." Remarkably, they further stated that "other camp commanders might well receive training under him." Charles Eberhardt of the U.S. State Department, who accompanied the International Red Cross inspectors, observed that Cherbonnier had "gained the confidence and good will of practically the entire camp" and that even the irascible von Arnim was "especially complimentary" of the treatment he had received from this new commanding officer.[58] Captain B. H.

Glymph replaced Cherbonnier in January 1946 and oversaw the closure of the camp and the departure of the prisoners in March 1946.[59]

Ultimately, the American reeducation program for German general officers never really came to fruition. U.S. War Department officials chose not to utilize the generals in Mississippi, Arkansas, or Louisiana for any special purposes, and the specially established camp for cooperative generals at Dermott did not turn out any better than the ordinary generals' compound at Clinton. Yet a collaborative relationship between American authorities and Wehrmacht prisoner-of-war generals did develop. But the generals who most interested Washington were not the ones who had been in American custody during the war. U.S. officials had designs on those Wehrmacht officers captured during the final days of the war in Europe or in the weeks immediately following Germany's surrender. These men, brought to the United States in the summer and fall of 1945, had the most to offer in regard to America's burgeoning postwar national security interests and were asked to play significant roles in American postwar planning.

5

Cold War Allies

On April 15, 1945, a German U-Boat embarked from Kristiansand on the southern tip of Norway. *U-234* carried Lieutenant General Ulrich Kessler, the German air attaché and head of the German Air Force liaison staff to Tokyo. Kessler led a "mission of specialists for the purpose of acquainting the Japanese with the latest developments in German radio, radar, V and other weapons, and aircraft and assisting them in reproducing such equipment, weapons, and aircraft for Japanese use."[1]

En route to Japan, *U-234* received word of Germany's unconditional surrender. Following a great deal of discussion about the best course of action, and after receiving a message from German grand admiral Karl Dönitz urging all U-boat captains to surrender, *U-234*'s captain, Lieutenant Commander Johann Heinrich Fehler, radioed his position to the U.S. Navy and unconditionally surrendered. The U-boat also carried two Japanese passengers, Lieutenant Commander Tomonaga Hideo and Lieutenant Shoji Genzo, serving as part of the Japanese liaison staff. The German officers allowed these men to destroy their documents and then buried them at sea after the two Japanese men entered the stateroom of *U-234* and committed hara-kiri. Arriving shortly thereafter, the U.S. Navy then escorted the submarine and its distinguished passenger to Portsmouth, New Hampshire, where Kessler was officially taken into American custody as a prisoner of war.[2]

Kessler later claimed that he had never intended to fulfill his mission to Tokyo. Rather, he planned to go ashore on the coast of Florida and contact American officials about the possibility of collaborating. This appears to have been a distortion of the truth. In fact, Lieutenant Commander Fehler later stated that Kessler argued adamantly against surrendering to the Allies, contending that the U-boat should be sailed to South America instead.[3]

Regardless, Kessler's capture marked a notable point in the American relationship with Wehrmacht generals. Rather than placing the general with his colleagues in either Clinton, Mississippi, or Dermott, Arkansas, American authorities sent him to Fort Hunt, Virginia, the secret U.S. military intelligence facility near Washington, D.C. Here the American staff interrogated and eavesdropped on Kessler in a manner that reflected British practices at Trent Park. The U.S. War Department's Military Intelligence Service had been engaged in this type of activity throughout the war, but this was one of the few instances when its operation focused on a German general officer. In fact, Kessler was the first German general to be targeted by this kind of activity on American soil since the departure of von Vaerst, Köchy, Borowietz, Bülowius, and von Quast from the other secret U.S. military intelligence facility at Byron Hot Springs in July 1943. Why, with the war in Europe over, would Washington now find it important to initiate interrogations and eavesdrop on high-ranking Wehrmacht officers when it had shown so little interest in the dozens of German generals and admirals who had been in its immediate custody for months?

With the war against Germany concluded, the United States could now turn its full attention to the war against imperial Japan. Kessler had maintained contact with Japanese navy pilots during the war. More importantly, as Germany's chief liaison to Japan for the past year, he was able to provide the Americans with a great deal of information about Japanese military capabilities, especially the type of German technology and training the Japanese had received from Berlin.

Kessler agreed to provide the War Department with information about "Japanese capabilities in regard to the use and employment of German technical equipment, technicians and other experts." Indeed, he detailed the German-Japanese liaison from its inception in the spring of 1941, including the number and type of officers exchanged between the two Axis powers and the specific types of information and technology provided, such as the German air defense system and 88-mm flak gun. American interrogators seemed particularly interested in Kessler's "Mission to Tokyo." More specifically, Washington wanted to know exactly what weapons and communications technology the Germans had shared with the Japanese. It greatly relieved the War Department to learn that Kessler had not been able to maintain a direct exchange of technology with the Japanese owing to some dispute over the route any potential flights would take. The Japanese objected to the most direct route over Russia out of fear of angering the Soviets, and thus the German cargo aboard *U-234* would have been among the first large shipments to arrive in Tokyo since earlier in the war.[4]

Kessler also offered the Americans information about German and Japanese relations with the Soviet Union. Fort Hunt interrogators expressed great interest in Kessler's assertion that "the relationship between Russia and Japan was not as cool as it appeared." Based on information received from the Japanese naval attaché to Germany, Rear Admiral Kojima Hideo, Kessler claimed that the Soviet and Japanese intelligence services had "collaborated against the Americans in Turkey by exchanging information." He pointed out that the Japanese never made this information available to the Germans, so he could not speak to its nature or credibility. The general also reported that the Japanese government had executed twelve German agents for working against the Soviet Union from within Japan. Despite Japanese claims that these agents had provided Japanese secrets to the Russians, Kessler believed that the Japanese executed these men to appease the Russians because "the reports on Russia received from these agents were considered to be of great value" to the German government.[5]

Incredibly, Kessler also stated that "the Japanese [had] approached the Russians as early as 1943 and carried on conferences as late as 1944 with the purpose of creating a new Axis, incorporating Berlin, Tokyo and Moscow." According to Kessler, the Soviets initially approved of the idea. It never came to fruition simply because Hitler "flatly declined any political solution" with the Soviet Union and declared that any "settlement with Russia would be accomplished by military force." Likewise, with victory in the east appearing likely by the fall of 1944, the Soviets too lost interest in any kind of reorganized Axis coalition.[6]

If accurate, these were astonishing claims; in fact, they were ones that might have contributed to Americans' suspicions of their Soviet allies. News that Russian intelligence had collaborated with the Japanese and that Moscow had at one point considered approving of an alliance with Germany and Japan during the course of the war must have given American intelligence pause. Moreover, Washington believed Kessler's information to be reliable, largely because of his past relationship with the Nazi regime. First, in September 1938 Hermann Göring had considered offering Kessler the position of chief of the general staff of the air fleet, a unit designed by the *Reichsmarschall* himself for the purpose of attacking Britain. He demanded that Kessler state "on his honor" his "conviction that Germany would smash England." When Kessler refused to give Göring what he wanted and even intimated that invading England might be ill advised, Göring decided against offering Kessler the position and allegedly never forgot his attitude of "inferiority toward the English."[7]

Of even greater weight, Kessler had ties to Carl Goerdeler. The former mayor of Leipzig and a long-time political opponent of Adolph Hitler, Goerdeler became involved in the July 20, 1944, assassination attempt against Hitler and was later tortured and executed for his role in the plot. Kessler's brother-in-law, Dr. Kurt Weber, maintained constant contact with Goerdeler because of their close friendship and similarly intense hatred of the Nazis. Goerdeler, who planned to serve as German chancellor once Hitler had been removed, had apparently slotted both Weber and Kessler for important posts in his administration. Kessler came under suspicion from the SD and later discovered that his mail was regularly monitored by German authorities. He used this to try to redeem himself politically after the July Plot in letters to his family, however, by referring to the would-be assassins as "vipers" and appearing to delight in their execution. This ploy appears to have been somewhat effective. Kessler had remained more aloof from Goerdeler than had his brother-in-law and he believed that the SD later dropped any serious suspicions. Kessler remained unpopular with other high-ranking Nazis, including Göring and Admiral Karl Dönitz, however, and his appointment to Japan appears to have been Göring's final attempt to get rid of him.[8]

As one of the first targets of renewed American interest in senior Wehrmacht officers, Kessler provided American intelligence with some valuable information. But Kessler was not the only German general who arrived at Fort Hunt during the summer of 1945. He eventually shared a room with Major General Heinrich Aschenbrenner. Aschenbrenner, former chief of intelligence for the German Air Command, served as commander of foreign personnel in the east at the time of his capture in May 1945. It is most likely this latter position, with responsibility for foreign personnel fighting the Soviet Army, that made Aschenbrenner most valuable to American intelligence.[9]

Overall, the conversations between Kessler and Aschenbrenner that were "overheard" by American microphones were of little intelligence value. Indeed, the conversations again support the notion that both men knew the Americans were listening. At times, the two men seemed to be "playing" the American eavesdroppers to some degree. On one occasion, American intelligence officers reported that the two prisoners spoke "in very low voices so that it [was] impossible to understand them."[10] On another occasion, in a discussion about the causes of the war and the reasons for Germany's defeat, Kessler boldly proclaimed that Hitler "alone made all the decisions and he made wrong ones," which sounds a lot like later German protestations of a "clean Wehrmacht." Kessler later made an even more curious remark by suggesting that he and Aschenbrenner "stop reading this nonsense in English and go over to Russian. Russian is the language of the future." Given Kessler's insistent pronouncements about American responsibility for the postwar world and the U.S. obligation to establish "a democratic Pan-Europe" to fight off the Bolshevist influence, this comment appears to have been either a joke or a well-placed prod to his American listeners.[11]

Like Kessler and Aschenbrenner, Major General Walter Vierow had likely also been brought to Fort Hunt because of his service on the Eastern Front. Vierow, a general officer from the German engineering corps, had been in charge of all road and bridge construction and repair on the south Russian Front between the eastern border of Romania and the Caucasus Mountains. Vierow had also served as the commandant of Kiev, Belgrade, and Pilsen, Czechoslovakia, where he was captured by the Americans. Vierow devoted most of his brief stay at Fort Hunt to preparing engineering studies for his American captors, including reports titled "Preparations for the Attack on Sevastopol," "The Road Net of Eastern Crimea," "Winter Road Service in the Crimea," "Crossings of the Don," "The Road Net between Rostov and the Caucasus," and "From the Dnieper to the Crimea." His reports illustrated "the importance of the road net in the planning and execution of campaigns and the difficulties of maintaining roads with local material of untested qualities." He also provided hand-drawn, detailed maps of the road networks in the areas under his command.[12]

The American operation at Fort Hunt quickly involved other German general officers as well. Indeed, it appears that most of the POW generals who arrived in the United States after the German surrender in May 1945 endured at least a few weeks of American interrogation and eavesdropping at the secret facility in Virginia. All of the generals who arrived at either Camp Dermott or Camp Ruston in the fall of 1945, including Generals Gallenkamp, Gaul, Hermann, and Pollert, appear to have come through Fort Hunt.[13]

The Fort Hunt operation also illustrated a significant change in the Anglo-American relationship regarding prisoners of war. Beginning in the months following D-Day, American military intelligence had gradually exerted more autonomy in its relationship with senior German POWs. After the war in Europe concluded, the conduit of intelligence information began to flow in the opposite direction. Whereas the British had typically taken the lead in interrogating high-ranking Wehrmacht officers throughout the war, they now relinquished this responsibility to the Americans. For instance, the Royal Air Force sent a memorandum to the U.S. Military Intelligence Service dated May 21, 1945, requesting details about the German-Japanese liaison, especially the Japanese development of airplanes and communications, from General Kessler.[14] Britain largely abandoned its interrogation and eavesdropping activities and now relied on the Americans to share any valuable information gleaned from the prisoners captured at the end of the war.

Despite significant Allied interest in Ulrich Kessler, the most prominent and potentially valuable German general officer to arrive at Fort Hunt in the summer of 1945 was Reinhard Gehlen. Brigadier General Gehlen served as chief of Fremde Heer Ost (German Eastern Front Intelligence Service) from April 1942 until near the end of the war. In this capacity, Gehlen's organization was responsible for collecting "all possible intelligence material dealing with the military, political and economic situation existing in the U.S.S.R. and the southeastern European countries." After Hitler relieved him of command in April 1945, Gehlen and his staff hid their most important intelligence documents before surrendering to the Americans on May 22, 1945. Unfortunately for Gehlen, the Americans did not at first realize whom they had captured. The general transited through five different locations, from Fischhausen, south of Munich, to Wiesbaden, west of Frankfurt, before the American Captain John Boker finally took an interest in him.[15]

Boker, whose suspicions about the Soviet Union had already been aroused, immediately saw Gehlen as a potentially valuable contributor to American intelligence. "The interrogations which I made of several high-ranking German officers who had commanded units on the Eastern Front and interrogations which were made at CSDIC (UK) had undoubtedly awakened what was already a more than latent antipathy toward the Soviets," Boker later stated. "It was clear to me by April 1945," Boker reported, "that the military and political situation would not only give the Russians control over all of Eastern Europe and the Balkans but that as a result of that situation, we would have an indefinite period of military occupation and a frontier contiguous with them." Convinced that Gehlen was able to provide essential information about the Soviet Union, Boker reassembled Gehlen's staff, retrieved a significant number of the hidden German intelligence documents, and alerted his superiors to Gehlen's potential value to U.S. intelligence.[16]

Boker initially fought an uphill battle. He believed that significant resistance existed in Washington toward gathering intelligence against the United States's Soviet allies and that Gehlen's work with American intelligence initially had to be kept secret, even from most American personnel. Eventually Boker convinced enough of his superiors in Europe of Gehlen's potential value that General Eisenhower's chief of staff, General Walter Bedell Smith, provided a plane to transport Gehlen, several of his subordinates, and their cache of German intelligence documents to Fort Hunt in August 1945. Yet, upon arriving in Virginia, Boker still had to persuade the officers in the Eastern European Order of Battle Branch at the Pentagon, to whom the "Gehlen Organization" had been assigned, that these prisoners of war were valuable to the United States. Boker later claimed that "everywhere in the Pentagon . . . there was considerable hostility to working with Germans in any way and the feeling that the Germans could be of no use to us in any current endeavor." But "the extent and value of the information that Gehlen's group possessed became at once apparent to the Eastern European O.B. Group" once they began working with the prisoners, according to Boker, and the American captors "became quite enthusiastic."[17]

U.S. military intelligence officials not only directly interrogated these men and bugged their rooms, as they had done with Kessler, Aschenbrenner, and the other generals at the facility, but they actually developed a collaborative working relationship with the Gehlen Organization. In ten months at Fort Hunt, Gehlen and his staff, who came to be known as the Bolero Group, under the supervision of the American Captain Eric Waldman from the Pentagon, produced numerous reports regarding various aspects of Soviet military capabilities. These included "Methods of the German Intelligence Service in Russia," "Development of the Russian High Command and Its Conception of Strategy during the Eastern Campaign," "Fighting Methods of the Russian Armies Based on Experience Gained from the Large-Scale Russian Offensives in the Summer of 1944 and the Winter of 1945," and "Development and Establishment of the Russian Political Commissars within the Red Army," as well as studies of the Russian army order of battle and surveys of Russian army units and equipment and of the organization of Russian commands and troop leadership. Having directed Hitler's intelligence network against the Russians for three years during the war, Gehlen now provided the same service for the U.S. War Department at war's end.[18]

Notably, by the time the U.S. Army transferred him back to Europe in early July 1946, Gehlen had "not only prepared reports based on German records but also had access to and commented on American intelligence reports." Moreover, Waldman, who accompanied the Bolero Group to Germany, observed that the reason U.S. Army intelligence repatriated the Gehlen Organization was "to allow this group of German officers to engage in collection of intelligence against the Soviet forces in Germany." This decision, according to Waldman, "was crucial since it marked a radical departure from the concept of writing [historical] studies based on old Wehrmacht files."[19] The Pentagon had progressed significantly from its initial skepticism of Gehlen to a full-fledged relationship with the man who eventually would lead the new West German state's intelligence apparatus in the mid-1950s, and all because of a mutual distrust of the Soviet Union.

The War Department's collaboration with the Gehlen Organization led to an even more collaborative relationship with a group of German General Staff officers. On September 25, 1945, a little over a month after Gehlen's arrival at Fort Hunt, twenty-seven German officers and eleven German enlisted men boarded the SS *West Point*, bound for the United States.[20] These prisoners of war had agreed to work for a coordinated U.S., British, and Canadian military intelligence project. Kept secret from the American public as well as from the other Allies, the "Hill Project" eventually expanded to almost two hundred prisoners of war who produced over thirty-six hundred pages of documents for the Western Allied governments. The story of these "hillbillies," as their Allied captors frequently referred to them, is a little-known aspect of the interesting postwar relationship between American military intelligence and various high-ranking Wehrmacht officers.

An informal agreement between Major General Clayton Bissell, the assistant chief of staff, G-2 (Military Intelligence), of the U.S. War Department, and Major General John Alexander Sinclair, the director of military intelligence in the British War Office, created the Hill Project as "a skeleton German General Staff organization formed for the purpose of conducting such research for the War Department General Staff and the British General Staff as may be directed." This agreement placed the operation at Camp Ritchie, Maryland, and received the approval of the U.S. Army chief of staff on April 22, 1945. Exactly one month later, on May 22, 1945, the two Allies concluded the Sinclair-Bissell Agreement. This Anglo-American military intelligence accord obligated General Bissell and the U.S. War Department to "provide necessary facilities near Washington (near the German Military Document Section) for the handling of key enemy specialist personnel" and delineated a fifteen-point research agenda titled "Subjects for Research of German Documents."[21]

Before the work of the Hill Project could begin, however, the documents library had to be assembled. This job fell to the U.S. Army's Document Control Section in Frankfurt, Germany, under the command of Lieutenant Colonel S. Frederick Gronich. Gronich and his staff collected and catalogued the majority of the German documents captured in the closing months of the war in Europe. Gronich's operation maintained a "detailed card index for all captured documents in Germany," allocated "priorities for research by various agencies," shipped large volumes of documents to either London or

Washington—later Camp Ritchie—and oversaw the operations of the U.S. Third Army, U.S. Seventh Army, and Austrian Document Centers as well.[22] Because of his involvement with the exploitation of captured German documents, Gronich quickly became involved in the U.S. relationship with the German prisoners working for the Hill Project as well.

As early as 1943, British and American military intelligence agreed to collect and maintain captured enemy documents. The armies in the theater of operations immediately used important captured documents for "timely and accurate information regarding the German order of battle and related intelligence data." The Allied militaries then transferred the documents to the Military Intelligence Research Section (MIRS) in either London or Washington for safekeeping and further detailed research. In the spring of 1945 the London MIRS was renamed the London Military Documents Center and became a "records control and transmission organization." The Washington MIRS, soon to be renamed the German Military Documents Section, became the primary "records depository."[23]

On July 14, 1945, two months after the formal German surrender and the conclusion of the war in Europe, the U.S. War Department and the British War Office jointly established the German Military Document Section (GMDS) at Camp Ritchie, Maryland. The camp's fairly secluded location

A view of the GMDS area at Camp Ritchie (Courtesy of the U.S. National Archives and Records Administration)

along the Maryland–Pennsylvania border about sixty-five miles northwest of Baltimore allowed the GMDS to remain out of the public eye. Its mission was to "establish and operate a library of captured German documents and publications" and to "conduct such military document research as is mutually agreed upon" by the Directorate of Military Intelligence of the British War Office and the assistant chief of staff, G-2 (Military Intelligence), of the U.S. War Department.[24]

The initial library holdings consisted entirely of previously captured German documents transferred from the Washington Branch of the MIRS, actually located at Fort Hunt, Virginia. The initial American staff of nineteen officers and fifty-three enlisted men at Camp Ritchie occupied themselves in the summer of 1945 with setting up the library and learning to file documents according to the German filing system, or *Einheitsaktenplan*, albeit with several "extensive" American adaptations. GMDS personnel even received the "full approval" of Dr. Luther H. Evans, the librarian of Congress, and his chief of processing, Herman Henkle, for their efficient filing system.[25]

The following month the GMDS staff continued their efforts in the "sorting and filing of captured German documents, publications, and periodicals, in preparation for future intelligence research on the German armed forces." The prisoners needed for the research project and the German General Staff documents that constituted the main focus of the operation, however, were yet to arrive. At this early stage, the GMDS began circulating some of the German documents and publications already on hand to other U.S. government agencies, including the Air Technical Service Command, the State Department, Army Ground Forces, the Federal Bureau of Investigation, and even the surgeon general, and the FBI attached a permanent liaison officer to the operation.[26]

Despite the presence of the GMDS Library at Camp Ritchie, the U.S. War Department did not officially notify the camp's administrative staff of the establishment of the Hill Project until September 8, 1945. By this time the German POW personnel for the project were slated to arrive in less than a month. This may explain some of the animosity that developed between the chief of the GMDS, the American Colonel George F. Blunda, who directed the intelligence operations, and Camp Ritchie's post commandant, Colonel Mercer Walter, who oversaw the actual prisoner-of-war camp.

Further complicating the two men's relationship was the divided control of the prisoners, which eventually undermined the productivity of the project and had to be addressed in early 1946. When the project began in the

Dr. Bloomfield, special consultant to the secretary of war, examines a document in the General Library of the German Military Document Section Library at Camp Ritchie, Maryland. (Courtesy of the U.S. National Archives and Records Administration)

fall of 1945, keeping the prisoner-of-war camp and the secret military intelligence project under separate command made sense. The research required special intelligence leadership and U.S. military intelligence rightfully took control of the extraordinary arrangement. Establishing, administering, and providing security for a POW camp, on the other hand, seemed best left to

"Col. G. F. Blunda, our new Chief." Colonel George F. Blunda commanded MIRS, later renamed GMDS. (Courtesy of the U.S. National Archives and Records Administration)

the Army Service Forces, who were responsible for all POW camps in the United States.

Unfortunately, the problems of divided command reached the boiling point within only a few months. Colonel Blunda sent a long letter to the War Department in Washington detailing numerous problems with the relationship between the Hill Project and Colonel Walter's administration of the prisoner-of-war enclosure and the guard unit assigned to it. Blunda requested that Walter be relieved of responsibility for the hillbillies, complaining that Walter would "not take any responsibility nor any steps to liberalize the handling of the Hill Project in order to insure complete cooperation and the highest efficiency of the personnel therein."[27]

Blunda provided the War Department with a list of grievances. Foremost among them was Colonel Walter's insistence that the Allied officers who served as research project chiefs escort prisoners from their compound to the research building when sufficient guards were not available. Blunda's prior request that the hillbillies be allowed to come and go without escort had "met with a flat refusal." The GMDS chief contended that "such a method [resulted] in a loss of work on the Project both in the chain of thought being disturbed and because of the psychological reaction whereby the Chief of the Project [tried] to get along without the member from the Hill rather than go fetch him."[28]

The underlying problem was a fundamental difference in how each of these two men viewed the prisoners at Camp Ritchie. Blunda, who worked directly with the Germans as chief of GMDS, saw these men as colleagues whose "complete cooperation [was] not only desirable but essential." Walter, by contrast, perceived the members of the Hill Project as "purely and simply prisoners of war." On one occasion a prisoner was "manhandled by the guard," causing "an adverse effect on all members of the Hill," according to Blunda. Moreover, Walter gave the U.S. personnel on base openly preferential treatment. For example, more than once Walter denied the Germans any butter or marmalade in the mess hall, despite the fact that the prisoners shared the mess with American personnel for whom these items were always available. The camp commandant refused to divide the items equally if sufficient quantities were not available for everyone in the dining hall. Blunda criticized this decision as "not conductive to good morale, particularly when it is known that the amount of butter drawn is based on the total strength of U.S. [personnel and prisoners of war] combined."[29]

The War Department's response to Colonel Blunda's allegations can be inferred from a memorandum addressed to the GMDS chief from Colonel Walter, dated February 7, 1946. Walter informed Blunda that "effective 11 February 1946 such prisoners of war as may be selected mutually by the Chief, GMDS [Blunda] and the Commanding Officer, PW Guard Detachment [Lieutenant Colonel Gerald Duin] will be granted parole privilege and will be authorized to move about the parole area while on official business during the period 0700 to 1830 hours on normal work days." The camp commandant also stipulated that with proper notification parole privileges could be obtained for work on weekends and holidays as well. Furthermore, he authorized special quarters outside the prisoner-of-war compound for the general officer prisoners, provided that a GMDS officer was "designated daily to be responsible for the General Officers during off duty hours."[30]

Despite these later administrative issues, for most of the month of September 1945 the American, British, and Canadian personnel occupied themselves conducting practice searches for "materials on specific subjects which [were] likely to be important fields of study" in order to "train new personnel in tracing a subject through the documents library and to test the current filing and indexing systems." The GMDS staff still awaited the arrival of both German documents and POW researchers, which were scheduled to be shipped to Camp Ritchie sometime during September. Not until the last day of the month, however, did five railcars arrive full of captured German documents from the Heeresarchiv (German Army Archive), the Oberkommando des Heeres (OKH; German Army High Command), and the Oberkommando der Wehrmacht (OKW; German Armed Forces High Command). The GMDS staff did not have adequate time to catalog these valuable German General Staff papers before the prisoners arrived as well.[31]

Among the twenty-seven German officers who had been assembled at Camp Bolbec in Le Havre, France, and made their way across the Atlantic Ocean were four general officers. The senior prisoner and nominal leader was Lieutenant General Walther Buhle, chief of the army staff within the OKW. Buhle had previously served under Colonel Claus von Stauffenberg and had been present on July 20 when von Stauffenberg's bomb had demolished the "wolf's lair" but left Hitler largely unharmed. Following the July Plot, Buhle had continued in the service of Hitler's General Staff and had eventually earned promotion to lieutenant general for his "energetic" work.[32]

His fellow general officers included Hellmuth Laegeler, who taught tactics at the *Kriegsakademie* and held various staff positions before assuming the position of chief of staff for the German Replacement Army near the end of the war. As members of the OKW, he and Buhle appear to have been the more important of the first four general officers to join the project. Franz Kleberger, director of the OKH and chief quartermaster and finance officer for the German Field Army, and Rolf Menneking, a member of the OKH staff, served less important functions.[33] Clearly, however, all of these men would have had intimate knowledge of the newly arrived General Staff documents and could offer valuable experience, having served in Hitler's high command organizations.

Yet the Western Allies compromised to a degree in choosing these men for the project. These officers had attained high enough positions in the General Staff to have experience and expertise of value to the Hill Project. But

Master Sergeant Gustav Blackett examines a document in the Armeeoberkommando (Army Corps) stacks of the Heeresarchiv. (Courtesy of the U.S. National Archives and Records Administration)

they were lower-profile officers, selected in part because they were unlikely to be tried for any war crimes or seriously questioned by the other Allies after their work had concluded. Lieutenant General Adolf Heusinger illustrated this point. Heusinger, a high-profile Wehrmacht officer, served as chief of the operations branch of the OKW for most of the war. He was originally scheduled to join the Hill Project in November 1945 but Allied lawyers called him to testify at the Nuremberg trials and he never made it to Camp Ritchie.[34] Thus Western Allied intelligence was compelled to choose perhaps less valuable officers in order to find men available for the operation.

Eight colonels, eleven lieutenant colonels, two majors, and two captains, almost all of whom were General Staff officers, completed the first parcel of hillbillies coming to Camp Ritchie. A few days before their arrival "arrangements [had] been made for the prisoners of the Hill Project to have the same ration and laundry service as enlisted personnel of the [U.S. Army] to permit them to perform more effective intelligence research work." Indeed, on September 27, 1945, the U.S. Provost Marshal General's Office transferred twenty-two German POWs already interned in the United States to Camp Ritchie to serve as support staff for the Hill Project. These men assumed responsibilities as supply sergeants, canteen operators, latrine orderlies, firemen, painters, officer's orderlies, and general clerks.[35] Between October 1945 and April 1946, dozens of additional enlisted German POWs found themselves at Camp Ritchie serving the growing number of German officer prisoners working for the intelligence operation.

Prior to the prisoners' arrival, Allied authorities also sought to ensure that any reports produced by the Hill Project and the GMDS would be of "maximum usefulness to the using agencies." Officers from the U.S. War Department Personnel Division (G-1), Military Intelligence Division (G-2), Organization and Training Division (G-3), Supply Division (G-4), Special Projects Division, New Developments Division, Army Ground Forces, and Army Service Forces formed an informal panel of advisors "to give the research personnel at GMDS guidance in their effort." This advisory panel planned to meet with the researchers at Camp Ritchie once every seven to ten days to discuss any new research questions they wished the operation to address and receive progress reports on existing research projects.[36]

Brigadier General R. C. Partridge, one of the panel members from Army Ground Forces, had studied at the *Kriegsakademie* in Berlin for almost a year, from November 1938 until August 1939, as part of an exchange with the U.S. Army's Command and General Staff College. Partridge had completed only one year of the curriculum when the outbreak of the Second World War abruptly curtailed his studies. Yet his experience provided him unique expertise and made him "especially helpful in developing reports of value to the War Department and the Ground Forces."[37] Curiously, Partridge departed the *Kriegsakademie* only a few years before Laegeler began teaching at the German military school.

Following their arrival at Camp Ritchie on October 8, 1945, the prisoners,

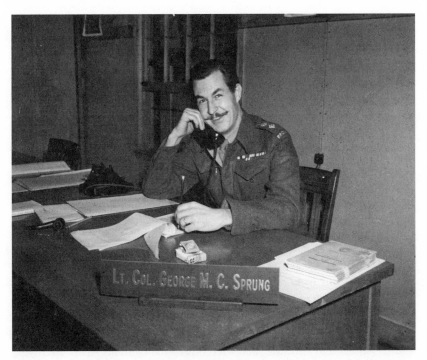

Lieutenant Colonel G. M. C. Sprung, a Canadian, chief of research at GMDS (Courtesy of the U.S. National Archives and Records Administration)

under the direction of Allied officers, quickly set to work. The organization of these earliest studies illustrated a remarkable level of collaboration between Allied officers and German prisoners of war as well as between the Allied officers themselves. The major research initiated in mid-October included a study of the German General Staff Corps led by American captain Robert C. Fitzgibbon. Canadian lieutenant colonel George Sprung and British lieutenant George Mowatt supervised a massive study of the German High Command involving General Buhle and twenty-five other German officers. Canadian captain Clarence Doerksen and American lieutenant Michael Tsouros also directed a study of German military personnel administration and German military training. Each report relied on the expertise of German officer prisoners as well as research in the GMDS documents by both German POWs and Allied officers and enlisted men.[38]

Another intriguing feature of the Hill Project research was that some of the reports were prepared at the behest of one of a number of Allied government agencies. For example, the GMDS prepared the first two special reports, on "Officer Efficiency" and "Officer Candidate Selection and Training," in response to queries from the U.S. Adjutant General's Office, and the first translations of German documents were specifically prepared for study by the U.S. Army Staff. This arrangement, in which military or civilian agencies made requests for specific research to be conducted by German prisoner-of-war researchers and writers, later featured prominently in the U.S. Army Historical Division's use of former Wehrmacht officers in Germany in the late 1940s and 1950s.[39] With both the Hill Project and later the Historical Division, Allied agencies requested specific information that could be put to use immediately.

The high level of collaboration between captors and captives as well as between the representatives of the three Allied governments continued for the duration of the Hill Project. Work began on several more major studies in November, including a series of bibliographical reports charting the possibility for further GMDS research projects, led by British major Horton Smith and American captain Homer Schweppe. The Hill Project and the GMDS staff also initiated research projects on "German Manpower and Mobilization," "Logistics on the High Command Level," "German Fortifications and Defense," "Organization and Methods of the German Army Archives," "German Military Administration," and "German Operational Intelligence," directed by four American officers and two British officers.[40]

The rapid expansion of the Hill Project's research agenda necessitated a restructuring of the program's administration as well as a significant increase in the number of personnel involved, both Allied and German prisoners of war. As of January 1, 1946, a new command structure supervised the program's activities. A new deputy chief of GMDS, British lieutenant colonel D. A. Prater, took over direct supervision of GMDS operations, and the coordination of all research projects now came under the direct supervision of the research chief, a new position awarded to Canadian lieutenant colonel George Sprung.[41] This new command structure highlighted the multinational nature of the project, with a Canadian research chief reporting to a British director of GMDS, who in turn reported to Colonel Blunda, the American commanding officer.

The structural reorganization of the project was accompanied by the continued expansion of its personnel. On December 20, 1945, eight German officers and nine enlisted men from the Pikesville, Maryland, prisoner-of-war camp joined the GMDS effort as translators. These men had been "screened for security and willingness to work and their translation ability

[had] been checked by a written examination." Less than three weeks later, on January 8, 1946, another eleven German officers and thirteen enlisted men from the prisoner-of-war camp at Camp Forrest, Tennessee, transferred to Camp Ritchie to serve as translators and lithographers.[42] The Hill Project researchers prepared all of their reports in German, since this was the prisoners' native language and the language of the documents in which they were conducting their research. Thus it fell to a large number of subordinate officers and enlisted men to translate these manuscripts into English, necessitating the transfer of dozens of qualified prisoners to Ritchie to serve in this capacity.

By January 1946, the number of German officer prisoners actively engaged in the research agenda of the Hill Project had grown to forty-one, including the arrival of two additional generals and twelve lower-ranking officers. The roster of hillbillies now included Brigadier General Herbert Gundelach, chief of staff for engineering and fortifications in the OKH. Gundelach brought additional expertise, having previously served as chief quartermaster of the First Army and chief of staff for the generals in Albania. In addition to Gundelach, Brigadier General Ivo-Thilo von Trotha, chief of the operations branch of the OKH, also was transferred to Camp Ritchie. Von Trotha had excelled in various General Staff positions. His experience in the Ukraine and later as chief of staff for Colonel General Gotthard Heinrici and Armee Gruppe Weichsel on the Eastern Front made him especially important to Western Allied intelligence.[43]

The final general officer to join the Hill Project did not arrive until March 16, 1946. Major General Wolfgang Thomale, one of the few hillbillies who was not a member of the General Staff, had extensive knowledge of panzer warfare. He served for the last two years of the war as chief of staff for Colonel General Heinz Guderian, after Guderian had been appointed inspector general of armored forces in 1943. Thomale, whom Guderian described as a "phenomenal panzer officer," contributed significantly to the project's research on panzer training and armored warfare.[44]

The final tally of hillbillies—the German prisoners directly involved with the work of the Hill Project—included 35 officers holding the rank of captain or above. All of these men had been chosen because they possessed "special knowledge." The list also included 22 more officers, largely lieutenants and captains, who were "selected for English language qualifications," 14 noncommissioned officers included because of their "familiarity with the available archives and records," and 108 enlisted prisoners chosen for "technical and language qualifications." Hundreds more German prisoners of war were transferred to Camp Ritchie to service the camp's POW enclosure and the requirements of the Hill Project inhabitants but did not actually take part in the research. The number of support staff members grew from 646 prisoners after the GMDS reorganization in January 1946 to as high as 1,572 prisoners at the end of March 1946, when the project was nearing completion.[45]

The most important question surrounding the Hill Project, however, regards the program's purpose. What were the main goals of this program and what kind of information did these research projects provide to Western Allied military intelligence? The Sinclair-Bissell Agreement's project outline offered three stated purposes for the Hill Project and the German Military Document Section: (1) research on "subjects which will aid in preserving military security in Europe," (2) research "in prosecuting the war against Japan," and (3) research "in improving intelligence organization and techniques and to other selected matters on which important lessons can be gained from studying German methods in detail."[46]

At the time the agreement was concluded in May 1945, obtaining information to aid the prosecution of the war against Japan had likely been paramount. But considering that the Wehrmacht POW officers who composed the Hill Project did not arrive in the United States until early October 1945, almost a month after the official Japanese surrender, this was obviously not one of the project's goals by the time its work began. In weighing the other two options, it is important to evaluate how the Allied agreement might have defined "subjects which will aid in preserving military security in Europe." Since no further definition was provided, one must suppose that preserving military security in Europe meant either the demilitarization of Germany to prevent the recurrence of yet another world war or, perhaps equally likely, preparation of an adequate defense against a potential invasion of Western Europe by the Soviet Red Army, something about which German General Staff officers would have had considerable information to offer. Regardless, the documents produced by Hill Project researchers suggest that the third option was the primary focus: that of "improving intelligence organization and techniques and . . . other . . . matters on which important lessons can be gained from studying German methods in detail."

Western Allied admiration for the prowess and efficiency of the German armed forces motivated the Allies to emulate the German military model. The Hill Project and the GMDS at Camp Ritchie, Maryland, produced, published, and distributed fifteen studies to numerous military schools and commands, including Headquarters, U.S. Forces European Theater (USFET); Headquarters, Mediterranean Theater of Operations, U.S. Army; the Brit-

Allied officers guiding the German General Staff Corps project in the fall and spring of 1945–1946. (Courtesy of the U.S. National Archives and Records Administration)

ish Joint Staff Mission; the U.S. Military Academy; the U.S. Command and General Staff School; the U.S. Air War College; the U.S. Naval War College; and the U.S. Office of Naval Intelligence, among many others. The majority of these documents were procedural studies that evaluated various aspects of the World War II German Army and highlighted lessons learned and successful practices that might be adopted by the Western Allied armies.

At least one of the studies found deficiencies in the German military system. The collection of publications included *German Operational Intelligence*, focused solely on the German intelligence effort against the Western Allies. This study detailed a variety of reasons for the "mediocre" performance of German intelligence in the Second World War. The authors concluded that "there [was] little the Allied intelligence services [could] learn from the Germans" but that "this general discussion of German methods [could] have at least the negative value to Allied intelligence of lessons in weaknesses."[47]

Other publications continued to laud "the high military efficiency of the German Army as a whole" while observing some peculiarities in the German command system that Allied leadership should not attempt to reproduce. For example, *The German General Staff Corps* found both strengths and weaknesses in this command structure. The report found that the German General Staff Corps had emerged during the Napoleonic Era and developed over a century and a half but had no direct equivalent in Allied armies. Likewise, a publication titled *The German Army Quartermaster and Finance Organization* studied the Heeresverwaltung, or German Army Administration, which was responsible for all quartermaster and finance functions, including "all cash transactions, rations, quartering, barracks and office equipment" and other responsibilities. The authors of this publication concluded that the Army Administration was "remarkably successful," despite the fact that it operated independently of the army command structure. Yet they again observed that "however well [the Army Administration] may have served in the German Army, [it] could not be imitated successfully by an Army with other traditions and habits."[48]

The Hill Project documents also included two operational studies. The first, titled *The German Operation at Anzio,* examined German defenses against the Allied invasion of the Italian coast west of Rome from January to May 1944. The second operational study, *Armored Breakthrough,* was the only one of the documents that dealt specifically with the German war against the Soviet Union. It was a translation of the war diary of the First Armored Group, which later became the First Panzer Army, during the planning phase of Operation Barbarossa. It focused on the first eighteen days of the campaign, when the First Armored Group was responsible for "following up the initial breach of Russian frontier defenses and effecting the strategic breakthrough."[49]

The main body of studies formally published and circulated by the Hill Project through the Military Intelligence Division in Washington, D.C., offered "important lessons" and a detailed view of German methods that the Western Allies might use to improve their own military organization and techniques. The "highly efficient mobilization of [German] forces in the summer of 1939" particularly impressed Allied researchers and their POW colleagues. *German Army Mobilization* detailed the development of German mobilization plans from 1921 through their implementation in 1939. The structure of the system, initially reminiscent of Frederick the Great's cantonal arrangement for recruitment, featured the same number of corps as *Wehrkreise* (military districts), with corresponding territorial administration. This allowed *Wehrkreis* headquarters to "direct the mobilization of all parts of the wartime Army to be formed in their areas" and made them "responsible for notifying all troops and Army installations within their areas."[50]

A special unit, the mobilization group, led by a General Staff officer took responsibility for the army mobilization plan. The group annually supplemented the existing plan with further detailed orders that "outlined the personnel and material plans for the current mobilization year." The *Wehrkreis* headquarters transmitted periodic reports to the mobilization group to aid in developing these orders and to regulate the personnel and supply situation by arranging transfers of men or material from one *Wehrkreis* to another to "satisfy the requirements of the overall plan." Timely briefing of personnel and regular mobilization exercises in which the essential elements of the process were rehearsed complemented the efficient planning and preparation. The only flaws in the German mobilization plan noted by the report—a lack of training in certain sectors of the field army and shortages of material—were not criticisms of the system itself but rather problems associated with the rapid activation of the army.[51]

A study, *German Training Methods*, also found much of interest in the Wehrmacht procedure, the system of wartime training in particular. "All fundamental training problems for the entire army (Field Army and Replacement Army) were worked out by the Training Branch of the General Staff of the Army." This branch prepared training manuals that were largely based on the combat experiences of the military's most decorated veterans and disseminated them throughout the various arms of the German military. Moreover, in the interest of providing essential new information to the troops as quickly as possible, the manuals were regularly supplemented with "instructional pamphlets, training hints, illustrated weapons pamphlets, and film and lantern-slide lectures." The individual military branches also issued monthly bulletins with specialized, branch-specific instruction, descriptions of pertinent combat experiences to spur further training ideas, and information about new weapons and methods of combat employed by the enemy.[52]

German Military Transportation provided a detailed analysis of the wartime German transportation system. The Germans largely relied on railroads, although they utilized inland waterways to some degree as well. This had much to do with historical development. Beginning with the Austro-Prussian and Franco-Prussian Wars of the 1860s and 1870s, the Germans built extensive rail networks and connected their four main rivers—Rhine, Weser, Elbe, and Oder—through a system of canals. Given that all of Germany's major rivers run generally south to north and that German fears of a two-front war necessitated rapid east–west transportation, the rail network took precedence from the beginning. Furthermore, thirty-five thousand miles of railroads that were mostly state-owned by 1938 and an abundance of coal and iron meant that even Hitler's "motorization" of Germany in the 1930s could not cause the railroad to be surpassed as the primary transportation medium, especially given Germany's lack of oil and natural rubber.[53]

Germany's dependence on rail meant that the transportation system itself offered few insights for the Western Allied governments, who relied much more heavily on automobiles and maritime transportation. However, what Western Allied intelligence did take an interest in was the manner in which German "civilian and military railway officials managed to cooperate very effectively." While noting weaknesses, such as "the inability of lower echelons to make major decisions" and the "uncertain relationship between the Operations Branch of the Army High Command and the military and civilian transportation authorities," the study concluded that the "German military transportation system functioned efficiently." In the east, the movement of troops and supplies remained relatively functional until near the end of the war. And even in the west, where American and British bombing pounded German rail networks, troop and supply trains continued running, although it required "ruthlessly cutting down civilian traffic."[54]

A series of seven special reports rounded out the publications of the Hill Project. Two of these reports, *Officer Efficiency Reports in the German Army* and *Officer Candidate Selection and Training in the German Army*, were requested by the Classification and Replacement Branch of the U.S. Adjutant General's Office in Washington, D.C. The British Army of the Rhine asked for the study *Ration Administration in the German Army*, and the Officers' Branch of the U.S. War Department General Staff's G-1 Division sought those titled *German Officer Courts-Martial* and *Screening of German Enlisted Personnel for Officer Appointments*. Of the final two special reports, *Infantry in the Sixth Year of the War* was a translation of an internal Wehrmacht study of the Twenty-Ninth Panzer Grenadier Division's experience in Italy. *German Chemical Warfare* was a bibliography of all important documents concerning German chemical warfare then in the collections of the German Military Document Section.[55]

In addition to these fifteen published studies and special reports, Hill Project researchers initiated ten other studies during their tenure at Camp Ritchie. Yet, for whatever reason, the Military Intelligence Division chose not to publish these manuscripts and essays. Some of them were never even translated into English, although at least one of them, a lengthy study titled "German Manpower: A Study of the Employment of German Manpower from 1933–1945," was later circulated on a very limited basis despite not being formally published.

Because of the exhausting, intellectual nature of the prisoners' work at Camp Ritchie, Allied personnel decided to offer the prisoners some intellectual diversions. These came in the form of weekly lectures presented in English, typically covering some period of English literature. The lectures were designed to complement the English-language classes held in the prisoners' enclosure four times each week. British and American officers offered four different levels of language instruction, ranging from beginner to advanced, and while the prisoners were not required to attend the courses, they almost always did. The language instruction served to raise morale among the prisoners, better prepare some of the advanced students to translate documents, allow the prisoners to speak with those Yanks, British, or Canadians who could not speak German, and "enable GMDS officers to form a clearer estimate of the individual [prisoners'] characters."[56]

This regular contact between Allied teachers and German students, not to mention that between fellow researchers in the Hill Project, fostered respect and concern between these former enemies. In fact, the American personnel in charge of the operation went to great lengths to help the German officers and NCOs in their custody. General Buhle, in his capacity as senior officer and spokesman for the prisoners, directly corresponded on at least three occasions and met once in person with American colonel John Lovell. Lovell, assigned to the War Department's Military Intelligence Division in Washington, D.C., served as overall chief of the GMDS operation and was the officer with whom Colonel Blunda, the director of the program at Camp Ritchie, coordinated his effort. Buhle provided Lovell with a list of each prisoner's immediate family members and their last known addresses. Lovell assured the German general that he would try to obtain the whereabouts and current circumstances of these individuals.[57]

Once contact with an individual prisoner's family had been reestablished, however, American authorities imposed some restrictions in an effort to protect the secrecy of the program. The prisoners' family members were instructed to send any mail intended for the Hill Project prisoner to a post office box in Frankfurt, Germany. From there, the letters or packages were then forwarded to Camp Ritchie through U.S. Army channels. A problem arose because many of the family members addressed their letters using the prisoner's military rank. Gronich feared that the post office box was being watched by the French and the Russians and that the Americans' receipt of letters addressed to a number of high-ranking German officers would arouse suspicion and lead to potential complications with their nominal allies. Clearly, the Americans were not prepared to reveal the extent and nature of their relationship with members of the German General Staff to any but the two Allies with whom they were already collaborating on the program. Thus the prisoners' families were asked to avoid using any military ranks in future correspondence.[58]

The Hill Project prisoners and their Allied supervisors and coworkers completed all twenty-five of their studies and reports by early April 1946. The only problem that intruded during their roughly six months at Camp Ritchie was the health of General Buhle. For unspecified health reasons, Buhle was transferred to the hospital compound at Fort George Meade, Maryland, in mid-March, where he remained until his repatriation to Germany in late April. In his absence, General Laegeler became the senior officer and, thus, the prisoners' leader and spokesman.[59]

With most of the Hill Project's work completed as anticipated, the operation was officially terminated and the bulk of the prisoners repatriated to Germany beginning on April 15, 1946. The prisoner-of-war enclosure at Camp Ritchie, established solely for the Hill Project and its support staff, was emptied and shut down by the end of the month, and Allied authorities coordinated procedures for returning the prisoners to civilian life in Germany. Considering that the hillbillies had been part of a top secret military intelligence project and, as mostly former members of the German General Staff, were high-profile prisoners, Allied military intelligence considered them a "potential security menace." Consequently, the prisoners' military personnel files, which included "as much detail as possible about family and business associations, residences, political affiliations, and a short security estimate of [each] man," were circulated to American and British military intelligence authorities in the European Theater. Allied operatives then kept these men under surveillance throughout their occupation of Germany. Allied officials also feared that information might be leaked by their own personnel who had worked with the GMDS at Camp Ritchie and took steps to impress upon these men the importance of keeping their work secret as well.[60]

The lengths to which American and British authorities went to stem any "potential security menace," not to mention the benefits they provided these prisoners of war during the course of the operation, testify to the Hill Project's importance to Western Allied military intelligence. This high level of secrecy also suggests that authorities in Washington, London, and Ottawa had greater concerns than simply gathering information for the war in the Pacific or improving Western Allied military operations. The Hill Project and the German Military Document Section were not simply historical endeavors. Had the operation been initiated simply to chronicle the German conduct of the war there would have been little need to keep the project's existence so confidential. The U.S. Army Historical Division's Operational History (German) Section, which utilized former Wehrmacht officers to write a comprehensive history of the Second World War, roused little if any resistance from the American public or local German citizens once the program became public knowledge in the years after the war. So why the shroud of secrecy surrounding the Hill Project?

Allied authorities feared that public knowledge of the German prisoners' participation in the Hill Project might compromise both captor and captive alike. In early March 1946, the Directorate of Military Intelligence in London learned that word of the operation might be brought before the House of Commons in a debate over a defense measure. This possibility stirred discussion among American and British authorities about the prospect of releasing an article themselves, detailing the "proper story" to the public to "vitiate possible adverse criticism." No evidence of such an article can be found, suggesting that either the matter was dropped before it reached the House of Commons, and thus no article was necessary, or the War Department simply decided against a preemptive public relations strike.[61]

Curiously, the proposed article would have contended that the Hill Project had been "undertaken from a strictly scientific point of view in order to determine the cause for the success of the German Military Operations in order that war in the future might be prevented." Yet, despite the ostensibly "scientific" nature of the endeavor, Allied personnel feared that the prisoners involved would be branded as traitors by the German public had information about the Hill Project been released.[62]

A letter from General Buhle to Colonel Lovell dated January 23, 1946, suggests that the hillbillies did harbor some qualms about working directly for an Allied intelligence project. Buhle describes the prisoners' quandary by saying that "the situation which emerges from this unorthodox and unparalleled method of work is as difficult to comprehend for our own officers as it would be for the officers of any other nation and it requires constant control over our minds to vindicate our conscience." This supports the notion that the clandestine nature of the Hill Project was intended, at least in some measure, to protect the reputations of the German prisoners involved.[63]

Despite the prisoners' concerns about working with their recent enemies, a number of reasons can be offered to explain their willingness to participate in the program. Given the choice between languishing in hastily prepared and often overcrowded prisoner-of-war camps in war-ravaged Europe or working for the Allies in a well-furnished camp in the United States with plenty of amenities, many a prisoner would have easily chosen the latter. Furthermore, the hillbillies gained a great deal from their service to the Allies, particularly in the manner in which the U.S. Army located and cared for most of their family members. The prisoners likely saw the potential to benefit their families and themselves early on and made continued attempts to better their situations throughout their time in the United States.

For instance, the former members of the German General Staff appear to have feared conviction as war criminals by the International Military Tribunal and insinuated that the Americans should correct any "misconceptions" about the "criminal-of-war question." Buhle expressed concern because "the gravest indictments [were] being raised in the public during the Nuremberg trial" against various elements of the German High Command, adding that "the claim has been uttered that they are to be considered collectively as criminal organizations." He continued by asking Colonel John Lovell, who was assigned to the War Department's Military Intelligence Division in Washington, D.C., and served as overall chief of the GMDS operation, if it would be possible, "on your journey to Nuremberg, to influence the appropriate officials to correct the view on war guilt of OKW, OKH and General Staff officers as a whole, which we feel is a misconception, so that a conviction of these groups will not be effected."[64]

The International Military Tribunal chose not to pursue the idea of collective responsibility for the German High Command organizations, and it is doubtful Colonel Lovell could have influenced them either way. But Buhle's request illustrates that self-interest also lay at the core of the hillbillies' willingness to participate in the program, despite their contention that their "only motive" was "the desire to throw light on the pertinent and historic development of German military leadership and organization" and to "contribute to world peace and thus save Europe and [their] country."[65]

The Western Allied general staffs also fostered the secrecy of the project because they did not wish for it to appear as if they and the German General Staff "were collaborating in preparation for a future war." This fear was predicated on a long-standing distrust between the Western Allies and their Russian counterparts in the Grand Alliance. Moscow harbored fears that American and British anticommunism would eventually compel the Western Allies to turn against the Soviet Union, possibly even siding with Nazi Germany if it best suited their interests. Considering the nature of the Hill Project, Soviet fears may not have been completely unfounded.

The overwhelming majority of the Hill Project publications offered "important lessons" and a detailed view of German methods that the Western

Allies could use to improve their own military organization and techniques. This, of course, satisfied the third item on the research agenda for the Hill Project, that of improving intelligence organization and techniques. The Japanese surrender had relieved the program of any need to address the agenda's second stated goal, that of research that would aid the war in the Pacific. This left only the first item, research on "subjects which will aid in preserving military security in Europe," to be addressed. A few of the project's documents, the study of the German General Staff Corps in particular, provided a greater understanding of the structure and command of the German Army that might have proved useful in the process of Allied demilitarization of postwar Germany. Only one, *Armored Breakthrough*, specifically examined the German war against the Soviet Red Army, however, and it dealt exclusively with the earliest stage of the German invasion in 1941.

Consequently, it might appear that the first goal of the program had gone unaddressed. Yet, unbeknownst to the hillbillies at Camp Ritchie, research into preserving security in Europe was being conducted nearby. After the Hill Project was officially terminated, a handful of these prisoners found that their route home diverted them through Fort Hunt, Virginia.

Lieutenant Colonel Gerald Duin, who was sometimes listed as the commanding officer of the prisoner-of-war guard detachment at Camp Ritchie and other times as the chief of the Hill Project, oversaw the camp's POW enclosure. He stated that "Colonel Lovell's idea in assembling the German Documents Center Project was to collect a representative German General Staff group and put them to work writing a comprehensive history of German Army experiences on *the Eastern Front* in all sectors and all branches of the service. Results of their work were to be complete studies of combat under all types of circumstances and conditions."[66]

Duin had first served in World War II as chief interrogator at the U.S. Interrogation Center at Fort Hunt, Virginia, code-named "PO Box 1142." The Fort Hunt staff interrogated the majority of the most important German prisoners in American custody during the Second World War, giving Duin invaluable experience for working with the hillbillies at Camp Ritchie. After "further wartime interrogation work in North Africa and Europe" and then service as chief interrogator for the Twelfth Army Interrogation Center, Duin was eventually assigned to the Hill Project at Camp Ritchie in October 1945. Clearly, Duin assumed a great deal more responsibility than simply commanding a POW guard detachment. He organized the entire Allied relationship with the prisoners and had been placed in this role because of his extensive military intelligence experience.[67]

Most revealing are Duin's statements about the connections between the Hill Project and the American relationship with the Gehlen Organization. Duin described numerous links between the work of the Gehlen Organization at Fort Hunt and that of the Hill Project at Camp Ritchie. First, Captain Boker, who was so instrumental in coordinating the American relationship with Gehlen, had once served as a subordinate officer to Lieutenant Colonel Duin when the latter had been chief interrogator at Fort Hunt. Thus these two men, highly involved in the two respective projects, had at the very least a long-standing working relationship. In addition to Boker, the GMDS "Record of Visitors" lists both Lieutenant Eric Waldman, the American officer in charge of the Gehlen group at Fort Hunt, as well as his superior officer, Lieutenant Colonel Dmitri Shimkin, as guests of the German Military Document Section at various times. Furthermore, the GMDS transferred numerous documents to Shimkin's custody during the course of its operations.[68]

Significantly, Duin revealed that the bulk of the German Eastern Front intelligence documents that Gehlen had spirited away at the end of the war and Boker had later retrieved and brought to the United States had been transferred directly to Camp Ritchie for use by the Hill Project. "Twenty packing cases of documents had accompanied [the Gehlen group] to the U.S.," according to Duin. These documents included "daily Eastern Front operational reports, daily situation maps, G-1, G-2, G-4 estimates, orders and reports, etc." While the "majority" of these documents went to Camp Ritchie, Duin related that "Colonel Gronich after some argument had permitted the group to keep certain documents which they considered the most important." When the Hill Project completed its work, these documents, along with the entire German Military Document Section, were sent to the basement of the Pentagon, where a member of Gehlen's group was allowed access to the documents and "permitted to select and take those documents which were of interest to 1142 [Fort Hunt interrogation personnel] for use by the Gehlen staff."[69]

During the Hill Project's operation "a very strict security wall was maintained between the group at 1142 [Gehlen's group] and the one at Camp Ritchie [Hill Project]," according to Duin. "It was specifically desired to keep the two groups from learning about the presence or work of each other, particularly the Ritchie group from knowing anything about the Gehlen [group] in order to prevent any information from reaching the Soviets in the event that any of the Germans elected to enter the Soviet zone after being returned to Germany."[70] American military intelligence viewed the hillbillies as the graver threat solely because of their numbers. Gehlen's staff at Fort Hunt consisted of only a handful of men, whereas the Hill Project roster reached close to two hundred, plus the numerous supplemental POWs not directly part of the secret project.

Further solidifying the ties between the Gehlen group and the Hill Project, Duin stated that on April 18, 1946, following the completion of the Hill Project operation and the closure of the POW camp, he personally escorted most of the prisoners from Camp Ritchie back to Germany. However, a few remained behind when the bulk of their colleagues were repatriated. These hillbillies were transferred to Fort Hunt for the purpose of continuing research in special areas of expertise. Upon his return to America in May, Duin assumed the position of chief of the interrogation and research unit at Fort Hunt, which included the Gehlen group. The prisoners of war under Duin's supervision at Fort Hunt now included the former members of the Hill Project who had been "attached to the Gehlen group" on April 15, 1946.[71]

The eleven prisoners obtained from Camp Ritchie included three general officers. General Thomale possessed special experience "in the field of training, organization, and development of equipment." In this regard, U.S. War Department personnel viewed him as "probably the best qualified officer in the German Army." They sought his expertise in writing several further reports, including a "German appreciation of United States armor." General Laegeler, because of his previous experience teaching tactics at the German *Kriegsakademie,* was considered a "valuable consultant in matters of major tactics and staff procedure in the field army." General von Trotha remained in the United States because of his "extremely wide experience in the field" as a staff officer and because the Americans viewed him as "without doubt one of the ablest young generals in the German Army."[72]

Accompanying these men were four colonels, two lieutenant colonels, a major, and a captain. Fort Hunt obtained these prisoners for various types of expertise. One man was described as having "knowledge of the German Staff College," while others were characterized as the "most able and experienced staff intelligence officer available," an "expert on all questions of the organization and methods of basic training," a "specialist in chemical warfare weapons," specialists in organization and personnel, and an "invaluable" consultant on "all questions of the constitutional status of the German Army." Duin claimed that two of these men, Colonel Kurt Rittman and Major Walter Lobedanz, had been members of Gehlen's organization prior to the end of the war in Europe and that one of the hillbillies, Colonel Johannes Haertel, had also been a member of Gehlen's group but for unspecified reasons was repatriated rather than being retained at Fort Hunt.[73]

The studies to be completed by these former members of the Hill Project now at Fort Hunt illustrate that the focus of the research now involved American preparation for a potential war against the Soviets. Thomale, seemingly the most important to the project of the men retained, prepared two papers titled "Panzer Warfare in the East." The first studied the effect of the "special characteristics of war on the Eastern Front" on the organization, handling, tactics, design, armor, and technical demands of panzer units and formations. The second dealt with issues of supply for armored troops on the Eastern Front. Thomale also undertook a "German appraisal of U.S. armor" and a study on "panzer casualties," while Laegeler analyzed the German "casualty reporting system" and von Trotha examined "tactics with an emphasis on the last phases of the war."[74]

The work of these men at Fort Hunt was kept secret, much as it had been at Camp Ritchie. When USFET cabled in late April to ascertain the names of any German general officer prisoners of war then interned in the United States, the Provost Marshal General's Office concealed the work of the former hillbillies still in America. The PMGO responded by including Laegeler's, Thomale's, and von Trotha's names on the roster it provided to USFET but listed them as being interned at Fort George Meade, Maryland, a common point of arrival and departure for German prisoners of war in the United States, rather than at the secret interrogation center at Fort Hunt, Virginia.[75]

Eventually, in June 1946, the U.S. State Department demanded that all German prisoners of war in the United States be repatriated by the end of the month. Despite protests by the War Department Military Intelligence Division, which wished to retain the Gehlen Organization and the attached hillbilly researchers, incoming secretary of state James F. Byrnes would not budge, insisting on the original deadline. Consequently, the eleven former members of the Hill Project along with the members of the Gehlen Organization held at Fort Hunt were returned to Germany at the end of June 1946.[76]

Following the Germans' repatriation, American officials feared the former prisoners' appearance before mandatory denazification and demilitarization courts in Germany. In November 1946 Lieutenant General Clarence R. Huebner, USFET chief of staff, informed Lieutenant General Lucius D. Clay, the U.S. military governor in Germany, that "possible disclosure of certain information by these people, which would be detrimental to United States interests, might be necessary should they have to appear before a German Court." Huebner was also concerned that "these persons might or might not succeed in obtaining pardons" if they actually went to trial. Consequently, in the spring of the following year General Clay granted amnesty to the returning hillbillies for "service in the interests of [their] own people."[77]

The Americans' primary concern in this circumstance was protecting U.S. national security interests. Presumably, this meant keeping the Soviets from learning about a secret project designed to better prepare the U.S. Army to protect Western Europe from any potential invasion by the Red Army. It is also noteworthy that the official rationale for granting amnesty was service to the German people. Given that the nature of the Hill Project focused on opposition to the Soviet military, and that Europeans, especially Germans, feared a Soviet invasion in the immediate postwar years, the hillbillies' work would have indeed been in the service of their own country.

It is also curious, however, that American occupation authorities were unsure whether their recent prisoners would be acquitted in denazification or demilitarization proceedings. Apparently German courts applied stricter standards than did Western Allied military intelligence.

This once again raises some interesting questions about American priorities and the Americans' stated goals of denazification and demilitarization. American occupation authorities made an extensive effort for several years after the war to find former National Socialist Party members and remove them from positions of leadership in the U.S.-controlled zone of Germany. Moreover, they sought to punish those in the Nazi regime who had committed the most heinous crimes during the war. Yet Washington allowed a free pass to men like General Gehlen and others who could have provided Allied authorities with a great deal of information about German atrocities.

Much as they allowed Nazi intimidation to undermine the reorientation effort at Camp Dermott, American authorities at times allowed national security concerns to eclipse their postwar denazification and demilitarization programs. German officers who could provide valuable information to American intelligence about Soviet capabilities had little to fear from postwar justice. Indeed, American authorities had seemingly little trouble reconceptualizing former Nazis as allies once they began to see their former Soviet colleagues in a different light.

During its operation at Camp Ritchie, the Hill Project produced over thirty-seven hundred pages of documents for American, British, and Canadian military intelligence (see appendices B and C). Interestingly, when the American Captured Records Section compiled a "List of GMDS Studies" in January 1954, the titles previously listed as being prepared by the hillbillies at Fort Hunt from mid-April until the end of June 1946 were not included.[78] These reports were either not satisfactorily completed or, more likely, were highly classified and not available for circulation at that time. Even without these documents, the studies prepared by the Hill Project at the German Military Document Section represent an impressive body of work, especially for prisoners of war employed by their recent enemies and completed within only six months.

The published manuscripts circulated fairly widely throughout American and British military channels. Yet there is no evidence that these documents had any impact on American strategic or operational planning in the immediate postwar world. Indeed, the impact of these documents on American military policy cannot be demonstrated in the way that the influence of the German military history series on the U.S. Army in the 1950s can be. Moreover, despite the fact that several of the studies are still available in the libraries of places like the U.S. Army Command and General Staff College, the Joint Forces Staff College, U.S. Army Europe, the U.S. Army Field Artillery School, the U.S. Naval War College, the U.S. Air Force Academy, and the Australian War Memorial, there is also no evidence that any of these documents ever appeared as part of the curriculum for the training of Western Allied military officers.

Thus it appears that these documents had very little long-term impact. Yet the significance of the Hill Project and the German Military Document Section becomes clearer when considered in the context of the developing Cold War. That Western Allied military intelligence utilized former Wehrmacht officers, even General Staff officers, after the conclusion of the Second World War to gain information about the Soviet Union and how to prepare a potential war against the Red Army is not a revelation. Moreover, the Werner von Braun Center and the Marshall Space Flight Center in Huntsville, Alabama, stand as testaments to the American utilization of former Nazis to gain an advantage—in this case in the space race—against their former Soviet allies. The Hill Project was just one previously unknown component of the larger postwar American effort to protect U.S. national security interests.

Following the termination of the project, Colonel Richard L. Hopkins, deputy chief of the War Department's Military Intelligence Service, evaluated the German Military Document Section, which by then included not only captured German documents but also the studies prepared at both Camp Ritchie and Fort Hunt by the Hill Project and the Bolero Group, respectively. His assessment illustrates the collection's importance to Western Allied intelligence. Hopkins's evaluation stated that the GMDS documents were "our richest source of factual intelligence on the U.S.S.R." and that "much of this information [could] never be secured from any other source." He concluded that "if the U.S. were to be forced to conduct strategic air operations against the U.S.S.R. the German document collection would constitute the chief source of intelligence upon which to base such operation."[79]

The eleven former hillbillies at Fort Hunt and the members of the Gehlen Organization were returned to Germany at the end of June 1946.[80] During its operation at Camp Ritchie, the Hill Project completed a body of work that studied German methods as a means to potentially improve the structure and procedures of the Western Allied armies. By contrast, the hillbillies and their counterparts in the Bolero Group at Fort Hunt assisted in preparing a defense of Western Europe against a potential invasion by the Soviet Army. In this fashion, two of the Anglo-American agreement's goals for the German Military Document Section—research "in improving intelligence organization and techniques and to other selected matters on which important lessons can be gained from studying German methods in detail" and research on "subjects which will aid in preserving military security in Europe"—were met.

Conclusion

Following the end of the war, British and American authorities agreed to hold their highest-ranking Wehrmacht prisoners until some semblance of order could be restored to Germany. Although the U.S. War Department returned all of its German prisoners of war, including all of the general officers, to Europe by the end of June 1946, the prisoners were not allowed to return home. Washington turned some of the generals over to the British and placed the remainder in various hastily established POW camps in Western Europe. London, in turn, established a new camp for German general officers in January 1946 called Special Camp No. 11, or Island Farm, at Bridgend, Glamorganshire, in south Wales, where many senior Wehrmacht officers languished for over two more years until they were all finally released by the spring of 1948.

The process of returning the generals from the United States to Europe was haphazard at best. There were no plush Pullman cars to transport the generals from camps in Mississippi, Arkansas, and Louisiana as there had been when they first arrived in America. The U.S. War Department decided to disallow the use of Pullman cars to transport prisoners of war after the war ended because the "period of redeployment and readjustment" severely taxed American rail facilities. Moreover, "first class accommodations [were] frequently not available for soldiers or American civilians," and therefore, Washington feared an adverse public reaction if it used the railcars to transport POWs, even general officers.[1]

"Squeezed together in trucks," recalled General von Sponeck, the generals "rode through the country from camp to camp, always carrying [their] heavy luggage." When he and his fellow prisoners arrived in New York City, they were "packed like sardines onto a liberty ship." After their trip across the Atlantic, the senior officers from Dermott arrived at Camp Bolbec in Le Havre, France. "Bolbec was an awful camp," von Sponeck remembered. It lacked protection from the icy winds and rain coming from the Atlantic and

the prisoners' only shelter was "a leaky old tent." But even worse, camp officials provided very little food and turned a blind eye to what von Sponeck
described as the "German bastards who had basically taken over this camp,"
referring to a group of hard-core Nazi sympathizers who intimidated and
harassed their fellow prisoners.[2]

Fortunately for the generals at Bolbec, they were quickly transferred
again. The prisoners endured yet another truck ride, this time from north-
western France to southern Germany. "We had the impression," recalled von
Sponeck, "that the drivers had been instructed to kill us by driving as fast
and reckless as possible." They arrived at a transit camp in Ulm in southern
Germany before moving a short distance away to Camp Dachau, the former
notorious concentration camp on the outskirts of Munich. From there, some
of the prisoners were called to testify at the Allied war crimes trials taking
place in Nuremberg, about one hundred miles north of the camp. Eventually
von Sponeck and his fellow prisoners were transferred again, this time to an
old German Army barracks at Garmisch, a little over an hour's drive south-
west of Munich.[3]

The American camp at Garmisch reflected a change in American priorities. The U.S. Army had begun to compile a history of American involvement in the war and sought information from the enemy side. The initial
idea of interrogating German military leaders had originated with the U.S.
War Department's Military Intelligence Division, Historical Branch. Dr.
George N. Shuster led a team of American military officers and academics
to Control Council Prisoner of War Enclosure No. 32, code-named Ashcan,
located at Bad Mondorf, a few miles outside Luxembourg. In July 1945 Ashcan held a large group of high-profile German prisoners, including Admiral
Karl Dönitz, General Alfred Jodl, Field Marshals Albert Kesselring and Wilhelm Keitel, and Reichsmarschall Hermann Göring. The Shuster Commission sought information from them to complement the American historical
record of the war.[4]

These initial interrogations quickly grew into a larger, more formal endeavor. By September 1945 the Historical Branch had been established as a
special staff division of U.S. military intelligence, headquartered at St. Ger-
main outside Paris and under the direction of the U.S. European theater historian. The new Historical Division, in turn, created the Operational History
(German) Section in January 1946 to exploit the "sources of combat information still available in the theater," and interrogate "German commanders
and staff officers who actively opposed U.S. Army operations" for historical
purposes. The German history program embarked on a full-fledged effort to

locate and obtain information from as many German generals as possible, starting with the distribution of questionnaires to every general officer that could be located. By May 1946 over one thousand German officers had been contacted and almost three hundred had written historical accounts for the program.[5]

The Historical Division quickly found its efforts hindered by the disparate geographic locations where German generals were held after the war. For instance, in June 1946 there were 328 German officers preparing operational reports in ten different locations in Germany, Britain, Belgium, Austria, France, and Italy. To make the program more efficient, the Historical Division obtained exclusive control of a U.S. Third Army prisoner-of-war camp in Allendorf, Germany, designated the Historical Division Interrogation Enclosure, and began transferring most of the general officers working for the German history program to this location.[6]

In December 1946 the 7734th USFET Historical Detachment established a secondary German history program at the prisoner-of-war camp at Garmisch, where von Sponeck found himself in early 1947. This program focused on World War II German operations outside of the western European Theater, namely operations in the Mediterranean and the Soviet Union. In July 1947 the Historical Division combined the Garmisch and Allendorf operations and the new program, labeled Operation STAPLE, eventually relocated to Neustadt, Germany.[7]

Von Sponeck had begun writing a history of the Battle of El Alamein while interned at Garmisch. Despite the proximity of his family and their periodic visits to the camp, American officials forced him to temporarily relocate to Allendorf to complete his work for the German history program. Von Sponeck was finally released and allowed to return home in November 1947 after finishing three reports totaling almost seventy pages.[8]

General von Choltitz also eventually found himself at Allendorf writing for the U.S. Army Historical Division. His journey home had begun much like von Sponeck's, with an initial arrival at Camp Bolbec followed by a transfer to New Ulm. But unlike von Sponeck, von Choltitz was transferred to a camp at Oberursel, which the general described as "one of the most bitter memories of imprisonment." "The treatment was cruel and lacked any human dignity," lamented von Choltitz. "We were spared no humiliation." One of the embarrassments von Choltitz most vividly remembered was that the American guards confiscated the prisoners' belts and suspenders and forced them to carry their meals and other items through the hallway. With both hands full, the prisoners often suffered the indignity of not being able to hold up their pants. After enduring this humiliation, von Choltitz was eventually transferred to Allendorf, where he authored two reports regarding his leadership of the Eighty-Fourth Corps in Normandy in June 1944. He completed his work and was released in April 1947.[9]

Including von Sponeck and von Choltitz, twenty-one of the fifty-five German generals previously held as prisoners of war in the United States contributed to the U.S. Army Historical Division's German history program.[10] These twenty-one former officers contributed forty-four reports totaling over thirteen hundred pages. While this made up only a fraction of the program's total output, over half of the reports written by the twenty-one former prisoners of the United States were prepared at Garmisch or Neustadt after the focus of the program had shifted to concerns about the Soviet Union. Curiously, American authorities had spent little if any time interrogating these men when they had been so readily accessible on American soil. For instance, Generals Gustav von Vaerst, Fritz Krause, and August Viktor von Quast spent almost three years in the United States and were interrogated for only about three weeks of that time. Following the war, when American priorities had changed, these men devoted considerably more than three weeks preparing the nine reports for which they were collectively responsible, suggesting that U.S. officials found these prisoners of war to be far more valuable in postwar Germany than they had been in wartime America.[11]

Yet the general who played the most important role for American authorities in postwar Germany was Reinhard Gehlen. Upon arriving in Germany, members of the Gehlen Organization reestablished their intelligence-gathering operation at Camp King, located just north of Frankfurt. Camp King consisted of three houses and some apartments in a secret compound surrounded by barbed wire. Gehlen and his subordinates worked under the supervision of the American intelligence officer Lieutenant Colonel John Russell Deane Jr. and reported to the American chief of intelligence for the European Theater, General Edwin Sibert. Their main responsibility was gathering intelligence on activities within Soviet-occupied Germany and Eastern Europe.[12]

American support for the Gehlen Organization directly reflected Washington's growing level of concern during the early years of the Cold War. During the organization's initial re-formation at Camp King, the majority of American officials had only begun to suspect Soviet intentions and consequently provided Gehlen so few resources that he and his staff had to obtain additional operational funds by selling some of the supplies they received from the U.S. Army on the German black market. Yet by December 1947, with U.S.-Soviet tensions escalating, American intelligence relocated the Gehlen Organization to Pullach, a small town located a short drive south of Munich, where the operation greatly expanded. Under the cover of being the headquarters for a large business, the Gehlen Organization turned Pullach into a "self-contained village," including housing for Gehlen's staff and their families, a kindergarten and school for the staff's children, and even a PX and infirmary.[13] In Reinhard Gehlen, U.S. Army intelligence embraced not only a former prisoner of war but a previously high-level member of Hitler's staff. By late 1947, denazification clearly took a backseat to anticommunism.

American interest in Gehlen's work only increased. As early as the fall of 1946, Colonel Deane requested to transfer responsibility for the Gehlen Organization from the U.S. Army to the infant Central Intelligence Group, soon to be the Central Intelligence Agency; the request was initially refused. By September 1948, however, in the midst of the Soviet blockade of West Berlin, CIA agent James Critchfield began studying Gehlen's work. With the United States increasingly engaged in the Cold War, the CIA formally adopted the Gehlen Organization as an umbrella agency on July 1, 1949. The CIA continued its support and supervision of Gehlen until West Germany fully gained its sovereignty in May 1955. The Gehlen Organization was then transformed en masse into the Bundesnachrichtendienst, West Germany's federal intelligence agency, on April 1, 1956, with Gehlen as its chief.[14]

Reinhard Gehlen utilized the intelligence network he built as Hitler's chief of Eastern Front intelligence during the Second World War to provide first the U.S. Army and then the Central Intelligence Agency with information about the Soviet Union during the early years of the Cold War. He parlayed his control of this organization, along with some powerful connections within the leadership of the new West German state, into the highest position in West German intelligence. In exchange for a decade of substantial support, Gehlen provided the U.S. military and CIA with information, as well as offering the United States intimate knowledge and contacts within the new West German intelligence apparatus.[15]

While lacking the same level of achievement as Gehlen in his rise from POW to West German intelligence director, two other Wehrmacht generals and former prisoners of war in the United States, Kurt Freiherr von Liebenstein and Hellmuth Laegeler, also assumed positions of leadership in the emerging Federal Republic of Germany. Von Liebenstein found himself back in Europe in the summer of 1946, where, like a number of his fellow prisoners, he was co-opted by the U.S. Army Historical Division to work on the German history program. He joined the Historical Division Interrogation

Enclosure at Allendorf, where he wrote four historical reports on German operations against American forces in North Africa. He relocated with the program to Neustadt, where he contributed one more report, this one belonging to the "NONET" group, which dealt with operations against the Soviet Union. He finally obtained his release in October 1947.[16]

Von Liebenstein returned home and served for over five years as director of the city transportation office in Göppingen, east of Stuttgart, before applying for a position in the newly created West German military. Von Liebenstein received his commission in the Bundeswehr in May 1956 and reentered the German military holding the same rank, brigadier general, that he had departed with in 1947. The reincarnated general served the Federal Republic of Germany for five years as commanding officer of Military District V, headquartered at Böblingen, also near Stuttgart. He retired in April 1960.[17]

Laegeler also returned to Germany in the summer of 1946, after his service to the Hill Project at Camp Ritchie and the Bolero Group at Fort Hunt, and was released three months later. He spent over five years as a sales representative for Zweckform, a stationery and office supplies corporation, before being admitted into the Bundeswehr in November 1955. Like von Liebenstein, he obtained the rank he had held as an officer in the Wehrmacht, also brigadier general. Laegeler capitalized on his previous military teaching experience and, in 1959, he obtained a position as commandant of the *Führungsakademie* in Hamburg-Blankenese. He served in this capacity for three years before retiring in 1962.[18]

Like von Liebenstein and Laegeler, Hermann Ramcke and Ludwig Crüwell also rose to prominence in the newly established West German state, although as political figures rather than reincarnated military officers. Ramcke emerged as one of the leading anti-Western voices in West Germany and Crüwell his most vocal opponent. Shortly after his New Year's escape from Camp Clinton, U.S. War Department officials sent Ramcke to Camp Shanks, New York, where they placed the general on a transport ship to be returned to Europe. Believing that he was being repatriated to Germany, Ramcke was quite disappointed when he arrived in the port city of Antwerp and was promptly sent to Camp 2226 in Belgium on March 17, 1946. After only four days in Belgium, Ramcke was then transferred to the London District Cage and interrogated about alleged German atrocities on the island of Crete. British authorities temporarily placed him in Special Camp No. 11 at Bridgend before then forwarding him to Lüneberg, a short drive southeast of Hamburg, to testify in the war crimes trial of General Kurt Student.[19]

Following Student's conviction, which incensed Ramcke, and his brief stay in the British transit camp outside Münster, Germany, British officials extradited Ramcke to France to stand trial himself for war crimes committed during his defense of the city of Brest in the summer of 1944. The German general endured fifty-seven months in a French prison awaiting his formal hearing. Exasperated, Ramcke finally escaped to Germany in an effort to see his family. He returned to France voluntarily, however, in early March 1951 in order to finally stand trial. A French military court convicted Ramcke of "war crimes against the civilian populace of Brest" on March 21, 1951, and sentenced him to five years of hard labor. But because he had already served almost five years in custody before the trial, French law allowed him to be released early. He returned to his hometown of Schleswig in mid-1951 after completing the final three months of his sentence in France. Ramcke claimed that upon his return he was greeted by some of his fellow paratroopers, the local band, residents offering him flowers and gifts, and the adoration of what he estimated to be ten thousand people![20]

Quickly, the "fanatical defender of Brest" emerged on the West German political stage, espousing his anti-Western views. At a meeting of the Fallschirmjägerverband, the German paratrooper veterans association, held in Braunschweig in July 1951, some of Ramcke's soldiers carried him into the convention on their shoulders. The former general then addressed the five thousand men in attendance by condemning what he saw as Western Allied defamation of both former German soldiers and the German people in general. He also made a plea for the release of German officers still imprisoned for war crimes, referring to these men as the "so-called war criminals." Not surprisingly, Ramcke's remarks prompted a negative reaction from the leftist press in Germany, France, and Switzerland and marked him as a potentially troublesome political figure among many officials in Bonn.[21]

Over a year later, he fully established himself as a thorn in Bonn's side by adopting a much more controversial public stance. On October 26, 1952, veterans of Hitler's Waffen-SS held their first postwar rally in the city of Verden, located about thirty minutes southeast of Bremen. As one of the more popular Wehrmacht general officers and the newly elected president of the Fallschirmjägerverband, "Papa" Ramcke was invited to offer a brief talk. The rally organizers asked him to simply offer greetings from the paratrooper veterans' organization and to limit his remarks to no more than three minutes. Upon taking the stage, however, the old general launched into a lengthy anti-Allied diatribe. "Who are the real war criminals?" he asked. "Those who by themselves made the fatal peace, who destroyed entire cities without tactical ground for doing so, who hurled atomic bombs on Hiroshima and now make new atomic bombs." Despite repeated written pleas passed to him by the organizers asking him first to curb his language and eventually to stop altogether, Ramcke pontificated for twenty-five minutes. He finally concluded by remarking that it was "an honor for us to have been on the black list of the enemy. Time will show that this list can again be a roll of honor." At this, to the horror of the rally's organizers, most of the four thousand SS veterans assembled in Verden erupted with chants of "Eisenhower schweinehund!"[22]

Following the scandalous speech, the former SS general Felix Steiner, who served as head of the veterans' organization, disassociated the organization from Ramcke's remarks. But he made no attempt to explain why virtually the entire assemblage had cheered and chanted at the conclusion of the controversial speech. Of graver concern for Bonn were the pointed responses from Washington, London, and Paris. In an effort to defuse the situation, numerous representatives of the West German government denounced Ramcke's position. Konrad Adenauer offered what *Time* magazine called the "understatement of the week" when he observed that Ramcke "should realize that his remarks cannot bolster Germany's reputation in the world." And the soon-to-be West German minister of defense, Theodor Blank, later stated in regard to the composition of the Bundeswehr that "the Ramckes . . . will not return. This is the type of National Socialist general whom the German people . . . do not want their sons to be entrusted with."[23]

Ludwig Crüwell's postwar political career took a decidedly different path from Ramcke's Nazi rabble rousing. The newly formed Afrikakorps-Verband, or Africa Korps veterans association, which dedicated itself to "the principles of moderation and democracy," elected Crüwell president in July 1951. Crüwell cooperated with the Bonn government in planning the group's first reunion in September 1951 and even sought contact with the veterans' former World War II enemies, namely veterans of the British Eighth Army, whom they had fought all across North Africa. Much to the delight of the new West German government and the Western Allies alike, Crüwell stated his hopes that the Afrika Korps reunion in Iserlohn, outside Düsseldorf, would "take the wind out of the sails of Bernhard Ramcke . . . and other sponsors of nationalist veterans' organizations."[24]

When West German rearmament became a reality and plans were underway for the establishment of the new Bundeswehr, Crüwell was considered for the position of commander in chief. While he never returned to the German military, likely because of his successful postwar business career, Bonn's consideration of him for the post speaks volumes. When the *New York Times* profiled Crüwell as part of a discussion about German rearmament in December 1954, it observed that the former general "personifies respectability," that he had a "spotless record," and that "he is conscious of the need to instill in the mind of the next generation of German soldiery a respect and understanding for the law." This characterization of Crüwell and his consideration for the highest military position in the new West German state was a far cry from the wartime British assessment of him as an idiotic Nazi.[25]

The experiences of Gehlen, von Liebenstein, Laegeler, Ramcke, and Crüwell are exceptional. The stories of most of the generals who returned from the United States are more pedestrian, largely involving the former prisoners simply returning home and attempting to rebuild a life for themselves and their families. In order to do this, however, they first had to navigate the Allied camp system in Europe for anywhere from a few months to a few years.

The most striking thing about both the American and British camps in Europe for returning POWs after the war is the level of disorganization and poor communication. This is perhaps understandable given the enormous tasks confronting the Allies at this time. With responsibility for providing food, shelter, and protection for millions of Europeans on a war-ravaged continent, organizing efficient camps and processes for returning prisoners of war was not their top priority. At times, however, it created some curious circumstances.

First, prisoners, even senior officers, could often be lost in the shuffle. The Allies often did not know which prisoners were in each other's custody. In fact, in many cases, one U.S. Army unit did not know which prisoners were in the custody of another. Frequently USFET, particularly the Historical Division, initiated searches in European camps for prisoner-of-war generals who were still held in the United States. At various times between November 1945 and March 1946, for instance, the U.S. Army Historical Division sought Generals von Aulock, Bieringer, von Choltitz, Elster, Neuling, Ramcke, Richter, Eberding, Daser, Rauch, Spang, Schuberth, and Badinski when most of these men could still be found at either Camp Clinton, Mississippi, or Camp Dermott, Arkansas, and Schuberth was deceased.[26]

Much of the confusion stemmed from the fact that the generals were sent to numerous locations upon their return to Europe. Indeed, Allied, particularly American, determination of which camp a particular POW general should be interned in appears to have been somewhat haphazard, at least until the Historical Division began requesting prisoners, first for Garmisch and then for Allendorf. Badinski, Stolberg, Spang, Ramcke, Richter, Elster, and Gallenkamp first arrived at Camp 2226 in Zedelgem, Belgium, one of the camps operated by the British Army of the Rhine outside Brugge. Daser found himself at Zuffenhausen, north of Stuttgart, and various others, including von Sponeck, Krause, von Liebenstein, and von Choltitz, were sent to Bolbec in France. This prompted USFET to cable Washington, requesting a list of the German generals who had been interned in the United States since the beginning of the war. Only adding to the confusion, the list that the Provost Marshal General's Office provided was incomplete. It provided the names of only forty-two of the German general officers who had been interned on American soil.[27]

U.S. Army Historical Division priorities seemed to dictate much about U.S. policy regarding the POW generals in Europe. The division initiated searches for Generals Erwin Menny and Franz Vaterrodt in February and March 1947, respectively, at a time when many of the generals were being released from the history program. Moreover, American officials released the generals at different times, depending upon their work for the program. Badinski, Bieringer, Bruhn, von Choltitz, Kessler, and Ullersperger departed Allendorf in April 1947, after each of these officers had completed reports for the Historical Division, while von Liebenstein and von Sponeck were retained as civilian internees to prepare further studies.[28]

For those generals not participating in the historical program, both the Americans and the British released the prisoners according to their date of capture, with the earliest captured being released first. Yet further restrictions applied. The Americans and British agreed immediately after the war that "a principal purpose of the Allies in occupied Germany [was] to prevent the renascence of the German Armed Forces and to destroy the German military spirit and tradition." It was for this reason that the generals had been kept out of Germany for so long after the war. Furthermore, the Allies defined a "militarist" as "any former regular officer of the German Navy, Army or Air Force . . . who by reason of his disposition, past activities and professional military knowledge is considered by the Military Governor as likely to foster or resuscitate the military ambitions of the German nation." Being classified as a "militarist" or "security suspect" meant the former general officer was subject to varying restrictions on travel and political participation, as well as other potential limitations.[29]

By April 1946, the British and Americans jointly maintained a "watch list" of German generals in Europe whom they deemed to be militarists and security suspects. This list included Alfred Gutknecht because of his "Nazi sympathies" and because he was a former police officer. The Allies believed former policemen might be tempted to rejoin police organizations and thereby "perpetuate military tradition and training under cover of police activities." Heinrich Kittel was also included because of his "Nazi sympathies." Notably, both of these men were soon to be working for the U.S. Army Historical Division. Remarkably, the list also included Wolfgang Thomale, who was characterized as having "Nazi sympathies" and being "very clever" as well as considered to be a potential resistance leader because he had joined the Freikorps in 1919. At the time the list was promulgated in April 1946, Thomale was an integral part of the Hill Project at Camp Ritchie and soon after joined the Bolero Group at Fort Hunt, Virginia.[30]

Clearly, as late as a year after the end of the war in Europe, American authorities appeared to be of two minds regarding their Wehrmacht general officer prisoners. On one hand, many of these men were deemed to be potential threats to the successful reconstruction of western Germany. Yet their American captors had also come to view some of these very same men as valuable sources of both historical information and military intelligence. Paradoxically, American officials trusted a number of German officers to accurately provide sensitive information but then harbored enough suspicions of these former enemies to keep them under surveillance for months after their repatriation.

Despite Western Allied fears, the prisoners could not be kept indefinitely. The U.S. Historical Division sought to retain prisoner-of-war status for the German historical program participants for as long as possible in order to gather as much information from these men as it could. Also, had the general officer prisoners been reclassified as civilian internees, they would have lost their military rank and accompanying pay along with rations of five hundred calories per day because German civilians were allotted less food than were POWs. But a U.S. European Command directive required that all prisoners of war be discharged by June 30, 1947, and the Historical Division was forced to comply. At the time of discharge, there were 767 German officers writing reports; 401 of these remained as "civilian internees" to continue the program.[31]

A number of generals remained in the German history program long after their conversion from prisoners of war to civilian internees. The program continued in a reorganized fashion under the direction of the Control Group, a select number of German generals led by one-time chief of the German General Staff Franz Halder. After again relocating, this time to Königstein, near Frankfurt, in May 1948, Halder and his staff entertained requests for special studies submitted by various U.S. government agencies through the U.S. Army Historical Division in Washington. Control Group members then chose qualified former generals to write the special reports, supervised their preparation, and served as liaisons between the former German generals, who wrote these reports from their homes, and the German history program authorities. Not surprisingly, an overwhelming number of these special studies dealt with issues related to the German war against the Soviet Union. Requests for special studies came from numerous U.S. government agencies, including the U.S. Army staff and officer training schools, U.S. Navy, U.S. Air Force, U.S. Army Corps of Engineers, and Joint Chiefs of Staff.[32]

The Control Group continued preparing historical reports and special studies until it was finally disbanded in 1961. During the German history program's fifteen years of operation, former Wehrmacht generals prepared over twenty-five thousand manuscripts totaling over two hundred thousand pages. Chief German coordinator and former general Franz Halder received the Meritorious Civilian Service Award from the United States for "a lasting contribution to the tactical and strategic thinking of the United States Armed Forces."[33]

British authorities retained their Wehrmacht generals as prisoners of war for almost a year longer than did their American counterparts. In October 1947 the British transferred a number of them, considered militarists and security suspects, to a camp in Adelheide, outside Bremen in northern Germany. Three former U.S. POWs were included in this group, Carl Köchy, Hans von der Mosel, and August Viktor von Quast. These men were retained at the camp until the spring of 1948. Once released, their names were added to a "stop list" that prohibited them from leaving Germany unless the military governor of the British Zone agreed to remove their restrictions. The names of numerous other generals appeared on the "stop list" as well, including Detlef Bock von Wülfingen, Knut Eberding, Erwin Menny, Ferdinand Neuling, Robert Sattler, Karl Spang, Christoph Graf zu Stolberg-Stolberg, Erwin Vierow, and Heinrich Aschenbrenner.[34] By the summer of 1948, however, British and American officials had repatriated all of their general officer prisoners with the exception of a few, like Ramcke, who remained in Allied prisons awaiting trial for war crimes.

During the six years in which the British and Americans held German generals as prisoners of war, the relationship between Anglo-American officials and the fifty-five Wehrmacht general officers considered in this study had evolved considerably. The transformation of this relationship, wrought by the developments of the war and the national security concerns of the immediate postwar era, illustrate two important points. First, despite some similarities, the respective priorities of British and American authorities regarding their POW general officers differed significantly. British officials consistently interrogated and eavesdropped on all of their senior officer prisoners. London primarily sought operational and tactical intelligence to aid the Allied war effort. The British believed that anything the generals could tell them about individual commanders, their histories and habits, soldier morale, or the weapons and equipment Wehrmacht forces used in the field would be useful in the war against Nazi Germany. Moreover, CSDIC took great interest in the possibility of organizing a Free Germany Committee like the one that emerged among the German officer and enlisted prisoners of war in the Soviet Union, even though it eventually determined that such a group would not be feasible among the prisoners in Britain.

Once Allied victory appeared likely in the fall of 1944, British intelligence also developed some interest in evidence of potential war crimes committed by the generals in its custody. Although few of the general officers in this study were tried by the Allies after the war, London was in the best position to assess which British prisoners should be investigated because of the time and resources it had spent gathering this type of information; Bernhard Ramcke may be a good example. CSDIC also unearthed evidence of collusion that violated international law between some of the general officers at Trent Park and at least one of the ostensibly neutral inspectors from the Red Cross. Furthermore, by the end of the war the British also showed considerable interest in the generals' views of the respective Allied powers and assessed each prisoner's willingness to collaborate with the Allies in the reconstruction of postwar Germany.

Yet CSDIC's interrogation and monitoring of the prisoners' activities and conversations ended immediately following Germany's surrender. In January 1946 London moved its general officer prisoners to Bridgend, where it held these officers for almost two and a half years and never again systematically sought any information from them. Clearly, the primary purpose of the British operation was to gather information that could help the Allies win the war. Once this had been accomplished, the operation no longer appeared necessary.

In sharp contrast to its British allies, Washington initially had little regard for the value of Wehrmacht general officer POWs. Despite briefly accommodating its first handful of POW generals at the luxurious Byron Hot Springs resort in California, the U.S. Provost Marshal General's Office quickly transferred these men to Mexia, Texas, where the generals voiced complaints about the insolence of American personnel. In response to these complaints, American officials assured the generals that accommodations more appropriate for prisoners of their high rank awaited them at Camp Clinton.

But the generals found life in Mississippi little different than it had been in Texas. Indeed, as late as August 1944, War and State Department inspectors condemned the quality of the personnel who guarded the generals at Camp Clinton, labeling them misfits and men collectively unqualified for the job of providing security for a high-profile camp of that nature. Moreover, for the duration of the war, U.S. War Department officials entrusted Camp Clinton's most distinguished prisoners to a commandant who believed these men should be treated like any other prisoners of war and regularly turned a deaf ear to their requests and complaints.

This early American neglect and disregard for German POW generals sprang from the U.S. War Department's initial lack of interest in these men. Most U.S. officials did not believe that the officers who had been captured in North Africa could offer them any intelligence of value to the coming invasion of northwest France. Besides, their British allies had a great deal more experience dealing with prisoners of war, including general officers, and CSDIC made what valuable information it gleaned from the generals in its custody available to American military intelligence. Thus Washington likely saw no need to expend its own precious resources. After the generals' first brief stay in California, the War Department did not make any further attempts to interrogate or eavesdrop on its general officer prisoners at Camp Mexia, Camp Clinton, Camp Dermott, or Camp Ruston. American authorities appeared only too happy to allow their British counterparts to take the lead in gathering information from captured Wehrmacht senior officers.

The War Department slowly began to develop a formal policy for dealing with its senior prisoners after the success of the Allied invasion of Normandy. American intelligence personnel began directly interrogating a select few prisoners who possessed particular kinds of operational, technical, or logistical expertise. Yet, despite this modicum of autonomy in their handling of German general officer prisoners, U.S. officials still continued to allow CSDIC to take the lead in interrogating most of the senior German officers captured before the end of the war in Europe.

Washington officials also finally began to reconsider the kind of relationship they were developing with the Wehrmacht generals in their custody. What prompted this reconsideration was the formulation of American ideas about what the United States wanted to do with postwar Germany, something about which it had had little concern prior to D-Day. Once American officials determined the importance of building a democratic, demilitarized postwar German state, they began to evaluate what, if any, role the generals in their custody might be able to play in this process.

Still, the development of American policy was slow and halting. It was anti-Nazi German POW collaborators who pointed out to the War Department the incongruity of using German general officers to "re-educate" lower-ranking and enlisted German prisoners of war when demilitarization was one of the primary goals of the process. Moreover, until the end of the war, logistical concerns like finding appropriate housing for the numerous German officers interned in the United States continued to take precedence over establishing any kind of bona fide reorientation camp for collaborative anti-Nazi senior officer prisoners, as the shifting arrangements at Camp Dermott attest.

Finally, by the end of the war a new concern occupied American military policy makers, one that demonstrated the confluence between postwar national security concerns and wartime POW policy for high-ranking officers. Admiration for the prowess of German officers and the German military tradition in particular, coupled with anxiety about Soviet intentions and the strength of the Red Army, drove Washington officials into a collaborative relationship with many of the Wehrmacht general officers in U.S. custody.

The second important point emerging from this study deals with this collaborative relationship. The evolution of America's national security concerns in the years immediately following the end of World War II had consequences for its policy governing the treatment of high-ranking prisoners of war. Seemingly overnight, U.S. officials came to view Wehrmacht POW generals as highly valuable sources of information. Indeed, these prisoners proved far more valuable to the United States *after* the war concluded than they had during the war itself.

American officials quickly came to rely on Wehrmacht generals for a variety of purposes. Following the end of the war in Europe, American military intelligence first sought information about the German-Japanese alliance that could aid the American war in the Pacific. German generals like Ulrich Kessler were now taken to Fort Hunt, Virginia, where American interrogators questioned and eavesdropped on these men in much the same manner as CSDIC had done throughout the war. During the final month of the war in Europe, American, British, and Canadian military intelligence began organizing the Hill Project, utilizing recently captured German General Staff officers to provide information about the German military that might help the Western Allied armies improve their own mobilization, logistics, training, and efficiency, among other things. And, given the U.S. Army's burgeoning interest in preparing for a potential war against the Soviet Union, a general like Reinhard Gehlen offered Allied military intelligence firsthand information and lessons learned from the German war against the Soviet military.

Driven by the needs of the war in the Pacific, American and British admiration for the German military model, and Western Allied fears of Soviet intentions, American authorities began to reconceptualize their German prisoners of war as potential "allies." Whereas only a year earlier American officials had found little use for the German generals in their custody, changing national security concerns in the immediate postwar era transformed Washington's relationship with Wehrmacht general officers. Similarly, as the generals were returned to Europe, the U.S. Army Historical Division solicited information from hundreds of German generals to supplement the American historical record of the war. Eventually, the reports these generals produced began to play a highly influential role in the development of U.S. Army policy in the late 1940s and early 1950s, particularly in plans to defend Western Europe from a potential Soviet invasion.

British authorities had taken on the lion's share of the effort to gather valuable military intelligence from Wehrmacht general officer prisoners during the war itself. But a change in national security concerns immediately following the war compelled American authorities to take the lead in developing a relationship with German generals in the early years of the Cold War. Remarkably, the relationship that Anglo-American officials forged with Wehrmacht generals following the Second World War endured. While driven by common fears of Soviet communism, the roots of the relationship sprang from British and American admiration for the German military. In June 1947, following a study of the attitudes of the German officers in Britain's remaining POW camps, London concluded that many British officers' admiration for their German counterparts heightened the potential danger of a possible resurgence of German militarism. British officials saw the need to disabuse their military officers of the idea that the German generals had become their allies and warned that "the reputation of the German Wehrmacht remains high, and the sympathy shown for its senior officers by British officers seems to increase with time. If the core of the German Army is not to be resurrected as a factor to be reckoned with, the complacency existing in many [British] minds will have to disappear, and the notion that the German generals and General Staff are necessarily 'on our side' should not be seriously entertained."[35]

A similar veneration of the German military existed among American officers and officials. The resources and time that American occupation authorities had spent tracking down German generals for the Historical Division demonstrated how important German views of the war were to the West. Moreover, respect and veneration of the military prowess of German officers had, in part, facilitated the formation of the Allied Hill Project, the work of the Bolero Group, and the influence of the German history program's reports on U.S. Army doctrine in the late 1940s and early 1950s.[36]

The comments of Heinz Guderian's grandson, Lieutenant Colonel Günther Guderian, epitomize the emulative nature of the Anglo-American relationship with German generals. After serving as the Bundeswehr liaison officer to the U.S. Army at Fort Bragg in the 1990s, Guderian stated, in reference to his grandfather, that "sometimes, I get the impression that in the United States Army, even more officers know the name [Guderian] than in the German army." He also recalled that one of the ranking officers of the U.S. Army's Seventh Corps had two large pictures hanging on his wall. "One was Patton," observed Guderian, and "one was my grandfather."[37] American perspectives of the importance of German general officers had obviously come a long way.

Acknowledgments

This book has played a role in my life for the past nine years. During this time, I have accrued considerable debt to many individuals who aided me in the process of researching and writing this manuscript. While insufficient, this acknowledgment of their contributions is an expression of my sincere gratitude.

First, my thanks to the Department of History at Texas A&M University, the Melbern G. Glasscock Center for Humanities Research, the German Historical Institute, and the Andersonville National Historic Trust, all of which provided generous financial support for this endeavor. I am also grateful to the many individuals who directly aided my research. Martin Gedra, Robin Cookson, and Paul Brown at the National Archives and Records Administration II in College Park, Maryland, all graciously helped me locate important American documents. Wolfgang Frey at the Bundesarchiv-Militärarchiv in Freiburg, Germany, spent considerable time helping me access the requisite German military records. And the archivists and staff at the British National Archives in Kew, England; the Mississippi Department of Archives and History in Jackson; and the Library and Archives at the Hoover Institution at Stanford University all proved extremely helpful with my work in their respective collections.

I wish to thank Anja Schwalen for her help in translating two of the German memoirs and Chad Daniels and Christy Calhoun at the Mississippi Armed Forces Museum, who proved incredibly gracious in providing me with pictures and documents from their collection. My thanks as well to all of the following individuals who aided me in various ways at some point in this project: Cornelia Cesari, Esther Krug, Terrence Winschel, Gunter Bischof, Ruediger Overmans, Susan Strange, Sabrina Bader, Robyn Rodriguez, Jeffrey Johnson, David Macri, Adrienne Lamberson, Walter Kamphoefner, Andrew Kirkendall, Kelly Crager, and Jeremy Toynbee and the staff and reviewers at the *Journal of Contemporary History*.

My thanks go to Stephen Wrinn and Allison Webster at the University Press of Kentucky. Your confidence in my work and your assistance in this process have been wonderful. I am also extremely grateful for all of the individuals who read and commented on the manuscript at some point in the process. The two reviewers selected by the press took valuable time to review my work and offered very helpful suggestions. My copyeditor, Joy Margheim, did a remarkable job helping me prepare the manuscript for publication. Joseph Dawson, David Vaught, Adam Seipp, and James Hannah all offered substantive comments and criticisms of the manuscript as well as challenged me to be a better historian and writer. Thank you all for your help and direction. Finally, I have enormous respect and appreciation for the contributions, both to this manuscript and to my career as a whole, of Arnold Krammer. Professor Krammer's guidance and mentorship have left an indelible mark on my work. His example will remain the standard I strive to emulate.

Last, but certainly not least, I wish to thank a special group of family and friends who have provided essential support for me and this project. I will forever owe a debt to Carol Burton, Amy, Anders, Chris, Lora, Andrew and Tashina, Richard and Abby, and all of the Feistel family. Roy and Chris Pilgrim, the late Gladys Hackworth, Jennifer and Brian Leatherman, Larry Blomstedt, and Rita Walker all offered invaluable support and encouragement. For special counsel and friendship, my thanks go to Chad Harvey and Albert Frieden, both of whom contributed far more than they know. For countless reasons, the contributions of Lenae and Jimi Steele; Alex, Wade, and Leah Hultz; Doug, Brenda, and Drew Mallett; and Donald and Judy Mallett are immeasurable. I doubt any of you know how important you have always been and will continue to be to my work. Aviaq Nielsen brought a glowing smile to my life and that has changed and inspired me in important ways. And, finally, I lack adequate words to express my gratitude for Tasha Wyatt and all that she brings to my life and work. Her valuable editorial contributions, challenging questions, engaging conversations, and inspirational words rank second only to her incredible love and support in making both me and my work better. Thanks for being my wife.

Appendix A

Wehrmacht General Officer Prisoners of War Held in the United States

Colonel General (Generaloberst)

Von Arnim, Hans Jürgen

Lieutenant General (General der Infanterie, der Artillerie, etc.)

Buhle, Walter
Crüwell, Ludwig
Gallenkamp, Curt
Kessler, Ulrich
Neuling, Ferdinand
Ramcke, Bernhard-Hermann
Von Choltitz, Dietrich
Von Vaerst, Gustav
Vierow, Erwin

Major General (Generalleutnant)

Aschenbrenner, Heinrich
Badinski, Curt
Borowietz, Willibald
Bülowius, Karl Robert Max
Daser, Wilhelm
Frantz, Gotthard
Kittel, Heinrich
Kleberger, Franz
Köchy, Carl Peter Bernard
Menneking, Rolf

Menny, Erwin
Pollert, Hermann
Rauch, Erwin
Seyffardt, Paul
Spang, Karl
Thomale, Wolfgang
Vierow, Walter
Von Heyking, Rüdiger
Von Sponeck, Theodor Graf

Brigadier General (Generalmajor)

Bieringer, Ludwig
Bruhn, Hans
Dunckern, Anton
Eberding, Knut
Elster, Botho
Gaul, Hans
Gehlen, Reinhard
Gundelach, Herbert
Gutknecht, Alfred
Hermann, Rudolph
Krause, Fritz
Laegeler, Hellmuth
Richter, Otto
Sattler, Robert
Schnarrenberger, Ernst
Schramm, Hans-Georg
Schuberth, Hans-Georg
Stolberg-Stolberg, Christoph Graf zu
Ullersperger, Wilhelm
Vaterrodt, Franz
Von Aulock, Hubertus
Von der Mosel, Hans
Von Hülsen, Heinrich-Hermann
Von Liebenstein, Kurt Freiherr
Von Quast, August Viktor*

---

*The Wehrmacht promoted von Quast to *Generalmajor* in August 1943, following his surrender to American forces in North Africa, but American military authorities refused to recognize this postcaptivity promotion.

Von Trotha, Ivo-Thilo
Von Wülfingen, Detlef Bock

Rear Admiral (Vizeadmiral)

Schirmer, Alfred**

Commodore (Konteradmiral)

Hennecke, Walter**
Kähler, Otto**
Meixner, Paul**
Weber, Carl**

**American and British authorities held these German Navy (Kriegsmarine) officer prisoners of war with the generals at various times and in various camps.

Appendix B
German Military Document Section Studies (Published)

Armored Breakthrough: War Diary of German First Armored Group (121 pages)

Bibliography No. 1b: German Chemical Warfare (11 pages)

German Army Mobilization: A Study of the Mobilization of the German Army (91 pages)

The German Army Quartermaster and Finance Organization (199 pages)

The German General Staff Corps: A Study of the Organization of the German General Staff (276 pages)

German Military Transportation (77 pages)

German Operational Intelligence: A Study of German Operational Intelligence (164 pages)

The German Operation at Anzio: A Study of the German Operation at Anzio Beachhead from 22 January 1944 to 31 May 1944 (128 pages)

German Training Methods: A Study of German Military Training (316 pages)

Special Report No. 1: Officer Efficiency Reports in the German Army (26 pages)

Special Report No. 2: Officer Candidate Selection and Training in the German Army (18 pages)

Special Report No. 3: Ration Administration in the German Army (20 pages)

Special Report No. 4: German Army Officer Courts-Martial (7 pages)

Special Report No. 5: Screening of German Enlisted Personnel for Officer Appointments (10 pages)

Special Translation No. 1: Infantry in the Sixth Year of the War (18 pages)

Appendix C

German Military Document Section Studies (Unpublished)

"German Administration of Occupied Territories" (265 pages) [not translated]

"German Appraisal of U.S. Armor" (7 pages)

"German Army Mobilization, 1921–1939" (656 pages) [not translated]

"The German High Command" (492 pages)

"German Manpower: A Study of the Employment of German Manpower from 1933–1945" (270 pages)

"German Permanent Fortifications" (305 pages)

"Hitler as Supreme Warlord, 1939–1945" (10 pages)

"Program 'Otto'" (10 pages)

"A Study on Anti-Partisan Warfare" (10 pages)

"Tactics" (Taktik) (240 pages) [not translated]

Appendix D

Wehrmacht Officer Prisoners of War in the Hill Project ("Hillbillies")

Lieutenant General (*General der Infanterie, der Artillerie,* etc.)

Buhle, Walter

Major General (*Generalleutnant*)

Kleberger, Franz
Menneking, Rolf
Thomale, Wolfgang

Brigadier General (*Generalmajor*)

Gundelach, Herbert
Laegeler, Hellmuth
von Trotha, Ivo-Thilo

Colonel (*Oberst*)

Berendsen, Friedrich
Engelter, Georg
Gaul, Hans
Haertel, Johannes
Kinitz, Franz-Josef
Kuehne, Rudolf-Theodor
Meyer-Detring, Wilhelm
Petri, Reinhard
Pollex, Kurt
Reissinger, Walter

Lieutenant Colonel (*Oberstleutnant*)

Bogner, Dr. Josef
Brix, Ernst
Euler, Richard
Fellmer, Reinhold
Klehr, Hans-Guenther
Linn, Hermann
Litterscheid, Friedrich-Franz
Mueller, Alfred-Johannes
Obermaier, Claus
Rittman, Kurt
Schaeder, Christian
von Brauchitsch, Hans-Georg
von Seydlitz-Kurzbach, Friedrich

Major (*Major*)

Lobedanz, Walter
von Luedinghausen, Horst

Lieutenant Commander (*Korvettenkapitän;* Kriegsmarine, or German Navy)

Schubert, Paul-Heinz

Captain (*Hauptmann*)

Cartellieri, Dr. Wolfgang
Dyckerhoff, Hans
Knieper, Werner
Lorenz, Reinhold
Zuber, Hans-Georg

First Lieutenant (*Oberleutnant*)

Benke, Heinz
Buehler, Eugen
Darsow, Hans-Jürgen
Koch, Hermann
Krueger, Herbert
Rahn, Helmut
von Berg, Karl-Ludwig

Second Lieutenant (*Leutnant*)

Achtelik, Walter
Gehrke, Hermann
Haeusing, Heiner
Jentsch, Dietrich
Mengler, Wolfgang
Meyer, Erwin
Naehler, Max
Oelze, Werner
Pflocksch, Gustav
Preckel, Karl
Wagner, Hans-Otto

Notes

Introduction

1. See Arnold Krammer, "American Treatment of German Generals during World War II," *Journal of Military History* 54 (January 1990): 27–46, for the only study of German prisoner-of-war generals in the United States.

2. War Diary, May 1943, WO 165/41, the National Archives of the United Kingdom, Kew, Richmond, Surrey, United Kingdom (hereafter TNA).

3. Richard B. Speed III, *Prisoners, Diplomats, and the Great War: A Study in the Diplomacy of Captivity* (New York: Greenwood Press, 1990), 98–100.

4. Ibid., 101–3.

5. Ibid., 31, 105.

6. For more on the United States serving as a protecting power during the First World War, see Speed, *Prisoners, Diplomats, and the Great War.*

7. Ibid., 123–26.

8. Ibid., 126–35.

9. Ibid., 156.

10. Ibid., 138.

11. Matthew Barry Sullivan, *Thresholds of Peace: Four Hundred Thousand German Prisoners and the People of Britain, 1944–1948* (London: Hamish Hamilton, 1979), 219–20.

12. F. H. Hinsley, *British Intelligence in the Second World War: Its Influence on Strategy and Operations* (London: H. M. Stationery Office, 1991), 2:32–51; War Diary, April 1943, WO 165/41, TNA.

13. Letter from P. H. Gore-Booth, March 14, 1944, FO 916/886, TNA.

14. Ibid.

15. Ibid.

16. Ibid.; Sullivan, *Thresholds of Peace,* 22.

17. CSDIC reports of interrogations and conversations between the German prisoner-of-war generals are housed in the Records of the War Office: Directorate of Military Operations and Intelligence, and Directorate of Military Intelligence; Ministry of Defense, Defense Intelligence Staff: Files (WO 208) at the National Archives of the United Kingdom; duplicate copies of some of the reports can be found in the files

of the U.S. War Department's General and Special Staffs at the National Archives and Records Administration in College Park, Maryland.

18. Letter from P. H. Gore-Booth, March 14, 1944, FO 916/886, TNA; War Diary, November 1943, WO 165/41, TNA.

19. For an examination of the German officer corps, see Karl Demeter, *The German Officer-Corps in Society and State 1650–1945* (New York: Praeger, 1965).

20. The last publicly accessible rank list for the World War II German Army is dated May 1, 1944. See Nikolaus V. Preradovich, "Die militärische und soziale Herkunft der hohen Generalität des deutschen Heeres am 1. Mai 1944," *Wehrwissenschaftliche Rundschau* 20, no. 1 (1970): 44.

21. Ibid., 45–55.

22. Ibid.; Nikolaus V. Preradovich, *Die militärische und soziale Herkunft der Generalität des deutschen Heeres, 1. Mai 1944* (Osnabrück, Germany: Biblio Verlag, 1978), 43, 51.

23. George A. Kourvetaris and Betty A. Dobratz, *Social Origins and Political Orientations of Officer Corps in a World Perspective* (Denver: University of Denver, 1973), 2–4, 21–22, 60.

24. Correlli Barnett, *Britain and Her Army, 1509–1970: A Military, Political and Social Survey* (London: Allen Lane the Penguin Press, 1970), 487–88; P. E. Razzell, "Social Origins of Officers in the Indian and British Home Army: 1758–1962," *British Journal of Sociology* 14 (September 1963): 253.

25. Garry D. Ryan and Timothy K. Nenninger, eds., *Soldiers and Civilians: The U.S. Army and the American People* (Washington, D.C.: National Archives and Records Administration, 1987), 7.

26. Edward M. Coffman, *The Regulars: The American Army, 1898–1941* (Cambridge, MA: Belknap Press of Harvard University Press, 2004), 50, 288; Kourvetaris and Dobratz, *Social Origins and Political Orientations*, 60.

27. Russell F. Weigley, *Towards an American Army: Military Thought from Washington to Marshall* (New York: Columbia University Press, 1962), 6.

28. Russell F. Weigley, *The American Way of War: A History of United States Military Strategy and Policy* (New York: Macmillan, 1973), 81.

29. Charles Robert Kemble, "Mutations in America's Perceptions of Its Professional Military Leaders: An Historical Overview and Update," *Armed Forces and Society* (prepublished April 4, 2007): 6–8, doi:10.1177/0095327X06293862, accessed via *OnlineFirst*, http://afs.sagepub.com; see also Charles Robert Kemble, *The Image of the Army Officer in America* (Westport, CT: Greenwood Press, 1973).

30. Kemble, "Mutations in America's Perceptions," 8–9; George MacMillan, "A Decade of War Novels: The Accent Has Been Political," *New York Times Book Review*, December 1951, 235.

31. Andreas F. Lowenfeld, "The Free Germany Committee: An Historical Study," *Review of Politics* 14, no. 3 (July 1952), 346–66. See also Bodo Scheurig, *Free Germany: The National Committee and the League of German Officers* (Middletown, CT: Wesleyan University Press, 1969).

1. *Afrikaner* and *Franzosen*

1. German Army and Air Force ranks for general officers equated to U.S. ranks as follows: *Generalmajor*—brigadier general; *Generalleutnant*—major general; *General der Infanterie, der Artillerie,* etc.—lieutenant general; *Generaloberst*—general; and *Generalfeldmarschall*—general of the army. See Andris J. Kursietis, *The Wehrmacht at War, 1939–1945: The Units and Commanders of the German Ground Forces during World War II* (Soesterberg, Netherlands: Aspekt, 1999), 7.

2. Paul Carell, *Foxes of the Desert: The Story of the Afrika Korps* (1960; repr., Atglen, PA: Schiffer, 1994), 168; Roger James Bender and Richard D. Law, *Uniforms, Organization, and History of the Afrikakorps* (Mountain View, CA: R. James Bender, 1973), 79; "Enemy Gets His First Taste of 'Unconditional Surrender': Germans in Bizerte Area Yielded to American General Who Offered No Terms and Vowed to Kill All Who Tried to Escape," *New York Times,* May 11, 1943.

3. Bender and Law, *Uniforms,* 62; John R. Angolia, *On the Field of Honor: A History of the Knight's Cross Bearers* (San Jose, CA: R. James Bender, 1979), 2:204–5.

4. Rick Atkinson, *An Army at Dawn: The War in North Africa, 1942–1943* (New York: Henry Holt, 2002), 371–72; Bender and Law, *Uniforms,* 89–90; Krammer, "American Treatment of German Generals," 30; Meixner was promoted to *Kapitan zur See* (captain) on April 1, 1943, and then to *Konteradmiral* (commodore) effective June 1, 1944. Hans H. Hildebrand and Ernest Henriot, *Deutschlands Admiral 1849–1945: Die militärischen Werdegänge der See-, Ingenieur-, Sanitäts-, Waffen- und Verwaltungsoffiziere im Admiralsrang* (Osnabrück, Germany: Biblio Verlag, 1988–1990), 462–63.

5. Bender and Law, *Uniforms,* 79–80, 134; Heinz Guderian, *Panzer Leader* (1952; repr., Costa Mesa, CA: Noontide Press, 1988), 107; Dermot Bradley, Karl-Friedrich Hildebrand, and Markus Rövekamp, *Die Generale des Heeres, 1921–1945* (Osnabrück, Germany: Biblio Verlag, 1993), 7:513–14.

6. Samuel W. Mitcham Jr., *Hitler's Legions: The German Army Order of Battle, World War II* (New York: Stein and Day, 1985), 409; John Thompson, "War Over in North Africa: Allies Capture 150,000; Seize Gen. Von Arnim," *Chicago Daily Tribune,* May 13, 1943; "Lecture for OATS Course," MSg 1/4133, Bundesarchiv-Militärarchiv, Freiburg im Breisgau (hereafter BA-MA).

7. Bender and Law, *Uniforms,* 68, 186; Mitcham, *Hitler's Legions,* 229, 377; Bradley, Hildebrand, and Rövekamp, *Die Generale des Heeres,* 6:183–84; Karl Friedrich Hildebrand, *Die Generale der deutschen Luftwaffe 1935–1945: Die militärischen Werdegänge der Flieger-, Flakartillerie-, Fallschirmjäger-, Luftnachrichten- und Ingenieur-Offiziere einschließlich der Ärzte, Richter, Intendanten und Ministerialbeamten im Generalsrang* (Osnabrück, Germany: Biblio Verlag, 1990), 1:309–10.

8. Correlli Barnett, ed., *Hitler's Generals* (New York: Grove Weidenfeld, 1989), 352, 335–41; Bender and Law, *Uniforms,* 127.

9. Barnett, *Hitler's Generals,* 342–49.

10. Ibid.; Atkinson, *Army at Dawn,* 489.

11. Barnett, *Hitler's Generals*, 351–52; Carell, *Foxes of the Desert*, 355, 362; Atkinson, *Army at Dawn*, 528–29.

12. Günter Bischof and Stephen E. Ambrose, eds., *Eisenhower and the German Prisoners of War: Facts against Falsehood* (Baton Rouge: Louisiana State University Press, 1992), 30; Sullivan, *Thresholds of Peace*, 221.

13. Combined Services Detailed Interrogation Centre (hereafter CSDIC) report, G.R.G.G. 2, May 24, 1943; CSDIC G.R.G.G. 3, May 24, 1943, WO 208/5016, TNA; Theodor Graf von Sponeck, *Meine Erinnerungen*, p. 173, MSg 1/3329, BA-MA.

14. "Gen. Von Arnim Taken to Palace at Gibraltar," *Los Angeles Times*, May 16, 1943; James MacDonald, "British Bells Hail Victory in Tunisia: Celebration at Its Peak When von Arnim, Axis Commander, Arrives as a Prisoner," *New York Times*, May 17, 1943.

15. Krammer, "American Treatment of German Generals," 28.

16. Patrick Campbell, *Trent Park: A History* (London: Middlesex University Press, 1997), 36–43.

17. The Knight's Cross was one of seven in a series of Iron Crosses awarded to members of the German military for acts of bravery. The first Iron Cross to be awarded for a single act of bravery would be the Iron Cross-Second Class, followed by the Iron Cross-First Class, for additional acts of bravery. Next came the Knight's Cross for still further bravery, then the Oak Leaves, followed by the Swords, Diamonds, and the Knight's Cross in Gold, each award contingent upon earning the previous one. Mitcham, *Hitler's Legions*, 363–64; Angolia, *On the Field of Honor*, 2:17–18, 45–46; Bradley, Hildebrand, and Rövekamp, *Die Generale des Heeres*, 2:480–82.

18. Bender and Law, *Uniforms*, 101.

19. B. H. Liddell Hart, *The Other Side of the Hill: Germany's Generals, Their Rise and Fall, with Their Own Account of Military Events, 1939–1945* (1948; repr., London: Cassell and Company, 1951), 243; Carell, *Foxes of the Desert*, 169; Sullivan, *Thresholds of Peace*, 223.

20. "Report of visit with General Crüwell, Cairo, September 9, 1942," "Report of visit with General Crüwell, Camp No. 11, September 28, 1942," PERS 6/114, BA-MA.

21. Sullivan, *Thresholds of Peace*, 221.

22. Ibid., 223; Sönke Neitzel, *Tapping Hitler's Generals: Transcripts of Secret Conversations, 1942–45* (Barnsley, U.K.: Frontline Books; St. Paul, MN: MBI, 2007), 26.

23. Richard Garrett, *P.O.W.* (London: David and Charles, 1981), 167.

24. Sullivan, *Thresholds of Peace*, 51–52; Neitzel, *Tapping Hitler's Generals*, 20.

25. Sullivan, *Thresholds of Peace*, 52.

26. CSDIC, S.R.G.G. 1, May 16, 1943; CSDIC, S.R.G.G. 5, May 16, 1943; CSDIC, S.R.G.G. 12, May 16, 1943; CSDIC, S.R.G.G. 18, May 16, 1943, all in WO 208/4165, TNA.

27. For further discussion of the guidelines issued by Ausland-Abwehr and the disregard for these rules by numerous German personnel, see Neitzel, *Tapping Hitler's Generals*, 25.

28. CSDIC, S.R.G.G. 12, May 16, 1943; CSDIC, S.R.G.G. 53, May 24, 1943, all in WO 208/4165, TNA.

29. CSDIC, S.R.G.G. 65, May 24, 1943; CSDIC, S.R.G.G. 67, May 26, 1943; CSDIC, S.R.G.G. 89, May 31, 1943, all in WO 208/4165, TNA.

30. See Neitzel, *Tapping Hitler's Generals,* 25.

31. Theodor Graf von Sponeck, *Meine Erinnerungen,* p. 176, MSg 1/3329, BA-MA.

32. "The Generals": Views of German Senior Officer P.W.'s, January 5, 1944, WO 208/5550, TNA.

33. War Diary, June 1943, WO 165/41, TNA; Theodor Graf von Sponeck, *Meine Erinnerungen,* p. 173, MSg 1/3329, BA-MA; As of June 1, 1943, the following thirteen generals were interned at Camp No. 11 at Trent Park: von Arnim, Crüwell, von Thoma, Cramer, von Sponeck, Frantz, Bassenge, Krause, Neuffer, von Liebenstein, von Broich, Schnarrenberger, and von Hülsen. Report on the German Senior Officer P/W at No. 11 P/W Camp for the Month of June 1943, WO 208/5622, TNA.

34. Report on the German Senior Officer P/W at No. 11 P/W Camp for the Month of June 1943, WO 208/5622, TNA.

35. Ibid.

36. Ibid.

37. Neitzel, *Tapping Hitler's Generals,* 15; Evaluation of Emil Ernst Schnarrenberger, February 12, 1943, Document No. 31, PERS 6/1876; Evaluation of Kurt von Liebenstein, October 1, 1942, PERS 1/294, BA-MA.

38. "The Generals": Views of German Senior Officer P.W.'s., January 5, 1944, WO 208/5550, TNA; For more on the historical social status of the German officer corps, see Demeter, *German Officer-Corps;* and Preradovich, *Die militärische und soziale Herkunft der Generalität.*

39. "The Generals": Views of German Senior Officer P.W.'s., January 5, 1944, WO 208/5550, TNA.

40. Ibid.

41. Ibid.

42. Index of Subjects Discussed by the Senior Officer PW at Camp No. 11, Published in the S.R.G.G. and G.R.G.G. Series from D-Day to December 31, 1944, G.R.G.G. 243, December 31, 1944, WO 208/5018, TNA.

43. Report on Information Obtained from Senior Officer PW, G.R.G.G. 171, August 5–8, 1944, WO 208/5017, TNA.

44. "Sattler," MSg 109, BA-MA; Hildebrand and Henriot, *Deutschlands Admirale,* 59–60; Report on Information Obtained from Senior Officer PW, G.R.G.G. 156, July 8–10, 1944, WO 208/5017, TNA.

45. Report on Information Obtained from Senior Officer PW, G.R.G.G. 152, July 1–2, 1944; Report on Information Obtained from Senior Officer PW, G.R.G.G. 156, July 8–10, 1944; Report on Information Obtained from Senior Officer PW, G.R.G.G. 159, July 15–16, 1944, all in WO 208/5017, TNA.

46. First Detailed Interrogation of Brig-Gen Bieringer, Ludwig, RG 165, Entry 179, Box 656, National Archives and Records Administration, College Park, MD (hereafter NARA).

47. First Detailed Interrogation of General of Infantry Neuling, Ferdinand, and First Detailed Interrogation of Brig-Gen Bieringer, Ludwig, RG 165, Entry 179, Box 656, NARA.

48. On Schuberth's and Badinski's commands, see "Schuberth," MSg 109, BA-MA; Milton Shulman, *Defeat in the West: Germany's Greatest Battles as Seen by Hitler's Generals* (1947; repr., New York: Ballantine, 1968), 206–7, 213; Report on Information Obtained from Senior Officer PW, G.R.G.G. 180, August 25–26 ,1944, WO 208/5017, TNA. On Menny, see Bender and Law, *Uniforms,* 73, 140, 114; Mitcham, *Hitler's Legions,* 101, 374; "Menny, Erwin," RG 242, T-78, rolls 883–95, NARA.

49. Report on Information Obtained from Senior Officer PW, G.R.G.G. 180, August 25–26, 1944, WO 208/5017, TNA.

50. Ibid.

51. Larry Collins and Dominique Lapierre, *Is Paris Burning?* (1965; repr., New York: Warner Books, 1991), 23–24; Telford Taylor, *The March of Conquest: The German Victories in Western Europe, 1940* (1958; repr., Baltimore, MD: Nautical and Aviation Publishing Company of America, 1991), 200, 203–4.

52. Collins and Lapierre, *Is Paris Burning?,* 25; Roger James Bender and Warren W. Odegard, *Uniforms, Organization, and History of the Panzertruppe* (San Jose, CA: R. James Bender, 1980), 53–54; Kursietis, *Wehrmacht at War,* 302–3; Shulman, *Defeat in the West,* 219.

53. Michael Veranov, ed., *The Mammoth Book of the Third Reich at War* (New York: Carroll and Graf, 1997), 525–27; Shulman, *Defeat in the West,* 219.

54. Collins and Lapierre, *Is Paris Burning?,* 192–94.

55. Report on Information Obtained from Senior Officer PW, G.R.G.G. 183, August 29, 1944, WO 208/5017, TNA; Collins and Lapierre, *Is Paris Burning?,* 180; Preliminary Report on Information Obtained from CS/211—General der Infanterie Dietrich von Choltitz, G.R.G.G. 181(c), August 25, 1944, WO 208/5017, TNA.

56. Report on Information Obtained from Senior Officer PW, G.R.G.G. 183, August 29, 1944, WO 208/5017, TNA; Collins and Lapierre, *Is Paris Burning?,* 312–14.

57. Report on Information Obtained from Senior Officer PW, G.R.G.G. 183, August 29, 1944, WO 208/5017, TNA; Confidential report from the Directorate of Military Intelligence, September 7, 1944, WO 208/5622, TNA.

58. Preliminary Report on Information Obtained from Generals Gutknecht, Eberbach and Schramm, G.R.G.G. 187, September 10, 1944, WO 208/5017, TNA; Report on Information Obtained from PW CS/221 Genmaj Gutknecht, S.I.R. 901, September 1, 1944, Report on Further Information Obtained from PW CS/221 Genmaj Gutknecht, S.I.R. 908, September 4, 1944, and Report on Further Information

Obtained from PW CS/221 Genmaj Gutknecht, S.I.R. 929, September 7, 1944, all in RG 498, Entry ETO MIS-Y, CSDIC, S.I.R., Box 4, NARA.

59. First Detailed Interrogation of: Baumgaertel, Friedrich, CSDIC West, September 13, 1944, RG 165, Entry 179, Box 656, NARA.

60. Report on Information Obtained from Senior Officer PW, G.R.G.G. 189, September 8–9, 1944, WO 208/5017, TNA.

61. Mitcham, *Hitler's Legions,* 127; Report on Information Obtained from Senior Officer PW, G.R.G.G. 190, September 10–11, 1944, WO 208/5018, TNA.

62. Preliminary Report on Information Obtained from Generalmajor Gutknecht, General der Panzertruppen Eberbach, Generalmajor Schramm and General der Infanterie Vierow, G.R.G.G. 187 (c), September 10, 1944, WO 208/5017, TNA; Bradley, Friedrich-Hildebrand, and Rövekamp, *Die Generale des Heeres, 1921–1945,* 1:126–27; United States Army, Third Armored Division, *Spearhead in the West, 1941–1945: The Third Armored Division* (Frankfurt am Main-Schwanheim: F. J. Henrich, 1945), 88; Preliminary Report on Information Obtained from Generalleutnant von Heyking and Generalleutnant Seyffardt, G.R.G.G. 192 (C), September 18, 1944, WO 208/5018, TNA.

63. Andreas von Aulock was called the "Mad Colonel of St. Malo" because of his refusal to surrender the heavily fortified citadel in St. Malo until the city had been largely destroyed.

64. Report on Information Obtained from Senior Officer PW, G.R.G.G. 200, September 22–23, 1944, WO 208/5018, TNA; von Arnim to the Legation of Switzerland, September 28, 1944, RG 59, Entry 1353, Box 24, NARA.

65. Preliminary Report on Information Obtained from Generalmajor Bock von Wuelfingen and Further Report on Information Obtained from Generalleutnant von Heyking, Generalleutnant Seyffardt and Konteradmiral von Tresckow, G.R.G.G. 199 (C), September 17–21, 1944, WO 208/5018, TNA.

66. Sullivan, *Thresholds of Peace,* 350; Richard Brett-Smith, *Hitler's Generals* (1976; repr., San Rafael, CA: Presidio Press, 1977), 146; James Lucas, *Hitler's Enforcers: Leaders of the German War Machine 1933–1945* (London: Arms and Armour Press, 1996), 119; Roger Edwards, *German Airborne Troops 1936–45* (Garden City, NY: Doubleday, 1974), 151.

67. Lucas, *Hitler's Enforcers,* 121–23.

68. Bender and Law, *Uniforms,* 151–54.

69. Edwards, *German Airborne Troops,* 151–52.

70. Shulman, *Defeat in the West,* 245; Lucas, *Hitler's Enforcers,* 127.

71. Lucas, *Hitler's Enforcers,* 127–28; Angolia, *On the Field of Honor,* 2:136; Shulman, *Defeat in the West,* 245. Ramcke would later claim that the United States treated German paratroops "shabbily" because it believed that only ardent Nazis would fight so fiercely; Lucas, *Hitler's Enforcers,* 128.

72. Angolia, *Field of Honor,* 1:93; Mitcham, *Hitler's Legions,* 417.

73. Report on Information Obtained from Senior Officer PW, G.R.G.G. 202, September 23–25, 1944, WO 208/5018, TNA.

74. Preliminary Report on Information Obtained from General der Fallschirmtruppen Ramcke and a Further Report on Information Obtained from Generalleutnant von Heyking, Konteradmiral von Tresckow and Generalmajor Bock von Wuelfingen, G.R.G.G. 198 (C), September 24, 1944, WO 208/5018, TNA; "Gen. Ramcke," CSDIC (U.K.), October 12, 1944, WO 208/5622, TNA.

75. Report on Information Obtained from Senior Officer PW, G.R.G.G. 206, October 2–4, 1944, WO 208/5018, TNA.

76. Report on Information Obtained from Senior Officer PW, G.R.G.G. 210, October 11–12, 1944, WO 208/5018, TNA; PW Generalmajor Elster, December 5, 1944, WO 208/5622, TNA; Christian Leitz, *Economic Relations between Nazi Germany and Franco's Spain: 1936–1945* (Oxford: Oxford University Press, 1996), 143; *The Thunderbolt Division: Story of the Eighty-Third Infantry Division* (U.S. Army, S.1, 1945), 7; Mitcham, *Hitler's Legions,* 121; "Elster, Botho," RG 242, T-78, rolls 883–95, NARA.

77. War Diary, September 1944, and War Diary, October 1944, WO 165/41, TNA; Report on Information Obtained from Senior Officer PW, G.R.G.G. 200, September 22–23, 1944, and Report on Information Obtained from Senior Officer PW, G.R.G.G. 216, October 26–28, 1944, WO 208/5018, TNA.

78. Mitcham, *Hitler's Legions,* 86; Shulman, *Defeat in the West,* 257; Report on Information Obtained from Senior Officer PW, G.R.G.G. 219, November 4–6, 1944, WO 208/5018, TNA.

79. Report on Information Obtained from Senior Officer PW, G.R.G.G. 220, November 7–10, 1944, and Report on Information Obtained from Senior Officer PW, G.R.G.G. 219, November 4–6, 1944, WO 208/5018, TNA.

80. Saul Levitt, "Capturing a Gestapo General," *Yank* 3 (January 12, 1945), 6–7.

81. Ibid.

82. Report on Information Obtained from PW CS/771 (Allgemeine) Brigadeführer (Major General) and General-Major der Polizei Anton Dunckern, S.I.R. 1613, April 13, 1945, RG 498, Entry ETO MIS-Y, CSDIC, S.I.R., Box 8, NARA.

83. War Diary, December 1944, WO 165/41, TNA.

84. Report on Information Obtained from Senior Officer PW, G.R.G.G. 2246, January 8–9, 1945, WO 208/5018, TNA.

85. Report on Information Obtained from Senior Officer PW, G.R.G.G. 240, December 27–28, 1944, WO 208/5018, TNA.

86. Report on Information Obtained from Senior Officer PW, G.R.G.G. 238, December 23–26, 1944, WO 208/5018, TNA; Report on Information Obtained from PW CS/937 Genmaj Vaterrodt, G.R.G.G. 239 (c), January 2, 1945, RG 165, Entry 179, Box 639, NARA.

87. These examples are cited in Reports on Information Obtained from Senior Officer PW, G.R.G.G. 147, 149, 151, and 152, WO 208/5017, TNA, as well as CSDIC, S.I.R. 483, RG 498, Entry ETO MIS-Y, CSDIC, S.I.R., Box 2, NARA.

88. War Diary, April 1945, and War Diary, May 1945, WO 165/41, TNA. The War Diary for May 1945 in the British National Archives actually lists a "Rüdiger von

Keyking" as one of the five generals transferred to American custody in April. However, considering that Rüdiger von Heyking had been at Trent Park for some time and there is no evidence of a "von Keyking," it can be assumed that this was simply a typographical error and that the transferred general in question was indeed von Heyking. War Diary, May 1945, WO 165/41, TNA.

89. Neitzel, *Tapping Hitler's Generals*, 18–19; War Diary, August 1945, and War Diary, October 1945, WO 165/41, TNA; Sullivan, *Thresholds of Peace*, 237.

90. Sullivan, *Thresholds of Peace*, 291.

2. Hitler's Generals Come to America

1. Krammer, "American Treatment of German Generals," 30; "v. Quast," MSg 109, BA-MA; Prisoner of War Circular No. 11, December 3, 1943, Stephen M. Farrand Papers, Box 1, Hoover Institution Archives, Stanford University, Palo Alto, CA; Memorandum from Provost Marshal General's Office to Commanding General, Fourth Service Command, November 2, 1943, RG 389, Entry 461, Box 2477, NARA; Inspection of Camp Clinton, Mississippi, by Lt. Col. M. C. Bernays and Mr. Bernard Gufler, May 5–7, 1944, RG 165, Decimal File, 1942–June 1946, 383.6 Reorientation, Box 590, NARA.

2. Major General Davidson to Major General G. V. Strong, June 1, 1943, RG 165, Entry 179, Box 364, NARA.

3. Ibid; War Diary, March 1943, WO 165/41, TNA.

4. For more on the American interrogation programs at Fort Hunt and Byron Hot Springs, see John Hammond Moore, "Getting Fritz to Talk," *Virginia Quarterly Review* 54 no. 2 (Spring 1978): 263–80.

5. Carol A. Jensen, *Images of America: Byron Hot Springs* (Charleston, SC: Arcadia, 2006), 103–14.

6. Memorandum for the Budget Officer, War Department, April 15, 1942, and Byron Hot Springs Project, August 12, 1942, RG 389, Entry 452C, Box 1410, NARA; Inspection of "Byron Hot Springs," undated, RG 389, Entry 439A, Box 3, NARA.

7. "Interrogation Center, P.O. Box 651, Tracy, California," Memorandum for Commander John L. Riheldaffer, RG 165, Entry 179, Box 364, NARA; Krammer, "American Treatment of German Generals," 29.

8. Interrogation of Unteroffizier Albert Karl Lauser, June 11, 1943, RG 165, Entry 179, Box 364, NARA.

9. Technical Apparatus for the Second Interrogation Center, April 27, 1942, RG 389, Entry 452C, Box 1410, NARA.

10. Room Conversation—Generals Borowietz and Von Vaerst, RG 165, Entry 179, Box 364, NARA.

11. Interrogation of General Gustav von Vaerst and Generalleutnant Karl R. M. Buelowius, June 28, 1943, RG 165, Entry 179, Box 364, NARA.

12. Ibid.; Notes on Information Derived from German Ps/W; Late Information from Ps/W (June 7–9), June 15, 1943, RG 165, Entry 179, Box 364, NARA.

13. Information and Views of Three German General Officers Recently Captured in North Africa, June 15, 1943, and Report of Interview with Generals Borowietz and Köchy, June 3, 1943, RG 165, Entry 179, Box 364, NARA.

14. Ibid.

15. Ibid.

16. Ibid.

17. Memorandum for Brigadier General B. M. Bryan Jr., June 29, 1943, RG 165, Entry 179, Box 364, NARA.

18. Room Conversation—Generals Borowietz and Von Vaerst, RG 165, Entry 179, Box 364, NARA.

19. PMGO to the Commanding General, Ninth Service Command, July 2, 1943, and Internal Security Division to Director, POW Division, July 8, 1943, RG 389, Entry 461, Box 2483, NARA; "Little Relief in Sight for Hot Texans," *Mexia (TX) Weekly Herald,* July 9, 1943, 1; "New Record Temperature Set Here by Saturday Heat," *Mexia Weekly Herald,* July 30, 1943, 6; "Hope Springs in Hearts of Heat Weary Sufferers," *Mexia Weekly Herald,* August 20, 1943, 3.

20. Inspection report, Camp Mexia, September 23–25, 1943, RG 389, Entry 461, Box 2667, NARA.

21. Ibid; Inspection report, Camp Mexia, August 19, 1943, RG 389, Entry 461, Box 2667, NARA.

22. Richard P. Walker, *The Lone Star and the Swastika: Prisoners of War in Texas* (Austin, TX: Eakin Press, 2001), 12; Inspection report, Camp Mexia, August 19, 1943, and September 23–25, 1943, RG 389, Entry 461, Box 2667, NARA.

23. Inspection report, Camp Mexia, September 23–25, 1943, and August 19, 1943, RG 389, Entry 461, Box 2667, NARA.

24. Ibid.

25. Letter to Commanding General, Eighth Service Command, August 23, 1943, and Donovan, CG, 8SC, to Provost Marshal General, telegram, July 30, 1943, RG 389, Entry 457, Box 1420, NARA; Inspection report, Camp Mexia, September 23–25, 1943, RG 389, Entry 461, Box 2667, NARA.

26. Inspection report, Camp Mexia, September 23–25, 1943, RG 389, Entry 461, Box 2667, NARA.

27. Arnold Krammer, *Nazi Prisoners of War in America* (1979; repr., Lanham, MD: Scarborough House, 1996), 27.

28. The Swiss legation, the protecting power for both German POWs in America and American POWs in Germany, discovered in September 1944 that German authorities paid American officer prisoners more than American authorities paid German officer prisoners and "urgently requested" that the U.S. government address this discrepancy. "The reports of the Protecting Power in Washington reveal that German officer prisoners of war in the United States receive monthly pay at the following rates," September 22, 1944, Farrand Papers, Box 1, Hoover Institution Archives.

29. Krammer, *Nazi Prisoners of War*, 50, 84.

30. General Officer Prisoner of War Camps, RG 389, Entry 457, Box 1420, NARA.

31. Inspection report, Camp Clinton, Mississippi, July 18–19, 1943, RG 389, Entry 461, Box 2658, NARA; Gene Wirth, "High-Ranking Nazi Generals Now Arm-Chair Strategists on Mississippi Hillside Here," *Jackson (MS) Clarion-Ledger*, October 31, 1943, 9, 14.

32. Gene Wirth, "High-Ranking Nazi Generals Now Arm-Chair Strategists on Mississippi Hillside Here," *Jackson Clarion-Ledger*, October 31, 1943, 9, 14. The author believes this general to have been either Gustav von Vaerst or Ernst Schnarrenberger because they are the only two who fit the description of the general in this October 1943 newspaper account. The American press was not allowed to print the generals' names for reasons of security, so this cannot be substantiated.

33. Ibid.

34. No archival sources from either the British or the American national archives regarding Frantz and Schnarrenberger's whereabouts from August 21 until October 6, 1943, could be found. It can be assumed that part of this time involved passage, likely by ship, across the Atlantic as well as a couple weeks' processing time at Ft. George Meade, Maryland, before transfer to Camp Clinton, Mississippi. However, this remains the author's conjecture and cannot be substantiated. Report of POWs Aboard Train, October 6, 1943, RG 389, Entry 451, Box 1258, NARA; "Two Nazi Generals Held Prisoners Here: 4 German Officers at Clinton Camp," *Jackson Clarion-Ledger*, October 9, 1943; Transfer of German General Officers, Prisoner of War, October 5, 1943, RG 389, Entry 461, Box 2477, NARA.

35. Inspection report, Camp Clinton, Mississippi, July 18–19, 1943, RG 389, Entry 461, Box 2658, NARA; Michael A. Allard, "A History of the Clinton Prisoner of War Camp, 1942–1946," M.A. thesis, Mississippi College, 1994.

36. General d. Pz. Tr. von Vaerst to War Department, October 13, 1943, and Army Service Forces, PMGO, to Commanding General, Fourth Service Command, November 2, 1943, RG 389, Entry 461, Box 2477, NARA.

37. Adjutants for German General Officer POWs, July 10, 1944, RG 389, Entry 461, Box 2477, NARA.

38. "Parole of German Generals Who Are Prisoners of War," November 1, 1943, RG 165, Entry 179, Box 364, NARA; "Prisoner of War Circular No. 11"—December 3, 1943, "The Administration of Prisoner of War Matters in the Continental United States during World War II so Far as They Were the Staff Responsibility of the Provost Marshal General's Office," historical monograph, United States Prisoner of War Operations Division, RG 389, Entry 461, Box 2477, NARA.

39. Ibid.

40. Inspection report, Camp Clinton, Mississippi, May 5–7, 1944, RG 165, Decimal File, 1942–June 1946, 383.6 Reorientation, Box 590, NARA.

41. Graham H. Stuart, "War Prisoners and Internees in the United States," *American Foreign Service Journal* 21 (October 1944): 530–31.

42. Memorandum from the Legation of Switzerland, February 18, 1944, RG 389, Entry 461, Box 2658, NARA.

43. Ibid.

44. "Memorandum on Visit Made 10–12 February 1944, Camp Clinton, Mississippi, by Dr. Edward Feer, Counselor of the Swiss Legation, accompanied by Mr. Bernard Gufler, of the Department of State," RG 389, Entry 461, Box 2658, NARA.

45. Ibid.

46. Ibid.

47. Ibid.

48. Ibid.

49. Ibid.

50. Ibid.

51. Inspection of Camp Clinton, Mississippi, by Lt. Col. M. C. Bernays and Mr. Bernard Gufler, May 5–7, 1944, RG 165, Decimal File, 1942–June 1946, 383.6 Reorientation, Box 590, NARA.

52. Ibid.

53. Ibid.

54. Ibid.

55. War Problems Memorandum, December 16, 1944, Farrand Papers, Box 1, Hoover Institution Archives.

56. Status of Training and Physical Condition of Men Assigned to Clinton, Mississippi, August 19, 1944, and Partial List of Enlisted Men Suffering from Mental Disturbances Employed by Prisoner of War Camp during Month of August 1944, RG 389, Entry 461, 2658, NARA.

57. Ibid.

3. The Seeds of the American Transformation

1. War Diary, June 1944, WO 165/41, TNA; Report of Visit to POW Base Camp on August 20, 21, 22, 1944, RG 389, Entry 459A, Box 1611, NARA.

2. First Detailed Interrogation of General of Infantry Neuling, Ferdinand, and First Detailed Interrogation of Brig-Gen Bieringer, Ludwig, RG 165, Entry 179, Box 656, NARA; Transfer of General Prisoner of War, August 30, 1944, RG 389, Entry 461, Box 2477, NARA.

3. Transfer of German Officer Prisoner of War, September 19, 1944, RG 389, Entry 461, Box 2477, NARA.

4. Von Arnim to Commanding Officer, P.O.W. Camp Clinton, October 5, 1944; Colonel McIlhenny to the Provost Marshal General, October 6, 1944; Army Services Force to Commanding General, Fourth Service Command, October 13, 1944, all in RG 389, Entry 451, Box 1259, NARA.

5. Swiss Legation to Brigadier General B. M. Bryan, September 26, 1944, and Colonel Francis E. Howard to Special War Problems Division, U.S. Department of State, October 25, 1944, RG 389, Entry 451, Box 1259, NARA.

6. Captain Heinkel's handwritten notes regarding Sinkel, September 28, 1944, RG 389, Entry 451, Box 1259, NARA.

7. Von Arnim to the Legation of Switzerland, September 28, 1944, RG 59, Entry 1353, Box 24, NARA.

8. Prisoner of War Officers, November 29, 1944, RG 389, Entry 459A, Box 1611, NARA.

9. Memorandum on Visit to POW Camp, Clinton, Mississippi, July 12–13, 1944, RG 165, Entry 383.6, Box 590, NARA.

10. Ibid.

11. Ibid.

12. Ibid.

13. Ibid.

14. Ibid.

15. Handwritten notes from Captain Walter Rapp, September 12, 1944, RG 389, Entry 459A, Box 1611, NARA.

16. Visit of Mr. Weingärtner and Mr. Mason to Prisoner of War Camp, Camp Clinton, Mississippi, July 19, 1944, RG 165, Entry 383.6, Box 590, NARA.

17. Ibid.

18. Memorandum on Visit to POW Camp, Clinton, Mississippi, July 12–13, 1944, RG 165, Entry 383.6, Box 590, NARA.

19. Ibid.

20. Major Howard W. Smith Jr. to Chief of Engineers, War Department, August 9, 1944, and Colonel Moses E. Cox, Corps of Engineers, to Chief of Engineers, September 18, 1944, RG 389, Entry 457, Box 1420, NARA; Report on Prisoners of War Camp, Clinton, Mississippi, August 5, 1944, RG 389, Entry 461, Box 2658, NARA.

21. Memorandum for the Assistant Chief of Staff, G-1, W.D.G.S., August 26, 1944, RG 389, Entry 459A, Box 1611, NARA; Memorandum for the Deputy Chief of Staff for Service Commands, August 19, 1944, RG 389, Entry 457, Box 1420, NARA.

22. Colonel James L. McIlhenny to Commanding General, Fourth Service Command, August 12, 1944, RG 389, Entry 457, Box 1420, NARA.

23. Memorandum for the Assistant Provost Marshal General, September 7, 1944, RG 389, Entry 461, Box 2658, NARA.

24. Report of Visit to POW Base Camp on August 20, 21, 22, 1944, RG 389, Entry 459A, Box 1611, NARA.

25. Memorandum for the Assistant Provost Marshal General, September 7, 1944, RG 389, Entry 461, Box 2658, NARA.

26. August Viktor von Quast was listed as a "General Major" in the inspection report, although the report explained that von Quast had been "promoted after he was captured. Rank therefore not recognized as 'of right.'" Prisoner of War Camp, Camp Clinton, Mississippi, January 10–11, 1945, RG 389, Entry 461, Box 2658, NARA.

27. Ibid.; Hildebrand, *Die Generale der deutschen Luftwaffe,* 1:309–10.

28. Memorandum for Director, Security and Investigation Division, June 15,

1945, RG 389, Entry 461, Box 2479, NARA; Stephen M. Farrand to the International Committee of the Red Cross, April 27, 1945, RG 389, Entry 451, Box 1340, NARA.

29. "High-Ranking Nazi General Dies Sunday at Clinton Camp: Autopsy Performed on Commander of Panzer Division," *Jackson Clarion-Ledger*, July 3, 1945; "Ex-POW Returns to Camp at Clinton," *Jackson Clarion-Ledger*, August 5, 1979; German Prisoners of War Interred in the United States, October 11, 1954, RG 389, Entry 467, Box 1513, NARA. Curiously, the official German records state that Borowietz's cause of death was a "fatal accident," although this was likely taken from the initial official reports coming from American camp authorities. "Borowietz," MSg 109/263, BA-MA.

30. Prisoner of War Camp, Camp Clinton, Mississippi, January 10–11, 1945, RG 389, Entry 461, Box 2658, NARA; Memorandum from General Blackshear M. Bryan regarding Glennan General Hospital, September 8, 1944, RG 389, Entry 457, Box 1422, NARA; Bradley, Hildebrand, and Rövekamp, *Die Generale des Heeres*, 4:506–7; "Gutknecht," MSg 109/886, BA-MA.

31. Homicide and Suicide Rates for Prisoners of War, April 24, 1945, RG 389, Entry 467, Box 1513, NARA.

32. Natural Death of German General Officer Prisoner of War, April 6, 1945, RG 389, Entry 467, Box 1513, NARA; "Nazi General Buried in Mississippi with Full Military Rites," *Jackson Clarion-Ledger*, April 9, 1945.

33. Prisoner of War Camp, Camp Clinton, Mississippi, January 10–11, 1945, RG 389, Entry 461, Box 2658, NARA; Handwritten letter from Charles Eberhardt to Bernard Gufler, January 14, 1945, RG 59, Entry 1353, Box 24, NARA.

34. Ibid.

35. Ibid.

36. Ibid.

37. Camp Clinton, Mississippi, Visited by Mr. P. Schnyder and Dr. M. Zehnder on February 1, 1945, RG 59, Entry 1353, Box 24, NARA.

38. German Generals in United States Custody, Memorandum, Special War Problems Division, August 8, 1944, Farrand Collection, Box 1, Hoover Institution Archives.

39. Ibid.

40. Ibid.

41. Krammer, *Nazi Prisoners of War*, 196–97.

42. Memorandum for Major Davison, September 28, 1944, RG 389, Entry 459A, Box 1611, NARA.

43. Ibid.

44. Ibid.

45. Ibid.

46. Reorientation, POW Camp, Clinton, Mississippi, September 8, 1944, RG 165, Entry 383.6, Box 590, NARA.

47. Reorientation of German Prisoners of War, Memorandum for the Assistant

Chief of Staff, G-1, February 3, 1945, RG 165, Entry 383.6, Box 590, NARA; Memorandum for the Deputy Chief of Staff for Service Commands, November 16, 1944, RG 389, Entry 459A, Box 1611, NARA.

48. Memorandum of telephone conversation, November 20, 1944, RG 59, Entry 1353, Box 24, NARA; Memorandum for the Assistant Chief of Staff, G-1, from F. M. Smith, assistant to Major General W. D. Styer, undated (likely October 1944), RG 165, Entry 383.6, Box 590, NARA.

49. Memorandum concerning the Special Projects Branch of the Office of the Provost Marshal General, December 16, 1944, Farrand Collection, Box 1, Hoover Institution Archives.

50. Temporary Duty of Captain Walter H. Rapp, November 15, 1944; Weekly Progress Report No. 1, Prisoner of War Camp, Clinton, Mississippi, November 27, 1944, RG 389, Entry 459A, Box 1611, NARA.

51. Weekly Progress Report No. 2, Prisoner of War Camp, Clinton, Mississippi, December 8, 1944, RG 389, Entry 459A, Box 1611, NARA.

52. Ibid.

53. Ibid.

54. Ibid.

55. Ibid.

56. Weekly Progress Report No. 1, Prisoner of War Camp, Clinton, Mississippi, November 27, 1944, RG 389, Entry 459A, Box 1611, NARA.

57. Ibid.

58. Ibid.

59. Ibid.

60. Weekly Progress Report No. 2, Prisoner of War Camp, Clinton, Mississippi, December 8, 1944, and Special Progress Report No. 1, Memorandum for Captain Walter H. Rapp, December 7, 1944, RG 389, Entry 459A, Box 1611, NARA.

61. Weekly Progress Report No. 1, Prisoner of War Camp, Clinton, Mississippi, November 27, 1944, RG 389, Entry 459A, Box 1611, NARA.

62. Ibid.; Weekly Progress Report No. 2, Prisoner of War Camp, Clinton, Mississippi, December 8, 1944, RG 389, Entry 459A, Box 1611, NARA; Theodor Graf von Sponeck, *Meine Erinnerungen,* p. 180, MSg 1/3329, BA-MA.

63. Weekly Progress Report No. 2, Prisoner of War Camp, Clinton, Mississippi, December 8, 1944, RG 389, Entry 459A, Box 1611, NARA.

64. Ibid.

65. Weekly Progress Report No. 1, Prisoner of War Camp, Clinton, Mississippi, November 27, 1944, RG 389, Entry 459A, Box 1611, NARA.

66. Memorandum for Deputy Chief of Staff for Service Commands, A.S.F., from Archer L. Lerch, Provost Marshal General, February 20, 1945; Memorandum for the Director, Prisoner of War Special Projects Division, February 9, 1945; and Memorandum for Record from Edward Davison, Director, Prisoner of War Special Projects Division, all in RG 389, Entry 459A, Box 1611, NARA.

67. Memorandum for the Director, Prisoner of War Special Projects Division, February 9, 1945, RG 389, Entry 459A, Box 1611, NARA.

68. Ibid.; Memorandum for Colonel Bernays from War Department General Staff, March 12, 1945, RG 165, Entry 383.6, Box 590, NARA.

4. Reeducating Hitler's Generals?

1. Transfer of German General Officer Prisoners of War, March 27, 1945, RG 389, Entry 461, Box 2477, NARA.

2. Memorandum for the Assistant Chief of Staff, G-1, from F. M. Smith, assistant to Major General W. D. Styer, undated (likely October 1944), RG 165, Entry 383.6, Box 590, NARA.

3. Inspection Report of Mr. Arthur M. Kruse, September 28–October 2, 1944, and Special Report on Visit to Prisoner of War Camp, Jerome, Arkansas, November 2, 1944, RG 389, Entry 457, Box 1421, NARA; Merrill R. Pritchett and William L. Shea, "The Afrika Korps in Arkansas, 1943–1946," *Arkansas Historical Quarterly* 37 (Spring 1978): 3–22.

4. Special Report on Visit to Prisoner of War Camp, Jerome, Arkansas, November 2, 1944, RG 389, Entry 457, Box 1421, NARA.

5. Theatre for Jerome Prisoner of War Camp, November 14, 1944, RG 389, Entry 457, Box 1421 and RG 389, Entry 459A, Box 1612, NARA.

6. Report on Visit to Prisoner of War Camp Dermott, Arkansas, December 17, 1944, RG 389, Entry 459A, Box 1612, NARA.

7. Ibid.

8. Field Service Report on Visit to Prisoner of War Camp, Dermott, Arkansas, March 15, 1945, and Report on Visit to Prisoner of War Camp, Dermott, Arkansas, March 12–14, 1945, RG 389, Entry 459A, Box 1612, NARA.

9. Field Service Report on Visit to Prisoner of War Camp, Dermott, Arkansas, March 15, 1945, RG 389, Entry 459A, Box 1612, NARA.

10. Ibid.

11. Report on Morale Status of War Prisoners at [POW Camp, Dermott, Arkansas], February 5, 1945, RG 389, Entry 459A, Box 1612, NARA.

12. Transfer of German General Officer Prisoners of War, March 27, 1945, RG 389, Entry 461, Box 2477, NARA.

13. Field Service Report on Visit to Prisoner of War Camp, Dermott, Arkansas, April 30, 1945, RG 389, Entry 459A, Box 1612, NARA.

14. Ibid.

15. Krammer, *Nazi Prisoners of War,* 200–202; Field Service Report on Visit to Prisoner of War Camp, Dermott, Arkansas, April 30, 1945, RG 389, Entry 459A, Box 1612, NARA.

16. Field Service Report on Visit to Prisoner of War Camp, Dermott, Arkansas, April 30, 1945, and Memorandum to the Prisoner of War Special Projects Division from Headquarters, Prisoner of War Camp, Dermott, Arkansas, September 12, 1945, RG 389, Entry 459A, Box 1612, NARA.

17. Memorandum for Director, Prisoner of War Special Projects Division, January 15, 1945, RG 389, Entry 459A, Box 1611, NARA.

18. Memorandum for Director, Prisoner of War Special Projects Division, January 13, 1945, RG 165, Entry 383.6, Box 590, NARA.

19. Ibid.

20. Ibid.

21. Ibid.

22. Comments of Colonel Truman Smith on Program for Reorientation of German General Officers, February 1, 1945, RG 165, Entry 383.6, Box 590, NARA.

23. Franklin M. Davis Jr., *Come as a Conqueror: The United States Army's Occupation of Germany, 1945–1949* (New York: Macmillan, 1967), 34.

24. Edward Peterson, *The American Occupation of Germany: Retreat to Victory* (Detroit: Wayne State University Press, 1977), 31–34; Robert Wolfe, ed., *Americans as Proconsuls: United States Military Government in Germany and Japan, 1944–1952* (Carbondale: Southern Illinois University Press, 1984), 53–54.

25. Ibid.

26. Peterson, *American Occupation of Germany*, 32–34.

27. Elster, Botho-Henning; von Liebenstein, Kurt (Baron); Graf von Sponeck, Theodor, POW Camp Dermott, Arkansas, May 16, 1945, RG 389, Entry 459A, Box 1640, NARA.

28. Report of Visit to Prisoner of War Camp, Dermott, Arkansas, June 4–6, 1945, RG 389, Entry 459A, Box 1612, NARA.

29. Memorandum from Headquarters, Prisoner of War Camp, Dermott, Arkansas, to the Provost Marshal General, September 12, 1945, and Report on Field Service Visit, August 29–30, 1945, RG 389, Entry 459A, Box 1612, NARA.

30. Memorandum from Headquarters, Prisoner of War Camp, Dermott, Arkansas, to the Provost Marshal General, September 12, 1945, RG 389, Entry 459A, Box 1612, NARA.

31. Prisoner of War Camp, Camp Dermott, Arkansas, October 17–20, 1945, RG 389, Entry 461, Box 2660, NARA; Report of Visit to Prisoner of War Camp, Dermott, Arkansas, October 17–18, 1945, RG 389, Entry 459A, Box 1612, NARA.

32. Prisoner of War Camp, Camp Dermott, Arkansas, October 17–20, 1945, RG 389, Entry 461, Box 2660, NARA.

33. Ibid.; POW Camp, Dermott, Arkansas, October 2, 1945, RG 389, Entry 461, Box 2593, NARA; Transfer of German Officer Prisoners of War, September 8, 1945, RG 389, Entry 461, Box 2478, NARA; Transfer of German Prisoners of War, October 15, 1945, RG 389, Entry 461, Box 2482, NARA.

34. Lord Russell of Liverpool, *The Scourge of the Swastika: A Short History of Nazi War Crimes* (London: Cassell and Company, 1954), 35–36; Josef Folttmann and Hanns Müller-Witten, *Opfergang der Generale: Die Verluste der Generale and Admirale und der im gleichen Dienstrang Stehenden sonstigen Offiziere und Beamten im Zweiten Weltkrieg* (1952; repr., Berlin: Verlag Gernard and Graefe, 1959), 169.

35. "Camp Ruston, Louisiana, has been designated for the internment of German Army Officers and enlisted men, POWs," RG 389, Entry 461, Box 2484, NARA; Field Service Visit to Prisoner of War Camp, Ruston, Louisiana, March 2, 1945, RG 389, Entry 459A, Box 1621, NARA.

36. Report of Visit to Prisoner of War Camp Ruston, Louisiana, May 20–21, 1945, RG 389, Entry 459A, Box 1621, NARA.

37. Report of Inspection of Prisoner of War Camp, Camp Ruston, Louisiana, August 9, 1945, RG 389, Entry 461, Box 2593, NARA. Curiously, Camp Ruston's commanding officer in 1945 is listed as Colonel Thomas A. Bay, a name amazingly similar to that of Colonel Thomas A. Bays, the commanding officer at Camp Mexia whom General von Vaerst had held in such high regard. It seems likely that these two were the same man, which might further explain the efficient operation at Ruston, although this has not been corroborated.

38. Theodor Graf von Sponeck, *Meine Erinnerungen,* p. 182, MSg 1/3329, BA-MA. Unfortunately, von Sponeck's memoir contains some factual inaccuracies. For instance, he wrote that he was accompanied to Dermott by General Krause, who actually remained at Camp Clinton for the duration of his time in the United States, and General von Broich, who remained in England for the duration of the war.

39. Report of Visit to Prisoner of War Camp, Ruston, Louisiana, October 15, 1945, RG 389, Entry 459A, Box 1621, NARA; Jason Kendall Moore, "Between Expediency and Principle: U.S. Repatriation Policy toward Russian Nationals, 1944–1949," *Diplomatic History* 24 (Summer 2000): 386.

40. Transfer of German Officer Prisoners of War, September 11, 1945; Transfer of German Prisoners of War, October 15, 1945; Transfer of German Officer Prisoners of War, October 23, 1945, RG 389, Entry 461, Boxes 2482 and 2484, NARA.

41. Transfer of German Officer Prisoners of War, April 12, 1945, RG 389, Entry 461, Box 2477, NARA.

42. Report from Colonel Callie H. Palmer, Director, Security and Intelligence Division, to Commanding General, Army Services Forces, August 29, 1945, RG 389, Entry 459A, Box 1614, NARA; Prisoner of War Branch Camp Clinton, November 3, 1945, RG 59, Entry 1353, Box 24, NARA.

43. Ibid.

44. Hermann Bernard Ramcke, *Fallschirmjäger: Damals und Danach* (Frankfurt am Main: Lorch-Verlag, 1951), 89–90 (translated for the author by Anja Schwalen).

45. Report on Information Obtained from Senior Officer PW, G.R.G.G. 184, August 30, 1944, WO 208/5017, TNA.

46. "4000 Veterans of SS Cheer Blast at Allies," *Washington Post,* October 27, 1952, 3.

47. American History Course and English Language Course in PW Officers' Compound, July 23, 1945, RG 389, Entry 459A, Box 1611, NARA.

48. Prisoner of War Branch Camp Clinton, November 3, 1945, RG 59, Entry 1353, Box 24, NARA.

49. Ramcke, *Fallschirmjäger,* 91–92.

50. Ibid., 92–94.

51. Ibid., 94–97.

52. Ibid., 97–99; Allard, "History of the Clinton Prisoner of War Camp," 119–21.

53. In his memoirs, Ramcke wrote that he chose to send one of his letters to "U.S. Senator" Byron Price because President Harry S Truman had appointed him "Commissioner for German Affairs." In truth, Price was never a U.S. senator, although he spent ten weeks studying American occupation policies in Germany in November 1945 at President Truman's behest and issued a report to the president upon his return. His previous responsibility as director of the U.S. Bureau of Censorship had ended when the office was closed in August 1945.

54. "Jackson Men Recall Duty at Clinton Camp," *Jackson Clarion-Ledger–Jackson Daily News,* February 20, 1983, 8F.

55. Ibid.

56. Terrence J. Winschel, "The Enemy's Keeper," *Journal of Mississippi History* 57 (Winter 1995), 331–32.

57. Colonel A. M. Tollefson, Director, Prisoner of War Operations Division, to Mr. W. K. Uhlenhorst-Ziechmann, November 9, 1945, RG 389, Entry 467, Box 1532, NARA.

58. Prisoner of War Branch Camp Clinton, November 3, 1945, RG 59, Entry 1353, Box 24, NARA.

59. Report on Visit to Prisoner of War Camp Clinton, Mississippi, March 1–2, 1946, RG 389, Entry 459A, Box 1621, NARA; Allard, "History of the Clinton Prisoner of War Camp."

5. Cold War Allies

1. Report from Captured Personnel and Material Branch, Military Intelligence Division, U.S. War Department, May 30, 1945, RG 165, Entry 179, Box 495, NARA.

2. Ibid.; "Mystery Man Arrives in Big German U-Boat," *Chicago Daily Tribune,* May 20, 1945; Joseph Mark Scalia, *Germany's Last Mission to Japan: The Failed Voyage of U-234* (Annapolis, MD: Naval Institute Press, 2000), 44–59.

3. Scalia, *Germany's Last Mission to Japan,* 44–46.

4. Report of Interrogation, No. 5193, May 22, 1945, RG 165, Entry 179, Box 495, NARA; Report of Interrogation, No. 5318, June 9, 1945, RG 337, Entry 15A, Box 69, NARA; Report from Captured Personnel and Material Branch, Military Intelligence Division, U.S. War Department, May 30, 1945, RG 165, Entry 179, Box 495, NARA.

5. Report from Captured Personnel and Material Branch, Military Intelligence Division, U.S. War Department, May 30, 1945, RG 165, Entry 179, Box 495, NARA.

6. Ibid.

7. Ibid.

8. Ibid.; Scalia, *Germany's Last Mission to Japan,* 92–95.

9. Hildebrand, *Die Generale der deutschen Luftwaffe,* 1:27–28. Aschenbrenner's

interrogation file from Fort Hunt is still security classified by the U.S. National Archives and Records Administration. A request for classification review under the Freedom of Information Act has been submitted and the material is currently being considered by NARA officials for possible declassification.

10. The comments of an American intelligence officer after listening to the POWs, who were housed in Room 1A, further suggest that the prisoners at Fort Hunt were aware that they were being listened to: "Judging from the meager monitoring results of 1A, it seems probable that [the prisoners] are carefully avoiding conversation on any topic that might be interesting to us!" Room Conversation, Vierow and von Tippelskirch, July 23, 1945, RG 165, Entry 179, Box 556, NARA; Room Conversation, Aschenbrenner and Kessler, June 24, 1945, RG 165, Entry 179, Box 495, NARA.

11. Room Conversation, Aschenbrenner and Kessler, June 21, 1945; Room Conversation, Aschenbrenner and Kessler, August 3, 1945; Report of Interrogation, No. 5440, June 3, 1945; Report of Interrogation, No. 5665, August 10, 1945, all in RG 165, Entry 179, Box 495, NARA.

12. Record of Interrogation, Walter Vierow, July 16, 1945; Record of Interrogation, Walter Vierow, August 25, 1945; Recommendations concerning Interrogation of P/W, W. Vierow, all in RG 165, Entry 179, Box 556, NARA.

13. The roster of senior Wehrmacht officers who were sent to Fort Hunt, Virginia, is difficult to accurately determine. Many of the transfer orders intentionally omit Fort Hunt as either a destination or point of departure for prisoners of war. The orders often substitute Fort George Meade, Maryland, because of a perceived need for secrecy. The rare exception is Rear Admiral Eberhardt Godt, whose presence at Fort Hunt can be verified more definitively because he was transferred out of the camp and then recalled for an unspecified reason. Complicating matters, there are no interrogation records for many of these men in the U.S. National Archives and, therefore, it is also difficult to determine what kind of information, if any, was gathered from these prisoners. Memorandum for Brigadier General B. M. Bryan, Return of Admiral Godt to Fort Hunt, January 11, 1946, RG 389, Entry 461, Box 2482, NARA.

14. Report of Interrogation, No. 5236, May 23, 1945, RG 165, Entry 179, Box 495, NARA.

15. Mary Ellen Reese, *General Reinhard Gehlen: The CIA Connection* (Fairfax, VA: George Mason University Press, 1990), 40–52; Biographic Data Report on Ex-General Reinhard Gehlen, RG 263, Entry 86, Box 17, NARA.

16. "Report of Initial Contacts with General Gehlen's Organization," by John R. Boker Jr., May 1, 1952, in Kevin C. Ruffner, ed., *Forging an Intelligence Partnership: CIA and the Origins of the BND, 1945–49: A Documentary History* (CIA History Staff, Center for the Study of Intelligence, European Division, Directorate of Operations, 1999), 1:19–34, NARA.

17. Ibid.

18. Report of Interrogation, No. 5725, August 28, 1945, Gehlen, Reinhard, vol-

ume I, RG 263, Entry 86, Box 17, NARA; Reese, *General Reinhard Gehlen,* 52–58, 71–75; preface to Ruffner, *Forging an Intelligence Partnership,* 1:xii–xxix, NARA.

19. "Debriefing of Eric Waldman on the U.S. Army's Trusteeship of the Gehlen Organization during the Years 1945–1949," September 30, 1969, in Ruffner, *Forging an Intelligence Partnership,* 1:45–50, NARA.

20. Memorandum from Col. R. L. Hopkins to Col. Sweet, September 24, 1945, RG 319, Entry 47C, Box 1294, NARA.

21. Memorandum, Establishment of German Research Group near Camp Ritchie, MD, August 1, 1945, RG 319, Entry 47C, Box 1292, NARA; GMDS, Report for the Month of January (1946), RG 242, Entry 282BC, Box 135, NARA; Memorandum to Commanding Officer, Camp Ritchie, MD, November 15, 1945, RG 319, Entry 47C, Box 1294, NARA.

22. Headquarters, U.S. Forces European Theater, Report of Operations, Period July 1—September 30, 1945, RG 498, Entry 681, Box 1, NARA.

23. Seymour J. Pomrenze, "Policies and Procedures for the Protection, Use, and Return of Captured German Records," in Robert Wolfe, ed., *Captured German and Related Records: A National Archives Conference* (Athens: Ohio University Press, 1974), 14–16.

24. GMDS, Report for the Month of June–July (1945), RG 242, Entry 282BC, Box 135, NARA.

25. Ibid.

26. Ibid.

27. Administrative Control of the Hill Project, Camp Ritchie, MD, January 14, 1946, RG 319, Entry 47C, Box 1294, NARA.

28. Ibid.

29. Ibid.

30. Memorandum for Col. G. F. Blunda, Chief, GMDS, Camp Ritchie, MD, February 7, 1946, RG 319, Entry 47C, Box 1294, NARA.

31. GMDS, Report for the Month of September (1945), RG 242, Entry 282BC, Box 135, NARA; RG 319, Entry 1206, Box 1, NARA. The collections held by the GMDS also eventually included *Wehrkreis* libraries V, VII, and XIII as well as the Nazi library. Documents Shipped and Ordered Crated for Shipment, Report of Operations, July–September 30, 1945, RG 498, Entry UD 681, Box 1, NARA.

32. Roster of Officer Escorts for Prisoners of War Enroute to War Department, Washington, D.C., September 20, 1945, and The "Hill Project," November 6, 1945, RG 319, Entry 47C, Box 1294, NARA; Peter Hoffmann, *Stauffenberg: A Family History, 1905–1944* (Cambridge: Cambridge University Press, 1995), 131.

33. Roster of Officer Escorts for Prisoners of War Enroute to War Department, Washington, D.C., September 20, 1945, and The "Hill Project," November 6, 1945, RG 319, Entry 47C, Box 1294, NARA; Personalakten: Das deutsche Militärwesen— Bundesrepublik Deutschland 1949–1990 (PERS 1), "Laegeler," files 103928 and 2885, BA-MA.

222 Notes to Pages 148–153

34. The "Hill Project," November 6, 1945, RG 319, Entry 47C, Box 1294, NARA.

35. Memorandum to Commanding Officer, Camp Ritchie, MD, November 15, 1945, RG 319, Entry 47C, Box 1294, NARA; "Prisoners of War," Memorandum to Col. Tollefson, Office of the Provost Marshal General, September 27, 1945, RG 389, Entry 461, Box 2482, NARA.

36. Memorandum from Col. Alfred McCormack, Director of Intelligence, MIS, September 25, 1945, RG 319, Entry 47C, Box 1294, NARA.

37. Timothy K. Nenninger, "Leavenworth and Its Critics: The U.S. Army Command and General Staff School, 1920–1940," *Journal of Military History* 58 (April 1994), 214; Memorandum from Col. Alfred McCormack, Director of Intelligence, MIS, September 25, 1945, RG 319, Entry 47C, Box 1294, NARA.

38. GMDS, Report for the Month of October (1945), RG 242, Entry 282BC, Box 135, NARA.

39. Ibid. For more on the use of this procedure and its implications, see Kevin Soutor, "To Stem the Red Tide: The German Report Series and Its Effect on American Defense Doctrine, 1948–1954," *Journal of Military History* 57 (October 1993): 653–88; and James A. Wood, "Captive Historians, Captivated Audience: The German Military History Program, 1945–1961," *Journal of Military History* 69 (January 2005), 123–48.

40. GMDS, Report for the Month of November (1945), RG 242, Entry 282BC, Box 135, NARA.

41. GMDS, Report for the Month of December (1945), RG 242, Entry 282BC, Box 135, NARA; GMDS, Report for the Month of January (1946), RG 242, Entry 282BC, Box 135, NARA.

42. Procurement of PWs for GMDS, December 20, 1945, and Procurement of PWs for GMDS, January 8, 1946, RG 319, Entry 47C, Box 1294, NARA.

43. POW Roster PW Camp, Camp Ritchie, MD, January 10, 1946, and Brief Notes on the Career and Background of the Twelve German Staff Officers Selected to Remain with GMDS, April 9, 1946, RG 319, Entry 47C, Box 1294, NARA; "Gundelach," MSg 109, and "v. Trotha," MSg 109, BA-MA.

44. "Troops Smuggle in Boy, 13, as Mascot," *New York Times,* March 17, 1946; POW Roster PW Camp, Camp Ritchie, MD, January 10, 1946, and Brief Notes on the Career and Background of the Twelve German Staff Officers Selected to Remain with GMDS, April 9, 1946, RG 319, Entry 47C, Box 1294, NARA; "Thomale," MSg 109, and "Thomale," PERS 1/957, BA-MA.

45. The "Hill Project," June 15, 1946, RG 319, Entry 47C, Box 1294, NARA; Prisoner of War Camp Labor Reports, Camp Ritchie, MD, January 15–March 31, 1946, RG 389, Entry 461, Box 2484, NARA.

46. GMDS, Report for the Month of January (1945), RG 242, Entry 282BC, Box 135, NARA.

47. *German Operational Intelligence: A Study of German Operational Intelligence,* p. 138, RG 242, Entry 282BC, Box 105, NARA.

48. Ibid.; *The German General Staff Corps: A Study of the Organization of the German General Staff*, RG 242, Entry 282BC, Box 106, NARA; *The German Army Quartermaster and Finance Organization*, pp. 1–4, RG 242, Entry 282BC, Box 119, NARA.

49. *The German Operation at Anzio: A Study of the German Operation at Anzio Beachhead from 22 January 1944 to 31 May 1944*, RG 242, Entry 282BC, Box 111, NARA; *Armored Breakthrough: War Diary of German First Armored Group, 5 February—10 July 1941*, p. i, RG 242, Entry 282BC, Box 122, NARA.

50. *German Army Mobilization: A Study of the Mobilization of the German Army*, pp. iv, 10, 34, RG 242, Entry 282BC, Box 112, NARA.

51. Ibid., 19, 36–37, 46.

52. *German Training Methods: A Study of German Military Training*, RG 242, Entry 282BC, Box 116, NARA.

53. *German Military Transportation*, RG 242, Entry 282BC, Box 116, NARA.

54. Ibid., 55.

55. *Officer Efficiency Reports in the German Army; Officer Candidate Selection and Training in the German Army; Ration Administration in the German Army; German Officer Courts-Martial; Screening of German Enlisted Personnel for Officer Appointments; Infantry in the Sixth Year of the War;* and *German Chemical Warfare*, all in RG 242, Entry 282BC, Boxes 121–22, 124, NARA.

56. The "Hill Project," November 6, 1945, RG 319, Entry 47C, Box 1294, NARA.

57. General der Infanterie Buhle to Colonel Lovell, December 15, 1945, RG 319, Entry 47C, Box 1294, NARA; "Statement of Lt. Col. Gerald Duin on Early Contacts with the Gehlen Organization," in Ruffner, *Forging an Intelligence Partnership*, 1:35–41, NARA.

58. Memorandum from Col. Hopkins to CHIEF, GMDS, January 15, 1946, RG 319, Entry 47C, Box 1294, NARA.

59. General Buhle, P/W Camp Fort Meade (Hospital), April 24, 1946, RG 165, Entry 179, Box 456, NARA.

60. Discontinuance of Prisoner of War Camps, May 9, 1946, RG 389, Entry 461, Box 2484, NARA; Procedures to Be Taken in Connection with Return of Prisoners for Hill Project to Germany, April 5, 1946, RG 319, Entry 47C, Box 1294, NARA.

61. Intra-Office Memorandum from Chief, MIS, to A.C. of S., G-2, March 14, 1946, RG 319, Entry 47C, Box 1294, NARA. No newspaper articles that directly mention the Hill Project could be found. Only one mentions the German Military Document Section at Camp Ritchie, Maryland, and it makes no mention whatsoever of the Hill Project or the use of German General Staff officers. See "Secret Nazi Papers Bare Economic Plans," *New York Times*, February 9, 1946, 7.

62. Intra-Office Memorandum from Chief, MIS, to A.C. of S., G-2, March 14, 1946, RG 319, Entry 47C, Box 1294, NARA.

63. General der Infanterie Buhle to Colonel Lovell, January 23, 1946, RG 319, Entry 47C, Box 1294, NARA.

64. General der Infanterie Buhle to Colonel Lovell, December 15, 1945, and General der Infanterie Buhle to Colonel Lovell, January 23, 1946, RG 319, Entry 47C, Box 1294, NARA.

65. General der Infanterie Buhle to Colonel Lovell, January 23, 1946, RG 319, Entry 47C, Box 1294, NARA.

66. "Statement of Lt. Col. Gerald Duin," in Ruffner, *Forging an Intelligence Partnership*, 1:36, NARA (emphasis added).

67. Ibid., 35.

68. "Statement of Lt. Col. Gerald Duin" and "Debriefing of Eric Waldman on the U.S. Army's Trusteeship of the Gehlen Organization during the Years 1945–1949," September 30, 1969, in Ruffner, *Forging an Intelligence Partnership*, 1:35, 45, NARA; GMDS, Reports for the Months of September, October, and November (1945), RG 242, Entry 282BC, Box 135, NARA.

69. "Statement of Lt. Col. Gerald Duin," in Ruffner, *Forging an Intelligence Partnership*, 1:39–41, NARA; "Final Report on GMDS," dated April 1, 1947, lists the "Foreign Armies East documents" as part of the German Military Document Section collections; no date for their arrival is given, however. RG 242, Entry 282BC, Box 135, NARA.

70. "Statement of Lt. Col. Gerald Duin," in Ruffner, *Forging an Intelligence Partnership*, 1:38, NARA.

71. Ibid., 37.

72. Data concerning POWs to Be Retained, April 15, 1946, RG 319, Entry 47C, Box 1294, NARA.

73. Ibid.; "Statement of Lt. Col. Gerald Duin," in Ruffner, *Forging an Intelligence Partnership*, 1:36, NARA.

74. German Military Document Section, MB 867, the Pentagon, June 7 and April 19, 1946, RG 242, Entry 282BC, Box 134, NARA.

75. German General Officer Prisoners of War Interned in the United States, May 7, 1946, RG 549, Entry 2202AC, Box 3, NARA.

76. "Statement of Lt. Col. Gerald Duin," in Ruffner, *Forging an Intelligence Partnership*, 1:36, NARA. Curiously, James Byrnes did not take office as secretary of state until July 3, 1946, three days after the imposed deadline for the repatriation of German prisoners of war.

77. General Huebner to General Clay, November 20, 1946, and General Keating to General Huebner, May 9, 1947, RG 260, Box 20, NARA.

78. List of GMDS Studies, January 29, 1954, RG 242, Entry 282BC, Box 137, NARA.

79. "Evaluation of GMDS Collection," summary sheet, Col. R. L. Hopkins to Chief of Staff, RG 242, AGAR-S, No. 1377, NARA.

80. "Statement of Lt. Col. Gerald Duin," in Ruffner, *Forging an Intelligence Partnership*, 1:36, NARA.

Conclusion

1. Transportation of Prisoners of War in Pullman Cars, June 30, 1945, RG 160, Entry 1, Box 36, NARA.

2. Theodor Graf von Sponeck, *Meine Erinnerungen,* pp. 186–88, MSg 1/3329, BA-MA.

3. Ibid., 189–91.

4. Kenneth W. Hechler, "The Enemy Side of the Hill: The 1945 Background on Interrogation of German Commanders," in *World War II German Military Studies: A Collection of 213 Special Reports on the Second World War Prepared by Former Officers of the Wehrmacht for the United States Army,* ed. Donald S. Detwiler, Charles B. Burdick, and Jürgen Rohwer (New York: Garland, 1979), 1:9–11, 20–25.

5. Ellinor F. Anspacher, Theodore W. Bauer, and Oliver J. Frederiksen, *The Army Historical Program in the European Theater and Command, 8 May 1945–3 December 1950,* Occupation Forces in Europe series (Karlsruhe, Germany: Historical Division European Command, 1951); Detwiler, Burdick, and Rohwer, *World War II German Military Studies,* 1:50–53.

6. Detwiler, Burdick, and Rohwer, *World War II German Military Studies,* 1:53–54.

7. Ibid., 1:81–82.

8. "Complete Listing by George Wagner of German Military Studies (ETHINT, A, B, C, D, P, and T Series) held at the U.S. National Archives, with Author Index," in Detwiler, Burdick, and Rohwer, *World War II German Military Studies;* Theodor Graf von Sponeck, *Meine Erinnerungen,* pp. 191–94, MSg 1/3329, BA-MA; "Von Sponeck," MSg 109, BA-MA.

9. Dietrich von Choltitz, *Soldat unter Soldaten* (Zürich: Europe Verlag, 1951), 279–84.

10. These twenty-one general officers included von Arnim, Badinski, Bieringer, Bruhn, von Choltitz, Cuno, Daser, Gallenkamp, Gundelach, Kessler, Kittel, Krause, von Liebenstein, von Quast, Richter, Schnarrenberger, von Sponeck, Stolberg, Ullersperger, von Vaerst, and Vaterrodt. "Complete Listing by George Wagner of German Military Studies (ETHINT, A, B, C, D, P, and T Series) held at the U.S. National Archives, with Author Index," in Detwiler, Burdick and Rohwer, *World War II German Military Studies.*

11. Ibid.

12. Ibid.

13. Ibid., 1:92–97.

14. Ibid., 1:90–92, 107–12. See also James H. Critchfield, *Partners at the Creation: The Men behind Postwar Germany's Defense and Intelligence Establishments* (Annapolis, MD: Naval Institute Press, 2003).

15. What is perhaps most remarkable about the American relationship with Gehlen is not that Washington chose to work with a former high-ranking member of Hitler's staff but rather that they chose one who appeared to be largely inept at

intelligence work. During the three years in which Gehlen served as chief of Fremde Heer Ost, his service was largely unremarkable, at times even incompetent. See David Thomas, "Foreign Armies East and German Military Intelligence in Russia, 1941–45," *Journal of Contemporary History* 22 (April 1987): 261–301.

16. Ibid.

17. PERS 1/103932, BA-MA.

18. PERS 1/103928, PERS 1/2885, BA-MA.

19. Ramcke, *Fallschirmjäger,* 101–13.

20. Ramcke, *Fallschirmjäger,* 254–61; "French Convict Nazi General," *New York Times,* March 22, 1951.

21. Alaric Searle, *Wehrmacht Generals, West German Society, and the Debate on Rearmament, 1949–1959* (Westport, CT: Praeger, 2003), 163–65.

22. Ibid., 168–69; "Ex-Nazi's Anti-West Blast Irks Bonn," *Christian Science Monitor,* October 28, 1952; "The Black Coats," *Time,* November 10, 1952.

23. "Ex-Nazi's Anti-West Blast Irks Bonn," *Christian Science Monitor,* October 28, 1952; "The Black Coats," *Time,* November 10, 1952; Searle, *Wehrmacht Generals,* 286.

24. "Reunion Planned by Afrika Korps," *New York Times,* August 29, 1951; Searle, *Wehrmacht Generals,* 165; "Afrika Corps Chief Plans to Organize German Vet Group," *Christian Science Monitor,* August 27, 1951.

25. "Bonn Army Chief Hinted," *New York Times,* October 9, 1954; "The New Look in German Generals," *New York Times,* December 18, 1954.

26. See the records of the U.S. Army, Europe, Historical Division, RG 549, Entry 2202AC, Box 3, NARA.

27. The list of German general officers interned in the United States omitted von Aulock, Bruhn, Cuno, Daser, Gallenkamp, Hermann, Heyking, Kittel, Pollert, Vaterrodt, and Buhle. Location of German PWs, August 14, 1946; Movement of PWs, May 14, 1946; Letter of Transmittal, May 4, 1946; German General Officer Prisoners of War Interned in the United States, May 7, 1946, all in RG 549, Entry 2202AC, Box 3, NARA.

28. Request for Location of Certain German Officers, February 10, 1947, and Memorandum to Commanding Officer, 7734 Hist. Det., March 5, 1947, RG 549, Entry 2202AC, Box 4, NARA; Parole of Cooperative Prisoners of War, April 2, 1947, and List of German Officers to be Retained with the Last Group to be Transferred to Allendorf, June 25, 1947, RG 549, Entry 2202AC, Box 6, NARA.

29. Report of Temporary Duty, Camp #11, February 28, 1948, RG 549, Entry 2202AC, Box 7, NARA; Suppression of the German General Staff and Officer Corps, June 3, 1946, FO 1038/136, TNA; Staff Minute Sheet, "The definition of a militarist," July 9, 1948, FO 1038/165, TNA; Classification of German Militarists, February 10, 1948, FO 939/194, TNA; Categorization of Ex-Members of the German Armed Forces, FO 1038/164, TNA.

30. Watch List of German Generals, April 3, 1946, RG 319, Entry 82, Box 3706, NARA.

31. Anspacher, Bauer, and Frederiksen, *Army Historical Program*, 55–56, 87–88, 100; "Editor's Introduction," in Detwiler, Burdick, and Rohwer, *World War II German Military Studies*, 1:1–2.

32. Ibid.

33. Ibid.

34. Category A (Security Suspects) for Transfer to Bremen for CIC Edelheide, October 8, 1947, FO 939/194, TNA; Nominal Role of Confirmed Category II (Militarists) by Review Boards at Adelheide as of January 1, 1948, FO 1038/164, TNA; Travel Control of Militarists/Stop List, October 11, 1948, FO 1038/165, TNA.

35. A Survey of the German Generals and General Staff, June 10, 1947, FO 393/40, TNA.

36. See Wood, "Captive Historians, Captivated Audience"; and Soutor, "To Stem the Red Tide."

37. For further study of the American admiration for German general officers, see Ronald Smelser and Edward J. Davies II, *The Myth of the Eastern Front: The Nazi-Soviet War in American Popular Culture* (New York: Cambridge University Press, 2008). The Guderian story and quotes appear on page 125.

Bibliography

Archives

Germany

Bundesarchiv-Militärarchiv, Freiburg im Breisgau
MSg 1, Das deutsche Militärwesen, Deutsches Reich, 1933–1945
MSg 109, Nachlässe und Militäregeschichtliche Sammlungen
PERS 1, Personalakten: Das deutsche Militärwesen, Bundesrepublik Deutschland 1949–1990
PERS 6, Personalakten: Das deutsche Militärwesen, Deutsches Reich, 1933–1945

United Kingdom

National Archives, Kew
Foreign Office
FO 916, Consular (War) Department, later Prisoners of War Department
FO 939, Control Office for Germany and Austria and Foreign Office, German Section: Prisoners of War
FO 1038, Control Office for Germany and Austria and Foreign Office: Control Commission for Germany (British Element), Military Divisions
War Office
WO 165, War Diaries, Second World War
WO 208, Directorate of Military Intelligence

United States

Hoover Institution Archives, Stanford University, Palo Alto, CA
Stephen M. Farrand Papers

National Archives and Records Administration, College Park, MD
RG 59, General Records of the Department of State
RG 160, Records of Headquarters Army Service Forces
RG 165, Records of the War Department General and Special Staffs
RG 242, National Archives Collection of Foreign Records Seized
RG 260, Records of U.S. Occupation Headquarters, World War II
RG 263, Records of the Central Intelligence Agency
RG 319, Records of the Army Staff
RG 337, Records of Headquarters Army Ground Forces
RG 389, Records of the Office of the Provost Marshal General
RG 498, Records of Headquarters, European Theater of Operations, United States Army (World War II), 1942–1946
RG 549, Records of the United States Army, Europe
Ruffner, Kevin C., ed. *Forging an Intelligence Partnership: CIA and the Origins of the BND, 1945–49: A Documentary History.* Vol. 1. CIA History Staff, Center for the Study of Intelligence, European Division, Directorate of Operations, 1999.

Memoirs

Choltitz, Dietrich von. *Soldat unter Soldaten.* Zürich: Europe Verlag, 1951. Translated for the author by Anja Schwalen.
Guderian, Heinz. *Panzer Leader.* Costa Mesa, CA: Noontide Press, 1988. First published 1952 by Dutton, New York.
Ramcke, Hermann Bernard. *Fallschirmjäger: Damals und Danach.* Frankfurt am Main: Lorch-Verlag, 1951. Translated for the author by Anja Schwalen.

Newspapers and Periodicals

Chicago Daily Tribune
Christian Science Monitor
Jackson (MS) Clarion Ledger
Los Angeles Times
Mexia (TX) Weekly Herald
New York Times
New York Times Book Review
Time

Published Primary Sources

Detwiler, Donald S., Charles B. Burdick, and Jurgen Rohwer, eds. *World War II German Military Studies: A Collection of 213 Special Reports on the*

Second World War Prepared by Former Officers of the Wehrmacht for the United States Army. Vol. 1. New York: Garland, 1979.

Levitt, Saul. "Capturing a Gestapo General." *Yank* 3 (January 12, 1945): 6–7.

Stuart, Graham H. "War Prisoners and Internees in the United States." *American Foreign Service Journal* 21 (October 1944): 530–31.

The Thunderbolt Division: Story of the Eighty-Third Infantry Division. U.S. Army, S.1, 1945.

United States Army, Third Armored Division. *Spearhead in the West, 1941–1945: The Third Armored Division.* Frankfurt am Main-Schwanheim: F. J. Henrich, 1945.

Secondary Sources

Allard, Michael A. "A History of the Clinton Prisoner of War Camp, 1942–1946." M.A. thesis, Mississippi College, 1994.

Angolia, John R. *On the Field of Honor: A History of the Knight's Cross Bearers.* 2 vols. San Jose, CA: R. James Bender, 1979.

Anspacher, Ellinor F., Theodore W. Bauer, and Oliver J. Frederiksen. *The Army Historical Program in the European Theater and Command, 8 May 1945–3 December 1950.* Occupation Forces in Europe series. Karlsruhe, Germany: Historical Division European Command, 1951.

Atkinson, Rick. *An Army at Dawn: The War in North Africa, 1942–1943.* New York: Henry Holt, 2002.

Barnett, Correlli. *Britain and Her Army, 1509–1970: A Military, Political and Social Survey.* London: Allen Lane the Penguin Press, 1970.

———, ed. *Hitler's Generals.* New York: Grove Weidenfeld, 1989.

Bender, Roger James, and Richard D. Law. *Uniforms, Organization, and History of the Afrikakorps.* Mountain View, CA: R. James Bender, 1973.

Bender, Roger James, and Warren W. Odegard. *Uniforms, Organization, and History of the Panzertruppe.* San Jose, CA: R. James Bender, 1980.

Bischof, Günter, and Stephen E. Ambrose, eds. *Eisenhower and the German Prisoners of War: Facts against Falsehood.* Baton Rouge: Louisiana State University Press, 1992.

Bradley, Dermot, Karl-Friedrich Hildebrand, and Markus Rövekamp. *Die Generale des Heeres, 1921–1945.* 12 vols. Osnabrück, Germany: Biblio Verlag, 1993.

Brett-Smith, Richard. *Hitler's Generals.* San Rafael, CA: Presidio Press, 1977. First published 1976 by Osprey Publishing, London.

Campbell, Patrick. *Trent Park: A History.* London: Middlesex University Press, 1997.

Carell, Paul. *Foxes of the Desert: The Story of the Afrika Korps.* Atglen, PA: Schiffer, 1994. First published 1960 by Macdonald, London.

Coffman, Edward M. *The Regulars: The American Army, 1898–1941.* Cambridge, MA: Belknap Press of Harvard University Press, 2004.

Collins, Larry, and Dominique Lapierre. *Is Paris Burning?* New York: Warner Books, 1991. First published 1965 by Simon and Schuster, New York.

Critchfield, James H. *Partners at the Creation: The Men behind Postwar Germany's Defense and Intelligence Establishments.* Annapolis, MD: Naval Institute Press, 2003.

Davis, Franklin M., Jr. *Come as a Conqueror: The United States Army's Occupation of Germany, 1945–1949.* New York: Macmillan, 1967.

Demeter, Karl. *The German Officer-Corps in Society and State 1650–1945.* New York: Praeger, 1965.

Edwards, Roger. *German Airborne Troops 1936–45.* Garden City, NY: Doubleday, 1974.

Faulk, Henry. *Group Captives: The Re-education of German Prisoners of War in Britain, 1945–1948.* London: Chatto and Windus, 1977.

Folttmann, Josef, and Hanns Müller-Witten. *Opfergang der Generale: Die Verluste der Generale and Admirale und der im gleichen Dienstrang Stehenden sonstigen Offiziere und Beamten im Zweiten Weltkrieg.* Berlin: Verlag Bernard and Graefe, 1959. First published 1952 by Bernard and Graefe, Berlin.

Gansberg, Judith M. *Stalag, U.S.A: The Remarkable Story of German Prisoners of War in America.* New York: Thomas Y. Crowell, 1977.

Garrett, Richard. *P.O.W.* London: David and Charles, 1981.

Hildebrand, Hans H., and Ernest Henriot. *Deutschlands Admiral 1849–1945: Die militärischen Werdegänge der See-, Ingenieur-, Sanitäts-, Waffen- und Verwaltungsoffiziere im Admiralsrang.* Osnabrück, Germany: Biblio Verlag, 1988–1990.

Hildebrand, Karl Friedrich. *Die Generale der deutschen Luftwaffe 1935–1945: Die militärischen Werdegänge der Flieger-, Flakartillerie-, Fallschirmjäger-, Luftnachrichten- und Ingenieur-Offiziere einschließlich der Ärzte, Richter, Intendanten und Ministerialbeamten im Generalsrang.* 3 vols. Osnabrück, Germany: Biblio Verlag, 1990.

Hinsley, F. H. *British Intelligence in the Second World War: Its Influence on Strategy and Operations.* Vol. 2. London: H. M. Stationery Office, 1991.

Hoffmann, Peter. *Stauffenberg: A Family History, 1905–1944.* Cambridge: Cambridge University Press, 1995.

Jensen, Carol A. *Images of America: Byron Hot Springs.* Charleston, SC: Arcadia, 2006.

Kemble, Charles Robert. *The Image of the Army Officer in America.* Westport, CT: Greenwood Press, 1973.

———. "Mutations in America's Perceptions of Its Professional Military Leaders: An Historical Overview and Update." *Armed Forces and Society* 34, no. 1 (October 2007): 29–45. Accessed via *OnlineFirst,* http://afs.sagepub .com, April 4, 2007, doi:10.1177/0095327X06293862.

Kourvetaris, George A., and Betty A. Dobratz. *Social Origins and Political Orientations of Officer Corps in a World Perspective.* Denver: University of Denver, 1973.

Krammer, Arnold. "American Treatment of German Generals during World War II." *Journal of Military History* 54 (January 1990): 27–46.

———. *Nazi Prisoners of War in America.* Lanham, MD: Scarborough House, 1996. First published 1979 by Stein and Day, New York.

Kursietis, Andris J. *The Wehrmacht at War 1939–1945: The Units and Commanders of the German Ground Forces during World War II.* Soesterberg, Netherlands: Aspekt, 1999.

Leitz, Christian. *Economic Relations between Nazi Germany and Franco's Spain: 1936–1945.* Oxford: Oxford University Press, 1996.

Liddell Hart, Sir Basil Henry. *The Other Side of the Hill: Germany's Generals, Their Rise and Fall, with Their Own Account of Military Events, 1939–1945.* London: Cassell and Company, 1951. First published 1948 by Cassell and Company, London.

Lockenour, Jay. *Soldiers as Citizens: Former Wehrmacht Officers in the Federal Republic of Germany, 1945–1955.* Lincoln: University of Nebraska Press, 2001.

Lowenfeld, Andreas F. "The Free Germany Committee: An Historical Study." *Review of Politics* 14, no. 3 (July 1952): 346–66.

Lucas, James. *Hitler's Enforcers: Leaders of the German War Machine 1933–1945.* London: Arms and Armour Press, 1996.

MacMillan, George. "A Decade of War Novels: The Accent Has Been Political." *New York Times Book Review,* December 1951.

Mitcham, Samuel W., Jr. *Hitler's Legions: The German Army Order of Battle, World War II.* New York: Stein and Day, 1985.

Moore, Jason Kendall. "Between Expediency and Principle: U.S. Repatriation Policy toward Russian Nationals, 1944–1949." *Diplomatic History* 24 (Summer 2000): 381–404.

Moore, John Hammond. "Getting Fritz to Talk." *Virginia Quarterly Review* 54, no. 2 (Spring 1978): 263–80.

Neitzel, Sönke. *Tapping Hitler's Generals: Transcripts of Secret Conversations,*

1942–45. Barnsley, U.K.: Frontline Books; St. Paul, MN: MBI, 2007. Originally published as *Abgehört: Deutsche Generäle in britisher Kriegsgefangenschaft 1942–1945* (Berlin: Ullstein Buchverlage GmbH, 2005).

Nenninger, Timothy K. "Leavenworth and Its Critics: The U.S. Army Command and General Staff School, 1920–1940." *Journal of Military History* 58 (April 1994): 199–231.

Peterson, Edward. *The American Occupation of Germany: Retreat to Victory.* Detroit: Wayne State University Press, 1977.

Preradovich, Nikolaus V. *Die militärische und soziale Herkunft der Generalität des deutschen Heeres, 1. Mai 1944.* Osnabrück, Germany: Biblio Verlag, 1978.

———. "Die militärische und soziale Herkunft der hohen Generalität des deutschen Heeres am 1. Mai 1944." *Wehrwissenschaftliche Rundschau* 20, no. 1 (1970): 44–55.

Pritchett, Merrill R., and William L. Shea. "The Afrika Korps in Arkansas, 1943–1946." *Arkansas Historical Quarterly* 37 (Spring 1978): 3–22.

Razzell, P. E. "Social Origins of Officers in the Indian and British Home Army: 1758–1962." *British Journal of Sociology* 14 (September 1963): 248–60.

Reese, Mary Ellen. *General Reinhard Gehlen: The CIA Connection.* Fairfax, VA: George Mason University Press, 1990.

Russell of Liverpool, Lord [Edward Frederick Langley Russell]. *The Scourge of the Swastika: A Short History of Nazi War Crimes.* London: Cassell and Company, 1954.

Ryan, Garry D., and Timothy K. Nenninger, eds. *Soldiers and Civilians: The U.S. Army and the American People.* Washington, D.C.: National Archives and Records Administration, 1987.

Scalia, Joseph Mark. *Germany's Last Mission to Japan: The Failed Voyage of U-234.* Annapolis, MD: Naval Institute Press, 2000.

Scheurig, Bodo. *Free Germany: The National Committee and the League of German Officers.* Middletown, CT: Wesleyan University Press, 1969.

Searle, Alaric. *Wehrmacht Generals, West German Society, and the Debate on Rearmament, 1949–1959.* Westport, CT: Praeger, 2003.

Shulman, Milton. *Defeat in the West: Germany's Greatest Battles as Seen by Hitler's Generals.* New York: Ballantine, 1968. First published 1947 by Secker and Warburg, London.

Smelser, Ronald, and Edward J. Davies II. *The Myth of the Eastern Front: The Nazi-Soviet War in American Popular Culture.* New York: Cambridge University Press, 2008.

Soutor, Kevin. "To Stem the Ride Tide: The German Report Series and Its

Effect on American Defense Doctrine, 1948–1954." *Journal of Military History* 57 (October 1993): 653–88.

Speed, Richard B., III. *Prisoners, Diplomats, and the Great War: A Study in the Diplomacy of Captivity.* New York: Greenwood Press, 1990.

Sullivan, Matthew Barry. *Thresholds of Peace: Four Hundred Thousand German Prisoners and the People of Britain, 1944–1948.* London: Hamish Hamilton, 1979.

Taylor, Telford. *The March of Conquest: The German Victories in Western Europe, 1940.* Baltimore, MD: Nautical and Aviation Publishing Company of America, 1991. First published 1958 by Simon and Schuster, New York.

Thomas, David. "Foreign Armies East and German Military Intelligence in Russia, 1941–45." *Journal of Contemporary History* 22 (April 1987): 261–301.

Veranov, Michael, ed. *The Mammoth Book of the Third Reich at War.* New York: Carroll and Graf, 1997.

Walker, Richard Paul. *The Lone Star and the Swastika: Prisoners of War in Texas.* Austin, TX: Eakin Press, 2001.

Weigley, Russell F. *The American Way of War: A History of United States Military Strategy and Policy.* New York: Macmillan, 1973.

———. *Towards an American Army: Military Thought from Washington to Marshall.* New York: Columbia University Press, 1962.

Winschel, Terrence J. "The Enemy's Keeper." *Journal of Mississippi History* 57 (Winter 1995): 323–33.

Wolfe, Robert, ed. *Americans as Proconsuls: United States Military Government in Germany and Japan, 1944–1952.* Carbondale: Southern Illinois University Press, 1984.

———, ed. *Captured German and Related Records: A National Archives Conference.* Athens: Ohio University Press, 1974.

Wood, James A. "Captive Historians, Captivated Audience: The German Military History Program, 1945–1961." *Journal of Military History* 69 (January 2005): 123–48.

Index

U.S. 458th Military Police Escort Guard Company, 68

U.S. 459th Military Police Escort Guard Company, 68, 130

U.S. Marine Corps, 9

U.S. Meritorious Civilian Service Award, 180

U.S. Military Academy, West Point, 8, 10, 11, 92, 109, 121, 122, 153

U.S. Naval War College, 153, 166

U.S. Navy, 14, 133, 180

U.S. Office of Naval Intelligence, 153

U.S. 7734th USFET Historical Detachment, 171

U.S. Seventh Army, 141

U.S.S.R. *See* Soviet Union

U.S. State Department: administration of prisoner affairs, 5; camp inspection reports, 70; inspections of Camp Clinton, 81–83, 87–90, 91, 93–94, 118; inspections of Camp Dermott, 120–22, 142, 182; memo on inability to find suitable guards for American POW camps, 75–76; Special War Problems Division, 5, 70

U.S Surgeon General, 142

U.S. Tenth Regiment, Fifth Division, 47–48

U.S. Third Army, 141, 171

U.S. 36th Infantry Division, 39

U.S. Twelfth Army Interrogation Center, 161

U.S. War Department: abandonment of Camp Dermott as a re-education camp, 123–24; administration of prisoner affairs, 5; camp inspection reports, 70; chooses Camp Dermott for reeducation camp, 107, 110, 111, 112; deference to British methods

of handling general officer prisoners, 2; discussion of moving the general officer prisoners to Camp Pryor, 96; failure to clearly define policy regarding German generals, 113–14, 116–17; "Partial List of Enlisted Men Suffering from Mental Disturbances Employed by Prisoner of War Camp [Clinton] during Month of August 1944," 75–76, 85, 90, 92, 93; perspectives of Camp Dermott and Camp Ruston, 125, 134, 139, 140, 141–42, 144–45, 159; promotions of German prisoners, 53; renovation and establishment of Camp Tracy, 55; requirement that the generals at Camp Clinton sign "paroles" in order to walk outside the camp, 69–70; returns German POWs to Europe, 169, 174, 182–83; selection of POW camp commanding officers, 74; temporary reduction in POW rations, 120–21

U.S. War Department General Staff, 140

U.S. War Department, Military Intelligence Division, 148, 154, 156, 157, 160, 164

U.S. War Department, Military Intelligence Division, Historical Branch, 170

U.S. War Department, Military Intelligence Service, 124–25, 134, 137, 166

U.S. War Department, New Developments Division, 148

U.S. War Department, Organization and Training Division, 148

U.S. War Department, Personnel Division, 148